To Susan,
Happy people and

Pull up Another Chair

Sept. 22/07

Memories of Old-timers

from Armstrong Spallumcheen

British Columbia

by Shirley Campbell

Trafford Publishing

Order this book online at www.trafford.com/07-0171
or email orders@trafford.com

Most Trafford titles are also available at major online book retailers.

Cover: *Pull up Another Chair*
        watercolour by the author
Remembering: poem by the author
Sketch maps by the author
Layout by Trafford Publishing

Note for Librarians: A cataloguing record for this book is available from Library
and Archives Canada at www.collectionscanada.ca/amicus/index-e.html

Printed in Victoria, BC, Canada.

ISBN: 978-1-4251-1709-2

*We at Trafford believe that it is the responsibility of us all, as both individuals
and corporations, to make choices that are environmentally and socially sound.
You, in turn, are supporting this responsible conduct each time you purchase a
Trafford book, or make use of our publishing services. To find out how you are
helping, please visit www.trafford.com/responsiblepublishing.html*

*Our mission is to efficiently provide the world's finest, most comprehensive
book publishing service, enabling every author to experience success.
To find out how to publish your book, your way, and have it available
worldwide, visit us online at www.trafford.com/10510*

 www.trafford.com

North America & international
toll-free: 1 888 232 4444 (USA & Canada)
phone: 250 383 6864 ♦ fax: 250 383 6804 ♦ email: info@trafford.com

The United Kingdom & Europe
phone: +44 (0)1865 722 113 ♦ local rate: 0845 230 9601
facsimile: +44 (0)1865 722 868 ♦ email: info.uk@trafford.com

10 9 8 7 6 5

For the *Storytellers*

Contents

Acknowledgements

My thanks go first to the eight storytellers who willingly shared their recollections of the early beginnings of our community. They spent hours recalling family lore and reworking my drafts of their stories until they accurately reflected their memories. In so doing they give us the gift of firsthand knowledge and a generous example of community spirit.

At the Armstrong Spallumcheen Museum and Art Gallery, Curator-Administrator Lisa Mori and archivists Jessie Ann Gamble, Louise Everest, Pat Brinnen, Marion Hope, Tiny Medhurst, and Bob Nitchie were unfailingly helpful. Ben McMahen's research on the Chinese community in Armstrong Spallumcheen was most useful. I appreciated too the assistance given by staff at the Enderby and District Museum and the Penticton Museum.

Judy Heaton and staff at Armstrong City Hall and Wendy Wallin at Spallumcheen Municipal Hall supplied information on local events, and former high school colleague Dick Lonsdale, on events of World War Two. Their support and assistance were timely.

Two of our earlier storytellers, Mat. S. Hassen and Ralph D. Lockhart made my hazy knowledge accurate. Their willingness to share a lifetime in our community eased my research and I am grateful.

Mary Jong assisted me throughout my conversations with her mother, storyteller Louie Non Chip Jong. Mary, Joan, and other members of the Jong family were essential to bringing their mother's story into the community memory.

I wish to thank E. Ruby (Caswell) Hitt for her description of the Edwin Chapple house on Salmon River Road, to which she and her husband, 'Young' Fred Hitt, a relative of storyteller Raymond Hitt, moved in 1946 and raised their three children, Lenore, Brian, and John.

I am grateful for the use of material by four family historians: Marjorie (Hitt) Gordon, Margaret (Maw) Duguay, Dolores (Harrison) Culling, and Doris Noble. Karen Hassard added memories of her aunt Doris (Harrison) Hassard and spent time with me after her aunt's death to finalize her story.

My thanks go to Jean Williamson for information about the McNair packing house, to Ben Lee for his knowledge of the Chinese community in Armstrong Spallumcheen, to Jake Wieringa for his assistance with regard to dairy quota, and to Edna Luxton for clarification of 4-H activities.

Jan Clemson gave permission to use photographs taken by his father, the noted photographer Donovan Clemson. Ernie Laviolette of Monashee Pictures in Lumby, B.C., once again prepared all photographs for publishing. Both men have my thanks.

Staff from Maglio Building Industries in Nelson, B.C., assiduously answered my inquiries regarding connections between that city and Armstrong Spallumcheen.

Lorna Carter kindly read the first proof of the book. I appreciated her patience and her eagle eye.

Our painting group – Amy Salter, Dagmar Watkins, and Linda Neden – helped me pull another chair onto the cover of the book, and Linda once again readied the computer disks for publication. Their advice and help were invaluable.

The community's enthusiastic reception of the first book of old-timer memories, *Pull up a Chair*, encouraged me to write this one, and I am grateful for the opportunity.

Finally, I wish to thank my husband, Kevin Campbell, for furnishing a writing space for me, googling computer answers to a range of questions, and giving constant encouragement. Our children and daughter-in-law always read the books.

Introduction

Pull up a Chair chronicled the memories of seven old-timers from Armstrong Spallumcheen in the Okanagan Valley of British Columbia. *Pull up Another Chair* continues to mine that treasure.

Three women and five men sat in their homes and spoke about the past and the present, how things began for their parents and grandparents, what it meant to grow up here or to make this place their home. Over a period of months, each storyteller approved a final draft of his or her story, selected a title for it, and received a copy to keep as a record. The author photographed each storyteller at home, and each supplied a photograph from earlier days.

On the surface each story is quite different. The similarities occur at a deeper level: the vigorous work ethic, the close observation of their environment, the courage to face and solve problems, and the humour to sweeten their days.

Two general themes surface in their memories:

The first is the importance of the family and the neighbourhood to their success as individuals and to the cohesion of the community. Their sense of 'neighbour' and 'neighbourhood' is keenly felt, and they recognize the need to nurture it.

The second is the recognition and handling of change in their own lives and in the community at large. Several have come to grips with the decline of familiar forms of agriculture, and many observe the influx of significant numbers of strangers into Armstrong Spallumcheen who are unaware of the roots of their adopted community. It is hoped that this book of old-timer memories, along with the former one, may reinforce the attachment of both longtime residents and latecomers to this valley.

Each story is a personal recollection, not an assemblage of facts, and bears the mark of the speaker's voice. Therefore, this book is *not* a history as that word is generally understood.

Instead, each story is one member's version of the family's history. Although, wherever possible, memory has been supported with research, I may have made errors that I leave to the next chronicler to correct.

The storytellers' words are in italic print. Pull up another chair, why don't you, listen to their stories, and feel at home.

Notes about usage:

One custom in the last century was to adopt the second name of a child for common use. For the sake of clarity, on occasion this nomenclature is reversed.

The current house number may follow a reference to a location.

Information about the teachings of the Chinese philosopher Confucius was obtained from *The Analects of Confucius,* translation and notes by Simon Leys, p xxviii-xxix. A reference for dragon symbolism was *A Dictionary of Symbols* by J.E. Cirlot, p 85-89. As used in the title of chapter eight, the dragon is both a symbol of power, strength and courage, and a symbol of the universal feminine guarding her treasure, her deepest realities. In addition, in Chinese numerology the number eight is lucky and indicates prosperity.

An apology:

In the first book of old-timer memories, *Pull up a Chair,* on Map 2, page 60, the name should read 'Fairfield Ranch.' The same error appears in the text on page 74.

Remembering

"I remember..." is a magic phrase.
It conjures up a door
To a world as real as this one is
Though gone for evermore —

A mother in the classroom
A father in the barn
An uncle knitting fish nets
A spare, reluctant farm

A glint of sea from windows
A sister, book in hand
Wild berries waiting capture
A wharf, a beach, the sand

Summer's careless idyll
Winter's gleeful sting —
A coloured kingdom in the soul
Remembers everything.

Chapter One

A Family and a Neighbourhood

Kenneth Craig McKechnie

McKechnie Neighbours to the East   Map 1

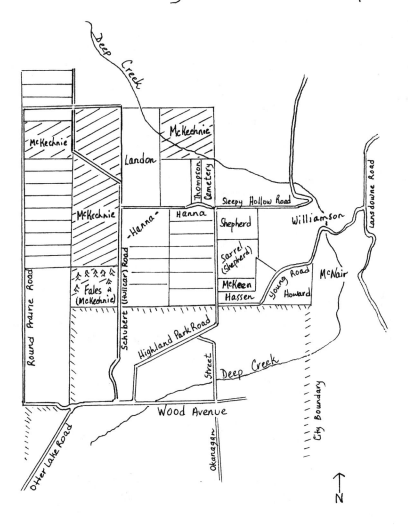

Round Prairie Neighbours   Map 2

Crawford Road

Salmon River Road

Deep Creek

Dodds Road

Docksteader

F. Hunter (Svenson)

Bullis (Seward)
Akitt (McKechnie)
Schubert Field
Dodds - Shaw

Maw Road

Hallam Road

Shultz

Babb (Cassidy) Road

Chapple (Sid Hitt)

Sid Hitt

Bosomworth

Billy Orr (Bigler, Smith)

Gus LeDuc

Duncan

Round Prairie Road

H.S. Maw

W. Hunter

Duncan

McKechnie

Swanson Mountain

Cail

Swanson

Hyde

Jennings

Swanson

Swanson

Schubert (Holliday) Road

Wood Avenue

Rifle Range

Noble Road

Fraser Road

Otter Lake Road

N

8

Neighbours North of Dodds Road   Map 3

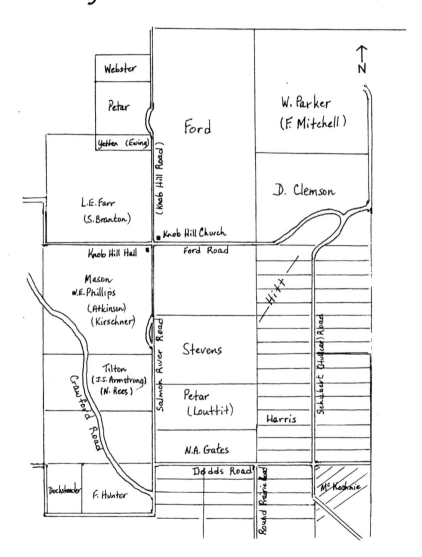

Neighbours West of Round Prairie   Map 4

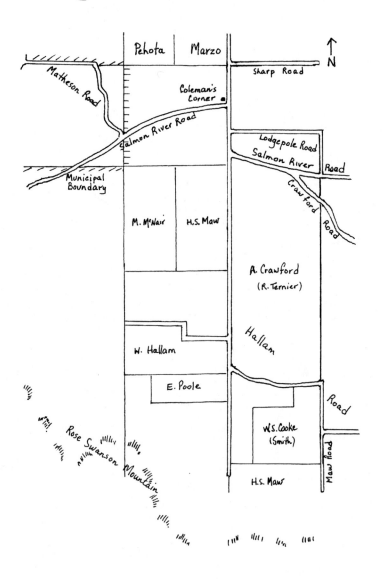

CNR Lease and Chinese Residents

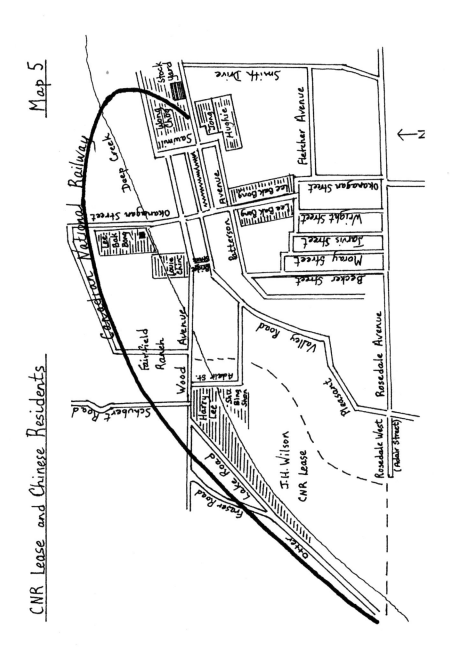

Map 5

*This farm was started by Gus and Catherine Schubert. I re-
member Dad saying their cabin was just inside the gate, and the remains of it were still here when our family arrived in 1920. I know in
Dad's diary of 1925 there's an entry: "We cleaned up the old house
today." That cabin is the only building it could have been. I have a
copy of an article their daughter Nora wrote about their trip here
by stage from Cache Creek, so I assume they built their house after
that, which is the house I grew up in.*

Craig is sitting at the kitchen table at 4376 Schubert Road in
a district known as Round Prairie. He is speaking about a founding family of Armstrong Spallumcheen, the Augustus Schuberts,
who with three children and a fourth en route, Rose, made a legend-
ary overland trip in 1862 from Manitoba to British Columbia. *Gus
spent a lot of time mining for gold in the Cariboo. He didn't come
here for about sixteen years – they lived in Lillooet. Then Catherine
got the job of housemother at the government boarding school in
Cache Creek. And that's where they were living – her and the kids
– when he got tired of mining and A.L. Fortune persuaded him to try
farming.*

*To my knowledge Gus and the two boys, Young Gus and Jim, ar-
rived on Round Prairie in 1879. Catherine with their younger children Charles and Catherine Henora (Nora) followed from Cache
Creek in 1883. They didn't get here in two and a half hours!* Nora
recorded that the trip took three days with overnight stops at Savona,
Kamloops, and Grande Prairie. *The [latter] name was changed to
Westwold when the railroad went through because there was already
a Grande Prairie in Alberta.* They arrived at O'Keefe Ranch in time
for dinner, and that afternoon the stage driver, Alex McDonald,

13

drove them to their new home. Nora's account of their journey to the Schubert cabin was uncomplimentary:

> I began to think we surely were entering a wilderness. I had never seen so many trees before, as Cache Creek was a dry belt with lots of sage bush and prickly pears. Then finally I saw what I thought was the roof of a house [but] Mr. McDonald said it was a straw stack. Of course, I didn't know what a straw stack was. He said that our house would not be that big, that it was quite small. Sure enough, when we got to the farm and I saw what a small house it was, I wondered where we would sleep. I had never seen a small building before, and after living six years in such a huge building as the school, I was very lonely leaving so many friends. I found the silence almost unbearable.

Nowadays the farm's rural quiet is broken by the strenuous cry of peacocks that wander the McKechnie place like chickens. *A few years ago a couple flew in from somewhere – they stayed around and produced more.*

Craig nods out the window at the farm buildings. *The old barn behind the grain silo is a Schubert construction – 30 by 40 feet – I would imagine they built that in the 1880s because, after all, you'd want a barn once you got a roof over your head. (The tin roof on the barn was added later.) There was a bit of orchard around here – everybody planted an orchard. The old shop beside the woodshed was actually made for apple storage, I'm sure, because the walls are thick – two sets of studs with sawdust between the studs of the outer wall. They built it instead of a root cellar. Dad said they forgot to insulate the floor – Grandpa must have put apples in there the first winter and the frost got in.*

One thing I always regret – the schoolhouse on the property burned – just some of the walls left. It was built in 1885 on one acre given by the Schuberts. The two young Schuberts along with other local children would fill the seats. *I remember reading that a work party started the building and then Schubert and his sons finished it. It was years before I happened to observe this statement was borne out by the construction, as the joints of the bottom two or three logs were all dovetailed; after that, the joints were 'arch and straddle' or something similar. Dovetailing is fancy axemanship – you end up with a real tight square corner. It was evident that the Schuberts used a different system and finished the building on their own. It was named Round Prairie School and Rose's husband, Thomas LeDuc, was the first teacher.*

A major consideration for the Schubert family was a consistent water supply. *It's something you've got to have. There is no water on this corner of Round Prairie, so at our gate this spring [2006], I was surprised to see a sinkhole forming deep enough that the head of a five-foot burdock growing in it was level with the ground. I got Raymond [Hitt] to dowse it, and he says there's a stream underneath over a hundred feet down. Actually, if it's quiet and you listen, you can hear a splash as if dirt were falling into water. It's a mystery! Grandpa McKechnie was well acquainted with Young Gus Schubert – Dad remembered him being around a lot – and the stories he told them make no mention of a well here. But I'm wondering if they tried to dig one here – it would make sense to try first near the house – and I'm going to get Marvin Hodge to clean the hole out carefully to see if the earth has been disturbed in comparison to the earth around it. If so, the Schuberts may not have been able to dig deep enough by hand to reach the water.*

We know for sure that farther up on a little bit of a hump, they dug a well seventy feet deep but got nothing – just rocks. (Rocks are still coming up there – whenever I seed alfalfa, I have to pick a few.)

Then on Deep Creek at the back of the property, they put in a hy-draulic ram. A ram is the nearest thing to perpetual motion that has ever been invented. It was a simple way of diverting a small amount of creek water to a household. *You have a little stream of water com-ing down a hill – it doesn't have to be much – and you've got an air dome and a few valves. Ten gallons of water comes swooshing into the air dome and is stopped by a valve closing – click – and the water builds up pressure and starts to go back, and a second valve shuts – click – and one gallon goes up a pipe to the house and nine gallons continues down the creek. Then you've got another rush of water and another click and away it goes again. The creek water is sustained and you just keep pushing the water... click... click... click... up the hill to your house – no electricity needed.*

Mat. Hassen told me one time that when he went into the real estate business with his dad, the first place he sold was the old Fred Shaw farm on the south side at the top of Schubert Road where it swings west, and they had a ram on the creek – all those places did. It was the '30s and the client was from Saskatchewan. He didn't have a car and Mat. drove him out there. Naturally anyone from the drought-stricken prairie wanted to know if there was any water around. So Mat. shows him the water – turn the tap and water comes out! – and then points out this weird-looking, clicking creature down below. The next day the guy walked the five miles from town back to the farm because he thought he was being put on – thought there was some hokey-pokey – and he wanted to get there unannounced and find out if the ram was still operating. Of course it was, and the deal went through. *Bill Skelton still has some rams around – nobody uses them anymore – they're curios. Ian Cameron wanders around the country quite a bit, and one time he told me he'd found this old box down in the ground in a certain place on the creek – he described it and wondered what it was. I told him it was probably the Schuberts' ram site.*

The Schuberts' hydraulic ram was a definite improvement over a well full of rocks, but the amount of water produced was insufficient. *So Schuberts made a deal with Bob Tilton, who owned the place a mile and a half up on Crawford Road. At the time his springs weren't registered.* Therein lies another story.

My water licence up on Tilton Springs was taken out in December, 1888, in the name of Schubert Brothers and Company. Gus told Grandpa that after they made the deal with Tilton, he headed off to Vernon the next day to register the springs with the

16

government agent, and as he was riding his horse along Otter Lake and past O'Keefe's, he noticed fresh hoofprints on the trail. He thought that was strange so early in the morning: "I just wonder if Tilton has had a second thought on this matter." So he took off fast on a shortcut and went directly to the government agent's house, and when the two of them reached the office, Tilton was waiting! The agent had to admit that Schubert was there first, so Schuberts got registered on the springs, and Tilton as well. With some ingenuity Schuberts had solved their water problem.

From my understanding Bob Tilton was a brother-in-law of Bill Miner. Bill Miner had a predilection for robbery that frustrated the law and fingered Tilton as a possible lead. *A policeman told Dad one time he was trying to make a connection between Bob Tilton and Bill Miner. Miner spent time in this country visiting his family although when he was in the area and stayed over at Hunter's place, he was known as George Edwards. Hunter lived below Maw's place, and Willis Hunter told my brother John he remembered as a boy Edwards' staying with them, and they'd go out squirrel shooting together. They didn't know he was on the run, of course.*

The Schubert sons did a good deal of to-ing and fro-ing among properties in these early days. *I really don't know how much land they owned around Round Prairie Road. There was a house built over here on Landon's place for Gus Junior when he got married, and then Jim bought the place on Otter Lake and later sold it to Gus, who moved down there and named it the Gumboot Ranch. Our farm ended up with Charles Schubert after his dad died in 1908, and in 1912 Charles traded it for the Okanagan Hotel, and the proprietor of the hotel – W.W. 'Billy' Rogers – got the farm. Neither of them was suited for the other occupation – things didn't go easy for either of them after the trade. And in 1920 Grandpa McKechnie bought it off Rogers and we arrived on the scene. The home farm was 120 acres minus the one acre for the schoolhouse.*

Somewhere we have two or three letters that Rogers wrote to Grandpa – wonderful letters with flowery language in 'Old Country' *script – describing the place. He said he'd like to get $20,000 for it, but Grandpa had John McCallan doing the deal for him – McCallan had lived next door to Grandpa in Vancouver – and he got $2,000 knocked off as "just a dream," and another $1,000 off for some other reason, and got it down to $17,000. In reality, it was still high for the times, but 1920 was a 'high' time. Certainly in comparison to ten years later [Depression], that price was as high as it got.*

In buying the Schubert farm, Dr. William Boyd McKechnie was eligible for assistance from the federal government. *Grandpa got this place by borrowing from the Soldier Settlement scheme that settled returning veterans on farms. It must have been a twenty-year agreement because I saw the letter that he sent around 1940 with the last payment, and he put in a little extra for the war fund.*

Fortunately, Dr. McKechnie knew something about agriculture. Born in 1867 in Bruce County, Ontario, he had grown up on a farm on the Saugeen River halfway between Port Elgin and Paisley. *100-acre farms were the norm in Ontario because they were laid out in 'concessions' whereas the norm here is a quarter-section – 160 acres. It wasn't a particularly good farm, and the curve of the river had cut it to sixty acres, so Grandpa and his brother John ended up buying the neighbour's place and adding it on.*

Grandpa took his high school in Walkerton, which was news-worthy in recent years for contaminated drinking water. He remem-bered a special ceremony in town one Sunday afternoon in 1885 because the local contingent was headin' off to fight the Northwest [Riel] Rebellion. He said by the time they got down to Southampton – a port on Lake Huron – word came through that the rebellion was over, so they all came home again! A successful student himself, William McKechnie taught school locally, and after a few years had saved enough to enter the faculty of medicine at the University of Toronto. It was 1891 and he was twenty-three, a late starter. *All these fine details – he told stories, but afterwards you think, 'What was he doin' there?' I know that for a summer job in 1894, he taught school in Manitoba because the kids went to school in the summertime, not in the winter. We have a little autograph book from that period and some letters that he got from his students after he'd left.*

A medical doctor-to-be was a most eligible man and deserved every assistance in finding a suitable wife. *I remember Grandpa telling me that him and a classmate, Tom Jeffs, boarded at the same place that last winter in medical school, and one day the landlady told them she had invited a couple of girls over for the evening. At this point Grandpa would have been twenty-seven, and you didn't have to be a rocket scientist to know what was going on.* The visit took place, and the women extended a reciprocal invitation. *Jeffs was quite smitten with the one girl, so they decided to accept. He was ten years older than Grandpa, a widower with a son, and at their door he got cold feet. Grandpa said, "I'm going in anyway," and Jeffs went back home. But after a while when his schoolwork was done at night, Jeffs would be off to see her, and so they were married. The name of the other girl was Annie Elizabeth Cowan. I remember Grandpa telling me a great story about a day trip they took over to Niagara Falls. He'd never been there and maybe she hadn't either. Anyway, he said, that's when Grandma latched onto him.*

Grandpa graduated in medicine in 1895 – he was nearly twenty-eight – set up shop in Harriston, Ontario – a retired farmers' town, he called it – decided life had *to be more exciting than this, and after only a few months headed west.* The larger family units and extensive networks of the times supplied way stations. *He spent Christmas of 1895 with his brother, a minister in Regina, and New Year's Day in Cowichan on Vancouver Island with Jeffs, who had moved out there. In January in Victoria he wrote the BC medical exam, which cost $100, which he didn't have, so he borrowed it off another brother who was working for Canadian Pacific Navigation on the west coast of Vancouver Island.* With that hurdle successfully behind him, he could practise medicine in the province. It had been a long ten years since Walkerton.

Now, of course, he had to set up a practice somewhere, and the news came down the pike (by way of the Methodist minister) that

"Revelstoke could sure use a doctor," so he borrowed another $50 off his brother for train fare. As his train came into town, he could see they were rebuilding the bridge across the river – low water – so he said to himself: 'If I don't get any medical business, I'm going down to get a job on the bridge' because he wasn't going back to his brother for more money. At that time Revelstoke was moving from 'Lower Town,' close to the river, to 'Upper Town,' closer to the railway station, and a lot of building was going on.

All the hotels had a horse and buggy at the station to pick up travellers, and Grandpa selected the Central Hotel, [run by] Abrahamson Brothers, and that afternoon word came up that the schoolteacher was sick, and Grandpa had his first customer. Back in Ontario he had charged $1 per visit, but he had heard that out here in the West, an office call was $2, and a house call, $2.50. "So I said $2.50 and the fellow paid it, and that was my first money made in BC!"

Dr. McKechnie's medical practice occasionally included a visit to Salmon Arm. *Before the turn of the last century, the town was served by either Kamloops or Revelstoke, and he'd come down on the train or flag a freight. One time a fellow met him at the station with a horse and sleigh. It was January, and the guy's farm was somewhere in Salmon Valley – three or four miles. Grandpa said it was cold, and sitting still on that sleigh was <u>mean</u> cold. When they got to the house and he did what he'd been called for, he figured he'd be warmer to walk back, as he had enough time to catch the eastbound train. But no, no, the fellow wouldn't have it – and Grandpa had to endure another ride.*

Grandpa lived in Revelstoke until March of 1900. In 1898 he was on the city's first council – his picture is up there in the council building – and he got married in May of 1899. Annie Cowan came out by train for the ceremony. One time I was in Revelstoke overnight, and in the morning I was wandering around looking at the mountains and thinking that it was quite a change for Grandma to come out here from Toronto – Toronto had streetcars, and she'd

20

never seen mountains before. It wasn't a big wedding. Grandpa said, "On my wedding day I got up at 4 o'clock, married at 5 o'clock, and boarded the train at 6 for a wedding boat trip down the Arrow Lakes." At this point he'd have been thirty-one and Grandma the same age. Grandpa's birthday was December 18th and Grandma's was December 28th. After she died, there was some discussion that she had been born the year before, but in those days you didn't want to be older than your husband! They moved to Vancouver where he did very well in the medical business. He was a general practitioner, but surgery was his specialty and he was good at it. He said he respected people that were good at their trade.

When the First World War came along, Dr. McKechnie had been practising medicine in Vancouver for about fifteen years and desired a change of pace. *He joined the army – he was forty-seven years old – and was assigned to the #5 Canadian Military Hospital in Salonika, Greece, which catered mainly to the fighting in the Balkans. It was a base hospital, not a MASH unit, so was not in the field. En route to Greece through the Mediterranean, the ship's alarm sounded – something suspicious had been sighted – possibly a submarine – and everybody was instructed to assemble on deck wearing a life jacket. Grandpa couldn't find his, and he was surprised when one fella appeared wearing two! The man said, "I'm a big person so I thought I'd better have two of them." Grandpa answered, "Well, I may be smaller, but I do need* one!!" *When they arrived at Salonika, the Greek government wouldn't permit them to land, so they went down to Egypt for a while until the French parked a couple of warships in the harbour – gunboat diplomacy – and they were allowed on shore. So that's where Grandpa was from 1915 to 1917.*

He told lots of stories about those years. One night a German zeppelin drifted overhead. They might have been spying or dropping a few hand grenades over the side. A French warship in the harbour got it in their searchlights and brought it down, and it landed on fire in the marshes of the Vardar River across from the base. "Let's go and have a look at it!" Grandpa was a man of rational thought and presence of mind – if you're going to look for some curios, and there's been a fire, the only thing that hasn't burned is metal, so you'd better have more than your fingernails to pry it off. So he goes to the shop and gets a hacksaw and a pair of pliers, and they get a Greek boy to row them across the river, and Grandpa came back from overseas with some leftovers. Now, how aluminum tubing ever survived the fire, I don't know, but Grandpa used it for small jobs around the farm for a long time. And he got away with some pulleys and cable that are now in the basement, but which from the time they moved here in 1920 until 1960 we used for the clothesline.

In 1917 the climax of the war had come, and conscription snared some reluctant recruits. *Grandpa spent 1917-18 with the Conscription Appeal Board. Conscripts that were appealing recruitment for medical reasons, he'd take a look at. He also seemed to be the secretary, as there are some records around here that are interesting to read – names of local people and the ailments they hoped would exempt them from service – anything from flat feet to hernias. Grandpa said he and a Dr. O'Brien from Grande Prairie were cronies because they were the older doctors – most of the others were just out of medical school – young enough to be his kids.*

In fact, in the nine years between 1900 and 1908, Dr. and Mrs. McKechnie had six children. *The first three were healthy and the last three were not. Two of those died in infancy – it was quite common for the times – but Dad [Kenneth], the second youngest, survived. We thought afterwards the deaths may have been caused by a blood problem: Dad was Rh-negative, and Grandpa was never tested – tests weren't done in those days. So there was a five-year gap between Dad and his next older brother, Ian. Don, the eldest of the children, was born in 1900 and was quite intelligent – he went to university at age fifteen, graduated at twenty as a mining engineer, and travelled extensively. His sister Mar [Martha] was one of the first women at UBC [University of British Columbia] to graduate in agriculture. She taught school and married Johnny McLeod, who taught at the high school in Armstrong in the mid-twenties before they moved to Vancouver. Ian was born in 1903, and he was the one*

Grandpa was going to make into a farmer, but Ian had other ideas. He was a rolling stone – came up here with them, stayed a couple of years and went back to Vancouver, principally in the sawmilling trade.

If Annie Cowan McKechnie as a young bride had found the contrast between Toronto and Revelstoke a shock, then her husband's decision at age fifty-three to leave his practice and go farming up-country was another. *After twenty years in Vancouver, to leave her friends and come up here with no electricity or other amenities, she was a remarkable woman.* But there was no question; this woman went along with her man. *I remember Grandpa saying that when he was looking for a farm, one of the places he viewed was halfway between Lytton and Lillooet, but he knew Grandma wouldn't like it, and Ian wouldn't live there at all! So he gave up on that one. That's when he got John McCallan to look around for him and ended up here.* McCallan lived on McLeery Road, presently the Konrad place.

We've added a couple of other pieces. Grandpa bought ten acres from Gus Schubert, all cultivated, which is still known to us as the Schubert Field. It had passed from his brother Charles to some 'gentleman' in London, England – I have his name on the deed downstairs – one of those deals where people were buying land and there's no rhyme or reason for it – and then Gus bought it back – it could have been nostalgia – and Grandpa rented it. I remember Dad saying they noticed Gus coming up Round Prairie Road with a horse and buggy one day, and he came down through the piece, and Grandpa was pretty sure what he was here for – he wanted to sell it. He did and Grandpa bought it. I think it was $700 in 1927. Land prices had decreased considerably.

One time Mother, Dad and I were visiting the Vernon Museum and noticed some photos lying out on a table beside the sign 'Do you know any of these people?' "Well," said Dad, "this one is Gus Schubert." So he called the clerk over and pointed him out. He laughed about what took place: "I think the guy was a little skeptical. He wrote on the back of the photo: 'Thought to be Gus Schubert.'" But there was no 'thought' about it – Dad knew it was Gus Schubert.

Gus Schubert appeared to enjoy betting on a sure thing. *Dad said he and Grandpa were coming along Otter Lake Road one day, and right at the corner with Otter Lake X Road – Gus's place took in that whole section – they saw a couple of guys and one of them was Gus, so they stopped to talk. He was kneeling on one knee writing something, and he got up and said to Grandpa, "I've just invested $1,000 in a machinery company this guy's promoting." Grandpa said, "It will be the last you ever see of it." Years later Gus said to Grandpa, "I sure wish you had come along fifteen minutes earlier!"*

Grandpa had had lots of experiences with such investments. As a doctor in Vancouver, he had had a bit of money. He'd invested in glue factories, fish mills, sawmills – actually, the Alberta Lumber Company didn't do too badly – a greenhouse – all kinds of deals. He lost money on many of them, and sometimes he ended up paying more than his share because he had some money and his partners didn't, and he paid to get out of hock. After any of these stories, he would say: "I'm telling you this so you'll know things and not make the same mistake!" And we would answer, "Well, you had lots of fun anyway!"

Dr. McKechnie's investments in additional acreage, however, were successful manoeuvres achieved by foresight and charm; for example, the W.E. Fales place. *From what I understand, Fales was a doctor at the Coast who bought the bush to the south of us prior to 1920. He died about 1930, and the son came up and had a look at it, went back and told his mother, "Forget about it – let it go." A number of local people were sitting around waiting for the tax sale, but Grandpa on one of his trips went out to see Mrs. Fales and offered her a deal. There was $100 in taxes owed by that time and he offered to pay the taxes plus $300. When Dad said to him one day that so-and-so was going to buy the Fales place, Grandpa responded, "I've* *got the title in my safety deposit box." Some people, Grandpa said, weren't too happy to hear the news, but he thought they were just parasites waiting for the tax sale to get it real cheap. He said, "I just went and talked to the lady." He bought another ten acres to the north of us the same way.*

As newcomers to Armstrong Spallumcheen, the McKechnies underwent some scrutiny before they were accepted. *Grandpa needed some straw for cattle bedding. Everybody that had threshed had a straw stack in the field. He could see across Round Prairie that Swansons had straw, so he goes over to ask Harry Swanson, Senior for some. 'No, he didn't think so.' A couple of weeks later Harry burned his straw stack. Well, Grandpa didn't think it was very neighbourly – his feelings were hurt. He ended up getting straw from Bill Sidney in Lansdowne. He said Bill sized him up first and then let him have some.*

Harry Swanson had pre-empted the place – they were the original people there. He may have had a temper. *I remember reading in an Okanagan Historical Report an account of a fellow being over in Lansdowne looking for work: "Well, Swanson needs somebody for threshing." So he came out here to Round Prairie and looked over toward Swanson's and he could see two guys running across the field. It was Swanson chasing his Chinese cook off the place.*

Harry Swanson was Rose Schubert's second husband. *She left Thomas LeDuc to marry him. For the times I imagine it created quite a stir. Their two sons, Young Harry and Donald farmed with their father. Donald was always known as Doug (pronounced Doog), but Grandpa always called him Dougal, as Dougal was a good Highland Scottish name. Mrs. B.F. Young, Junior taught school in Lansdowne and Armstrong (that's where she met her husband), and she said that Doug was a smart kid. Grandpa got along well with the Swanson boys – both bachelors – never married.*

Dad used to quote Old Harry Swanson whenever it rained in haying season and the hay wasn't good. Harry used to say, "Come

January, it will look better than snowballs." And it's very true. It may look bad when you're putting it in the barn, but when you're feeding it in mid-winter and there's no other hay around, it looks greener.

Harry lost a leg in a farm accident – I believe Grandpa was called in for a consultation before the operation – and he died in 1925.

Dad and I visited the Swansons one day in 1966 after they had moved to town – Doug, Harry, and their sister, Dolly. Dad wondered whether it was a hand-held pitchfork or the big hayfork dropping down from the loft that had hit their father and caused the amputation of his leg. Dolly said, "Well, you know, medicine wasn't what it is today," and the question was passed off. In either case, likely the reason was infection. I remember a television interview with an old doctor that Dad knew, Dr. Anderson, who retired many years ago and lived in Kelowna: "What is the biggest advancement that you have seen in your lifetime?" "Oh," he said, "antibiotics!" As a young doctor in Montreal, Anderson could recall seeing guys come in with a small wound and get an infection, couldn't fight it off and ended up dying. Mother nursed, and she said if somebody came to the hospital with a ruptured appendix and you saved them, that was really something because the stuff went all through the body.

Dolly Swanson – Mrs. Clara Gregory – was a nurse too and came back to the farm in the 1930s. She was the only reason the boys held onto the place all those years. It was tough sluggin', and she whipped them into shape and kept them in shape, which was a full-time job. A fellow told Dad one time: "I was workin' over there, and Doug had brought home a bottle of something and she came in: 'What's the idea of spending money on this when the creditors are at the gate!' And she grabbed the bottle and knocked the neck off it and poured the stuff down the sink." The fellow was disappointed: "It had already been paid for – we might as well have drunk it!" Dolly outlived both the boys. When she became frail, she entered Willowdale [Pioneer Square] in Armstrong where she suddenly came to life again. She was with a bunch of older people that she could help, and helping people had been her life. She had a gay old time running around looking after them all. It took ten years off her age.

If some of Dr. McKechnie's neighbours appeared eccentric, so did he. *Until about the mid-fifties the telephone line came up here and around the corner to Colin Harris's, where it ended. The first thing Grandpa did when they moved into the Schubert house was take out the phone for a while – he had retired.* (Apparently, so had his wife.) He had contributed to society. He wasn't going to be bothered day and night by stomach aches and nasal drip. He was going to have some fun. *Before he arrived in the fall of 1920, Grandpa got a fellow to plough the front field here with a tractor. It must have been one of the early ones because he and Dad ploughed with horses for the next twenty-three years – Grandpa's preference except for breaking alfalfa – you had to get a tractor in for that. Grandpa thought there was nothing like ploughing with horses for a day – it was great exercise for mind and body.*

A Donovan Clemson photograph places him in his element – a tough old farmer in his field of stooked grain. He is leaning on a long-handled pitchfork against a wide sky of cumulus – *Donovan loved clouds* – and the sheaves are waist-high. *They've got that picture in the archives in Victoria – Clemson won prizes with it – it appeared on the cover of a lot of magazines.* A large framed copy hangs in the McKechnie kitchen.

I remember him saying that first fall he got seed wheat off Floyd Hunter for $80 a ton, and that was high. But it was a high price that fall. The next fall he sold six tons of seed wheat to O'Keefe Ranch. I don't know what he got for it, but it wasn't $80 a ton – the price was low that year. I remember Dad saying Old Mrs. O'Keefe made the deal. He told me that Tierney O'Keefe and two other fellows – he half-recalled they might have been Indians [natives] – came up one morning with three teams of horses and wagons for the wheat and got loaded up – two tons in each wagon. Mrs. O'Keefe had sent them with lunches, but Grandma wasn't going to hear of these guys *sitting out in the yard eating lunches – she had them in for dinner – and a couple of days later a letter from Old Mrs. O'Keefe came along thanking Grandma for her hospitality. They probably ate their lunches on the way home.*

Dad told me he and Tierney were somewhere around the same age, so I always pictured Tierney at the time of the story in at least mid-teens. It wasn't until Tierney died that I had occasion to see his dates, and I realized that he must have been ten years old! Now, of course, some people said, "Well, that was nothing. You can drive a team of horses when you're ten." Of course, you can, but Dad never deemed it important enough to mention – it was never part of his story. Dad himself would then have been twelve, coming thirteen, and Tierney just a boy, but to Dad, Tierney was here with two help-ers. It's interesting what a society expects people of a certain age to do.

I was talking to Bill Whitehead one day about getting the farm work done, and he said, "I suppose the boys can help you now." And I said, "Yes, Ian is quite a help this year – I got him baling hay." I was working in the field too, and I'd told Ian, "If something goes wrong, just stop the tractor." Well, he did real well at it, so I said to Bill, "Yes, he was quite a help. He did a lot." And Bill said to me, "How old is he?" "He's fourteen." "Well,…." And I knew exactly what he was thinking: 'He's fourteen now, he's a man, he should *be able to do a day's work!'*

Today's culture is different. Yet it's amazing what some people have done at a young age. Cam Clayton tells this story about his grandfather: Old Frank Clayton, the founder of the machine shop, had a saying that there were too many feet <u>under</u> the table for the amount of food <u>on</u> the table, so at age thirteen he picked up and moved out – and he'd been on his own ever since. There were opportunities, of course, in those days. You could always get a job on a farm – you got room and board – $30 a month was big wages – $15 was more usual. Life expectancy was also a factor in the early assumption of adult responsibilities. *Start young because you end young. You just have to* *wander the Lansdowne Cemetery to see the graves of the infants.*

There's a lot of history in a cemetery. When you get to the point that you know more people in the cemetery than you do on the street, then it's a sign you've been around a long time. I walked Highland Park Cemetery with Dad a lot – I didn't marry until later, so I was at home longer and worked the farm with him. Now I can ramble around the cemetery in the summer and look at the stones of people long past in time and remember hearing his stories about them. Sometimes I see a stone and say to myself, 'I thought that person was still alive.' Then there are others whose deaths I hear about, and it's a shock to learn they're about ten years younger than I am right now! I've had those moments too.

Annie Elizabeth McKechnie predeceased her husband by seventeen years and is buried in this cemetery. *Grandma died in 1948 when I was not quite four, and I'm left wondering if I actually remember the incident or if I was told about it. I vaguely recall lying on a sack in the backyard when the hearse came to get her. I didn't even identify it with Grandma – I just remember it driving across the yard to the house.*

While she had her health, the McKechnies did some travelling. *Grandpa and Grandma got in the habit of going to California in the winter. One of Grandpa's schoolmates from Toronto lived in Fresno, and they bunked in with him. I can remember Grandpa talking about the oranges – how big they are right off the tree – and one year he packed a bunch of them home to us. They were bigger than we were used to, but he said they'd shrunk since they'd been picked. One thing he said you didn't talk about in California is the weather. The weather is the same yesterday, today, and tomorrow. You want to go on a picnic? One day is as good as another – it's always sunny.*

In 1930 they went on a trip to the eastern Mediterranean and up through the Dardanelles. I remember him telling me about a cane that he bought off a street pedlar in Istanbul. He didn't really want it – he just made the mistake of asking the guy what he wanted for it. Grandpa kept walking along, the fellow making offers, until they got back to the boat, and the guy said, "Oh, you're a poor man, you take it!" and he hung the cane over Grandpa's arm. So he bought it. I remember recounting this to Dad just after Grandpa died, and Dad said, "You take the cane because you heard the story."

Born in 1944, Craig's early memories are of a neighbourhood that had remained fairly static over a long period. When the McKechnies arrived on Round Prairie, the three-quarter section to the west had been neatly divided into forty-eight ten-acre lots – three rows of sixteen lots each.

It was done around 1910 for fruit-growing, but in Round Prairie it's heavy clay [not sand], and with the exception of the bit up on the hill where Maw's and Hitt's farms are, it's not fruit-growing land. So over the years these ten-acre lots were dispersed as farmland, and forty years ago the whole 480 acres was held by a few people. We own three of the lots, and Bigler had four. Four men had seven lots each: Swanson, LeDuc, Duncan, and Horn – he farmed here about thirty-five years. Bosomworth bought Horn's place in the '50s and farmed Duncan's place, and then he owned that too for a time. The rest were ten and twenty acres.

Ron Heal said one time that he never saw any place like Round Prairie for everybody knowing what everybody else was doing. It was just the geography – a saucer with no trees. If you opened your eyes you could see what Swanson or Bosomworth or LeDuc was doing. You certainly knew everybody too. And everybody was farming. They may also have had another job – they probably had to in order to survive. Even so, they probably had a cow or two, some pigs and chickens, produced a little bit – some asparagus, or whatever they were raising. At least they were producing something for themselves – they had endeavours going on that were farming activities. Everyone helped out a bit – there were sharing arrangements: Duncan and Landon owned a manure spreader together; we owned one with Shepherd.

Forty years ago there used to be no one living on the flat. I look out of the front room now and the whole of Round Prairie is back into ten-acre lots. In 1954 there were ten houses. Today [2006] there are forty-one. As the demand for land has increased, suddenly every ten-acre lot has a house on it, except for Neil Bosomworth, who has [only] three houses on nine of these lots, continues to farm, and is up to about the same number of years as acres. And that's part of the change that comes with the times – there's a whole mass of people out on Round Prairie now that I don't know, and the real tragedy is, I don't have much contact. You don't lean across the fence and talk to people as you used to. Neighbours used to have farming in common. *Nowadays most people keep a few horses or something, and that's about it.*

I've driven the school bus on a spare-time basis for thirty years now, and sometimes I think, 'What are we running this bus for? It's only half full.' The reason is that if everybody who was entitled to ride the bus got on, it would *be full, but since everybody has one or both parents going to town, the kids go to town with them. So you've got this dilemma – a fluid population. But in 1970 Dad could still say, "I can stand out there on Round Prairie and look around, and after fifty years I'm still a newcomer." Maw, Docksteader, Hitt, Harris, Landon – people that he knew – had been there much longer than he.*

In addition to Round Prairie, a map of the Township of Spallumcheen, June, 1922, indicates ten-acre lot sizes on each side of Schubert Road between Dodds Road and Ford Road, and to a lesser degree east of McKechnie's and north of the city boundary. Craig uses this map to locate the neighbours whom his family knew, or knew of, when he was a youth. The earliest property owner that Craig recalls is named first, and the names of some, not all, subsequent owners are bracketed. The accompanying sketches at the beginning of the chapter are *interpretive* only, not drawn to scale.

[See Map 1.] Landon *was our next-door neighbour to the east and arrived in 1919, just the year before our family did. Nelson*

Landon came into the country in 1910. He was the manager of the De Hart Ranch, which was A.L. Fortune's place. He lived in the old Fortune house, and the new Fortune house, where the Heals live now [1042 Fortune Road], was next door. Mr. Fortune used to take the Landon kids to Sunday school. Farther east, Grant Thompson *lived west of the cemetery and owned another piece off Sleepy Hollow Road. In the 1950s as I recall, he had a hatchery – Rhode Island Reds. He had an incubator in the basement of the house – not too many chickens by today's standards, but still his business.* Fred Hanna *lived across the road to the southeast of us. I think Mrs. Hanna was a cousin of John Shepherd's.* Shepherd *was farther east south of Sleepy Hollow Road, and* Sarrell *owned land south of him. Sarrell retired in the '50s and eventually Shepherd owned the whole block here.* Mat. Hassen *was on the corner of Young Road and Highland Park Road, and* McKeen *was immediately north.* Art Howard *was east of Hassen and south of Young Road,* Eric and Rich Williamson *had farms north of Young Road, and the* W. McNair *family owned several properties east to Lansdowne Road along with the earliest packing house in town. Melvin McNair was the chief farmer.*

[See Map 2.] The McKechnie farm fronted on Round Prairie. *At the bottom of the first row of lots immediately west of us and south of Dodds Road,* Carl Jennings *owned the first twenty acres and* Hyde, *the next ten – he came in the '50s.* Duncan *had thirty acres. The next four lots out there in the centre we always referred to as the* Billy Orr *place even though he died in the 1930s and it was bought by* Bigler *and later passed to* Al Smith, *his son-in-law. After Billy Orr died, Dad said that he was in town one day and Sage, the under-taker, spoke about him. He said, "Billy Orr belonged to a group of people vanishing from the face of the earth – those who paid their bills and minded their own business."*

Dad took a photo of Billy Orr's headstone and sent it to Billy's niece in Scotland because Grandpa and Grandma had visited her on their trip in 1930. Dad had bought a camera at the drugstore in the 1920s. Three cameras were on display. "What's the difference?" "Well," the fellow said, "you can drive to Vernon in a Chevrolet, a

Buick, or a Cadillac – they'll all get you there." So Dad bought the
Buick.

First Dodds *and later his companion* Mrs. Shaw *owned twenty
acres north of Billy Orr. North again lay the* Schubert Field, *which
Grandpa bought from Gus Schubert, and a further twenty acres
which Dad bought in 1942 from* Akitt. *He was a minister and had
been a schoolmate of my grandmother McKechnie; she rediscovered
him when she moved here. The ten acres immediately south of Dodds
Road was occupied by several owners.* Judd Bullis *lived there in the
'20s. Bullis was the engineer in the country. He dug the basement
for the Consolidated School – moved several buildings around. But
in my memory* Clarence Teward *bought that property in the 1950s.*

West of Round Prairie Road lay the second row of ten-acre lots.
Neil Bosomworth, *who owned seventy acres here, worked for the
Pea Growers and grew seed, told this story: A lot of hand weeding
was necessary to keep the plants clean, and he had hired Mrs. Shaw
and others to do the job. Mr. Steve Heal, Senior, the owner of the Pea
Growers, came out one day to see how things were going. It came
time for tea, and everybody quit weeding except Mrs. Shaw. He said
to her, "Aren't you going to have some tea?" And she said, "I was
paid to pull weeds, not drink tea!" She had a strong work ethic and
a voice to go with it. She may have had rickets in her youth because
she walked bowlegged. I never saw her doing farm work in anything
other than a dress – even to coiling hay.* Duncan *owned the forty
acres below Bosomworth, and the bottom five lots were owned by*
Dolly Swanson *and farmed by her brothers as part of the Swanson
place. Swansons were the big landowners.*

Immediately east of Salmon River Road was the third row of
lots. *The* Swanson *brothers had the bottom two lots that adjoined
the Swanson farm. The next ten acres in my day belonged to* Cail.
Gus LeDuc, *the youngest son of Rose Schubert and Tom LeDuc,
owned the seventy acres north of Cail, and the top sixty acres belonged to* Sid Hitt. *Across Salmon River Road, Hitt had bought
out* Chapple, *who had enlarged his place with twenty acres bought*

from Willis Hunter. *A son-in-law of Sid Hitt,* Lester Babb, *lived on the old Wilson place, now* Art Cayford. *The Hopkins property belonged to* Schultz. *Their neighbour to the north of Hallam Road was* Docksteader. *Docksteaders were there before 1910. My mother remembered Old Man Docksteader in the '20s hauling wood to them in town. Edgar Docksteader was his grandson, and after his death the farm came to Ted, who sold the place just a few years ago.* Floyd Hunter, *the brother of Willis, was Docksteader's neighbour to the east. In my earliest memory, in 1952 Floyd sold to* Bob Svenson *and moved to town. Svensons were there for fifty-three years until they sold out in 2005.*

[See Map 3.] *North of Dodds Road,* N.A. Gates *is Frank Gates's father. Like all Gateses, Old Gates was a blacksmith. Grandma told Dad one time that Grandpa took a ploughshare up to Gates to be sharpened, and she sat in the car and watched. He charged Grandpa fifty cents, and Grandma's comment was, "Boy, that was a lot of work for fifty cents!"* Petar *had the piece north of him, and later in my time it was Dora Petar's place. When she died, her nephew* Donald Louttit *bought it. Just east of Petar,* Colin Harris *had his ten acres. His daughter Jean (Harris) Gill has lived here now for eighty-six years. I remember Dad saying she won the Cutest Baby competition in the [Armstrong] Fair in 1920, the year we came. Colin reported, "As soon as the judge announced it, he ran away because he didn't want to face the other mothers!"*

Despite gravel roads and bush trails, connections among early settlers survived time and distance. *There was a family called* Stevens *moved in up on Knob Hill for about ten years in the twenties and early thirties. A.H. Stevens had originally come from Scotland after the First War and lived in Summerland and New Zealand. That's where he met his wife – she was Australian – and they ended up here. They had an orchard and Depression times were tough, so they returned to New Zealand. When I was on holiday in New Zealand in 1971, I went to visit Mrs. Stevens because she used to write to Gertie Louttit, our next-door neighbour, and I got her name.*

34

I was the first person to come from Canada to see her. She was eighty-six and staying in a seniors' complex on her own. We had a great visit. Her eyesight was poor, and she sat up real close looking at me for family resemblance. She had a little autograph book that had been passed around here at a farewell party, and she said she'd never let anyone else write in it. So we sat on the couch that day and I read out the names in the book – people in the whole Knob Hill area and round about – and we reminisced about them. It was kind of fascinating because a lot of them had died before I was born, but I knew stories connected with them and where they lived.

Knob Hill School, *later* Knob Hill Hall, *was on the corner of Ford Road and Salmon River Road. Dodd's Road to the south represented a type of boundary: south of Dodd's Road the residents associated themselves with the town people, and north of it they felt closer to Knob Hill settlers; for example,* Raymond Hitt, *on Schubert Road north of us, talks about Christmas parties at Knob Hill Hall whereas we were more associated with the town. When our family first came in 1920, Dad had the option of attending school at Knob Hill or in town. Knob Hill School closed the next year when the Consolidated School opened.*

Our water comes from the J.J. Armstrong *place, formerly* Tilton, *on Crawford Road.* Nigel Rees *still owns it. North of him* W.E. Phillips *owned the* Mason *property too. Phillips is a grandfather of Eric Hornby. Then the place was sold to* Atkinson, *and, a couple of owners later, to* Kirschner, *who came in the very late '50s.*

S. Branton *bought* L.E. Farr*'s place west of Knob Hill Road in the '30s.* Tom Yetten *was just ten acres in the corner of it. I remember a couple that lived there in the 1950s –* Ewing *was the name – they knew Mother and Dad through the church – and I still remember the old house – a wood heater in the living room. It was probably a cold old hole, really, but cozy as long as you were close to the stove.* Petar *owned the property north of Ewing.*

I remember talking to Mrs. Stevens about Charlie Webster, *who*

*had an apple orchard on his place north of Petar. Apparently he stut-
tered quite badly. Oh, yes, Mrs. Stevens knew Charlie. He used to
stop in on his way home. One time when he came she had visitors,
and she introduced them as Gotobed, an English name. Charlie had
never run across it. She went outside with him when he left – he
didn't stay long – and he was laughing and stuttering at the same
time because the name totally cracked him up. She said, "I can hear
him laughing yet as he was going out the gate."*

To the east of the old Ford *place, were two farms:* Donovan
Clemson *in the south; and north of him* W. Parker, *who sold to* Fred
and Eileen Mitchell.

[See Map 4.] *Willis Hunter's neighbour to the west was* H.S.
Maw *who was up the hill along the base of Swanson Mountain.
North of Maw, Dad spoke of* W.S. Cooke, *who was associated in
the early twenties with* E. Poole *in the packing house east of the
flour mill; in my time* Kenny Smith *was on the Cooke property. Mrs.
Kenny Smith was a Hunter, and their daughter is Mrs. Nigel Rees.
North of Hallam Road* Alex Crawford *owned a large property. Mrs.
Art Maw and Mrs. Gus LeDuc were Crawfords. Around 1950* Ternier
bought the Crawford place.

*Where Caravan Stage Company is presently located north
of Matheson Road,* Pehota *was an early resident of Armstrong
Spallumcheen. They were there in the '20s and came in earlier
[1910]. Old Man Pehota got busted one time during Prohibition for
making wine and selling to the Indians [natives], which was taboo.
So he spent a little time in the lock-up and reported it was the most
fun he'd ever had. He'd been put in charge of making loganberry
wine! I remember Dad said he went to see Charlie Pehota [son]
about something – the only time he was ever into the place. You
had to go down the driveway and the house was in the back. He
didn't see anybody – got out of the car – and thought, 'What a place
to have a still!' Then Charlie appeared: "I guess you're wondering where my land is." And Dad had to catch himself because he
wasn't thinking of that at all! Charlie and Martha were characters*

– brother and sister. Martha provided the *Armstrong Advertiser* with unofficial weather reports.

I remember Jack Jamieson saying he had some acquaintance in the newspaper business from Toronto visiting his office one day. The first person who walked in was Ralph Rosoman. He wanted to know when the paper was due. You remember Ralph? He had a loud voice and an unusual gait, and he toted a burlap bag over his shoulder to hold the bottles and cans he picked up along the road. Not long after he left, in came Martha Pehota announcing the weather because she had just read a pig spleen. The visitor from Toronto was mesmerized.

As new houses and new faces proliferated, the community modernized. *In this day and age you've got to have specific addresses for the fire department. You can't say, "Well, I'm out here somewhere north of town." As I remember, in the '60s roads received proper names. Earlier, where roads started and stopped was more variable. Some roads had no names at all – others were nicknamed by the local people.* [See Maps 3 and 4.] *For example, I grew up on Hullcar Road. Our old address – if there was an address at all – would show as Hullcar Road because the road we lived on went north to Hullcar, and a lot of traffic came along that way. Now we live on Schubert Road. Schubert Road used to be just the little piece within the City limits.*

I still think of Salmon River Road as Knob Hill Road. Today Salmon River Road runs all the way from downtown, and Knob Hill Road is just the stretch between Knob Hill School and Hullcar Hall.

Kenny Matheson had a little bit of trouble with his road. We saw Matheson Road as running roughly from the Matheson place all along the base of Hullcar Mountain to Hullcar Hall. When that road was renamed Hullcar Road, Matheson Road ended up being just the little bit from Salmon River Road to the junction. And since most of it passes outside the municipality through Indian reserve, these resi-

dents have added a second signboard on it – Williams Road. Kenny Matheson was the son of Donald Matheson, who was the first president of the Armstrong Fair and died in a buggy accident one night going home from a meeting in town. It was a long trip.

[See Maps 1 and 2.] When they named the road past the cemetery, they called it Cemetery Road. I remember when they were putting up the sign, Dad said, "That's the last road!" But then somebody decided they didn't want to live on 'Cemetery Road' so the name was dropped, and that piece became an extension of Highland Park Road.

Dodds Road was an obvious choice – Dodds lived on it and had been there a long time. For sleigh riding we always referred to it as Dodds Hill. Then there was the road south of Dodds. What are you going to call that one? Horn Road? Duncan Road might be more appropriate, as he owned land on both sides of it. So they solved the problem by calling it Round Prairie Road because it runs right down the middle of Round Prairie.

Some roads were broken in early days to solve topographical problems. Crawford Road was just a trail people used to avoid the steep hill on Knob Hill at the Phillips property. Horse traffic don't want steep hills, so this road follows the contour and has less grade. If Dad was going west, he'd use this road – if he was going north, he'd use Hullcar Road. About forty years ago they straightened the piece that caused the trouble on Knob Hill but didn't bother getting rid of the hill, as it wasn't a problem for motorcars.

Some roads disappeared altogether. A lady lived up at the corner of Parkinson Road and Salmon River Road – what we called Coleman's Corner – and I remember Dad driving her home along a trail called Lodgepole Road [See Map 4], but if you drive up there now, you won't find it. It's a road allowance but the road isn't there. Another road allowance extends east from the end of Dodds Road along the back of our property, but that road's not there either. Jack Heal once made some reference to Pineridge Road. I'd never heard *of it. I finally twigged that Heal had owned property along Ford Road in the '30s and the family had given it the name. Pineridge Road is now Ford Road, and Pineridge Road is to be found off Larkin X-Road.*

If street and road maintenance was important in the early days, so was attention to the weather. Settlers spent a good deal of time living with and outwitting by strenuous labour the effects of a variable climate. For example, living arrangements on the McKechnie farm in its early decades included cutting ice in winter for refrigeration. *The icehouse was right beside the old shop, and they hauled ice from Otter Lake. I remember Dad saying how great it was when they put through the section of Otter Lake Road between Fraser Road and Wood Avenue [1928]. Coming from Otter Lake on the level saved the horses' pulling a load of ice on a sleigh up the hill on Fraser Road.* The incline on Fraser Road was steep but short enough for the team with encouragement to manage the weight. Schubert Road's long, venomous tilt was another matter. *They just couldn't pull the whole load up the hill. You'd have to unload half of the ice at the bottom of the hill, drive up the hill, take the remaining half off, go back down and get the other half, drive up the hill again and reload the sleigh.* Time, patience, strong backs, and gritty horses supplied the essential mix.

Unlike the farming community, people in town had some access to electricity generated from the powerhouse on Fortune Creek. At times of low water, or the cost involved in running the generator, service might be discontinued between eleven at night and six in the morning. The story is told of a frantic telephone call to the powerhouse late one evening from the site of a local card game: "For god's sake don't turn off the power yet – I'm playing for a big pot!"

Rural electrification in the district didn't happen until 1948, but Grandpa had it brought to the farm about 1930. At the time the line came up from town in the Highland Park area and stopped just past the cemetery. The agreement was he would pay ten dollars a month for the next five years – and then he talked it down to nine dollars by supplying the poles and digging the holes. The poles he got from Deep Creek, and he and the boys did the digging. I remember Dad saying the holes had to be two feet square and five feet deep, and it was two-thirds of a mile to the house. Today they use fewer poles and string the wire farther.

Since Grandpa had to pay nine dollars a month whether he used that amount of electricity or not, he bought a combination electric-wood stove. It had the regular electric elements, baking oven and warming oven, but the chimney wrapped around a second baking oven, and the whole thing could heat the house – we used it for years. Grandpa didn't have a refrigerator then, but Dad had built a cooler room on the house, and they had an icebox. The principle for both units was essentially the same. *The cooler room was well insulated – you made sure the doors were kept closed – and it had shelving to hold whatever you wanted to keep cool. The ice sat on a tray near the ceiling and melted into a trough that could hold four milk cans, and then the overflow drained away outside. The icebox was just a box in the kitchen that held ice in a compartment on top, and it melted down between the walls and kept things cool inside.* However, you had to remember to empty the water occasionally from the drain pan.

In the late forties the Ice Age passed. I vaguely remember digging about the last block of ice we cut, since at Christmas time, 1948, we got a refrigerator, and that year Dad also built a deep-freeze. People 'round here will know what that means because Raymond Hitt has one in his basement, Neil Bosomworth has one in the old house, and Maw has one. You built the box – 50 cubic feet – but the refrigeration unit, insulation and shelving had to be bought. That thing cost him $600!

The weather too was making natural ice unpredictable. *The Curling Club got artificial ice around 1954 saying they'd never be able to curl otherwise. The winter of 1956-57 when I was in grade 7, I joined the Curling Club at school. I would never have gone myself – I was never a forward person – but my brother David was a joiner and he had played the year before and talked about it. I was the only grade 7 kid on a team with grade 13s – the last year they had grade 13 here – all classmates of my brother John. So they knew who I was, of course – "John's younger brother." I was put on a team with Wayne Smith, Donna Duggan, and Lenore Hitt. But when the bonspiel came along in the spring, Wayne Smith had quit school, and I was transferred to Jack Lee's team. (Jack was the third youngest of Lee Bak Bong's eleven children.) We curled Saturday mornings in the Curling Club – somebody must have opened the door for us – there wasn't any teacher around – no sponsor, just the kids. There was no heat – we'd light up the wood stove. In that vintage it was no big deal – everybody knew how to light a fire. There were no washrooms in the building either – but in the daytime if you had to go, you used the washroom in the back of Frank Harrison's grocery store south of the Armstrong Hotel. I don't remember there being a rush on – we survived somehow.*

Then when I was in grade 8, the Curling Club decided they didn't want high school kids curling, so we played in the Open league. At that time curling teams played nightly games twice a week, and the nights varied depending on the schedule. For high school students this system presented a problem. *So what we did was this – we had two teams acting as one team in the league, and one night four of us would play, and the second night the other four would play. I can remember me and Richy Landon – he was two years older – walking into town at night for the nine o'clock draw and walking home at eleven. But the next year wiser heads at the Curling Club prevailed – if they wanted to keep curling alive, they had to let the kids play. So when I was in grade 9, a lot of players joined, but only the small group of us had any experience. I discovered I was now a skip. Once again I was the youngest person on my team.* But with a difference. *I skipped my team for the next four years.*

In my grade 7 year we did have natural ice in the arena, but never after that in my school time. I was looking in the Weather Book – we've recorded weather here since the 1920s – and to note those temperatures for the late '50s was really interesting, as I remember Dad saying we could never make ice – it wasn't cold enough. We talk about mild winters now, but they were mild too. And there was certainly no ice until 1968-69 when it was really cold and there was ice all winter here. So for those years before 1968, there was a mild spell with lots of snow.

The Weather Books are a series of narrow ledgers that were dispensed by the federal department of agriculture to record temperature and precipitation. They were titled *Canadian Monthly Meteorological Service Illustration Stations*, the name of the operator and the station to be filled in appropriately. The McKechnie Weather Books are a source of factual information about local weather over eighty years – 1926 to the present – and are currently being used by the provincial department of the environment in a water and ground water survey of the Deep Creek water basin. *They are like diaries – recorded every day as opposed to looking back thirty or forty years and recalling what your memory tells you.* Each page allowed space for one month's temperature and precipitation and was written in duplicate. *We used carbon paper. Each month we sent in the white copy and the yellow copy remained in the ledger.*

At one point I went through the Weather Books and made a chart of the precipitation over the years. We went through cycles – something like a cycle of fifteen to twenty years' dry weather and then a change. It was dry in the '30s. The farm had enough water – not in abundance – but they knew to look after it. I remember hearing them talking that 1942 was a wet year – what stuck in their mind was they lost hay that year – it got rained on heavily in July. My memories of growing up in the '50s is hot and dry in summer. Then as you come into the '60s, we had a lot of wet years. I well remember that '64 was wet. It rained three inches a month in June, July, August and September. It just went on... and on... and on.... It was a nightmare for haying. The Swansons sold out. Doug Swanson was sixty-four and Harry, about seventy, and they were farming around 250 acres over there. They'd been struggling along but the summer of 1964 finished them. They just couldn't cope and moved downtown.

We hayed the whole time and everything got rained on. The hay was tough and the grain was tough. Mud everywhere. We packed it in. In my diary I've got a note: "Hauled in the last of the hay today. Burnt it." October came on nice. Grain harvest got finished. They brought in dryers.

Advice on coping with unseasonable weather was sought and valued. *Jock Patterson told me this story: George Heggie managed Stepney Ranch and later, the L&A Ranch. He lived on the road to Silver Star in an older house just past Butcher Boys store. When he retired, Jock Patterson took over managing the L&A Ranch and during his first winter on the job he began worrying about the fall wheat. He had sown a lot of it, and that winter of 1941-42 had very little snow – only about eleven inches. You always worried about winterkill, and Jock had the opportunity of looking at his bare fields all winter! So he went in to see George. Jock said he never forgot his advice: "The time to worry about your wheat is in April when you can do something about it. If it's there, fine; if it isn't, work it up and plant barley."*

Although the Schubert family figured largely in the McKechnies' early history, the Wilsons, Craig's maternal relations, knew them too. John Halfpenny Wilson, his wife, Alice, and their baby daughter Lily had moved to Armstrong Spallumcheen from Manitoba in 1910 and lived in town.

Old Gus Schubert was dead by this time, but my mother [Lily] remembered Catherine Schubert as an old lady sitting on the porch of a house on Railway Avenue [Pleasant Valley Road] where she lived, the present Brown Derby Café [3425]. Her daughter Nora and her husband, Harry Fraser, lived in a house on Mill Street where the police station is now. Harry Fraser taught school and was mayor of the town for a while. When they had their 50th wedding anniversary, Mother went down for the occasion and Mrs. Fraser said to her, "What do you do with that room on the east side of the house?" Well, in my time we didn't use it for much. It was a big room – 12 feet by 24 – Dad had an office at one end. Mother said, well, actu-

ally, she'd just been cleaning it that morning. And Mrs. Fraser said, "That's where we were married."

John Halfpenny Wilson's biography in the local history *Historic Armstrong and its Street Names* reads like a saga of Scottish fervour and unshakeable purpose. His diaries, a full page for every day, reveal that despite precarious health he was a doer in both church and state. Entries refer to church governance, city council meetings, civic organizations such as the Red Cross and the hospital board, family outings, social interests and, from 1928 to 1953, the business of his packing house. *Grandpa McKechnie wrote diaries in fits and starts – he wrote in doctor longhand, which makes exciting reading! But Grandpa Wilson began in 1919 and wrote up till he died in 1956.* His handwriting is spare and clear. *As a general rule he was very discreet in what he wrote – he skirted some topics – alluded to circumstances but didn't name names – and steered away from other topics altogether.*

From the time of his arrival in the area, Wilson was employed with the fruit and vegetable packing industry. *Grandpa Wilson first worked for Jean Williamson's grandfather, William McNair, who had a large packing house west of the flour mill on the spur line west of Okanagan Street and a second packing house in Ashcroft. McNair shipped mainly potatoes and wheat, and bought from growers around Kamloops, Monte Creek, and Malakwa. They'd grade the vegetables when they came in and load boxcars on the sidings. Grandpa's next job was as manager of the Armstrong Growers Exchange on the north side of Railway Avenue [later the BC Pea Growers site], and then in 1928 he went out on his own.*

Born in 1915, Mat. S. Hassen recalls the J.H. Wilson packing house as a grey [block] building located along Railway Avenue west of McDonald's packing house and almost directly opposite the train station. He says, *The east end of his building reached about the middle of the station. The stockyards were located [first] between Wilson's and McDonald's and later moved east to the junction of the CNR [Canadian National Railway] and CPR [Canadian*

Pacific Railway]. The coal sheds for local consumption were east of McDonald's. The seal of the Armstrong Growers Exchange [where Wilson worked] was in our [insurance] office for years after the organization became defunct.

In assessing the contribution of packing houses to the economy of Armstrong Spallumcheen, Craig McKechnie takes a moderate view. *The packing house business was vibrant in its day. The story we hear, though, is of five or six packing houses operating in the district at the same time and all running... busy... busy... busy... but I don't think it was that way at all – they tended to come and go. They didn't work all the time, you know, maybe shipped only a couple of times a week. [At some point] once you got over the seasonal rush, the orders were divvied out, and some were working and others weren't.*

Grandpa couldn't do physical labour – he had the Spanish Flu in 1919 and basically it wiped him out. He lived three doors down from the Anglican Church. His diaries state he always drove a car from home to the office, and it was a crisis in winter when the car wouldn't start. At that time the printing office was in the OK Garage building on Railway Avenue [Pleasant Valley Boulevard] – he'd have to stop in and talk to Jamieson – he couldn't reach the office without a rest. It was a five-minute walk.

At the time of the flu epidemic, Dr. McKechnie was practising medicine in Vancouver. *Grandpa McKechnie used to say, "If the war didn't get you, the flu did. More people died of the flu than had died in the war. It seemed to be the bigger and stronger you were, the faster you went down. Somebody would come home from work able-bodied at 5 p.m. and you'd carry them out at 8 o'clock the next morning." He saw it in so many houses where, incredibly, one person was still in good shape and looking after everyone else. He himself would have been past the usual age to get sick – apparently age eighteen to twenty-five was the dangerous period. Dad was ten and got it, but it was nothing – his brother Ian was fifteen and even that was okay.*

But Grandpa Wilson's health took a beating. I remember Mother saying one time he was shipping potatoes for McNair somewhere in the Kamloops area and came back by train to Salmon Arm. One of the McNair boys picked him up and brought him home quite late at night and he was sick. Grandma didn't know he was comin'. They were living on Patterson Avenue at the time across the street from their later home. And Mother said that because he was sick, Grandma put him in the spare bedroom in the back of the house, which wasn't heated, and Mother always felt guilty they hadn't given him her room instead. But there was no cure – you just lived with it. Some diary entries tell of his having to give up curling because he had no strength to sweep; other entries mourn various unsuccessful treatments of his afflicted kidneys until eventually Dodd's Kidney Pills were his only recourse.

The diaries tell a story of life in the early community of Armstrong Spallumcheen; in particular, the yearly routine in a packing house. Filling orders for vegetables and fruit meant creating relationships with growers and wholesalers, hiring men to build crates and load boxcars within a specified time frame, storing tons of vegetables at the packing house in anticipation of sales, and pre-ordering fertilizer, seed, waxed paper, and sacks from various sources for both his business and growers. At the local level a key concern was competition from other packing houses in town. *Who were the shippers Grandpa mentions in his diaries? Wong Chog was a grower and shipper on his own land down by the stockyards (that dates me!) at the junction of the CP and CN Railway. McDonald's packing house was just west of Mill Street – he specialized mainly in the express business. He went to the Prairies in winter and rounded up orders for fruit and vegetables.* His clever specialty for the treeless prairie towns was fragrant bundles of cedar branches for Christmas decorations. *Cuthbert grew vegetables where Highland Park School is now – his packing house was named Fairfield Ranch and was located on the west end of the present Pellet Plant property; Poole's packing house was on the east end with Hoover's Inland Flour Mill [Buckerfield's in 1946] separating the two; Landers was from Vernon and I'd never heard of him until I read the diaries.* Competition from growers in the Prairies, the Lower Mainland, and the United States, however, would become a larger problem.

In the following entries from the year 1938, excerpted phrases or summaries may replace Mr. Wilson's complete sentences; occasional references to 1939 augment seasonal information, and author's italics draw attention to the weather. Notations from 1938 illustrate that, except for asparagus, the growing season was a disaster. The summer was a scorcher and no rain fell for months. Competition for shipping business was soured further by the Depression that had dragged on for nearly a decade. Jobless men rode the trains into town looking for work. As a new city alderman, Wilson had the thankless task of dispensing local welfare relief. In the 1930s the Japanese occupation of China dismayed local Chinese, who had relatives back home. Early omens pointed to a bad year:

Wed.Jan.5.	Ice sweating badly last night making [curling] difficult.
Fri.Jan.7.	Some berry growers are insisting that I go into the berry business this year and handle their tonnage; I am reluctant, as this commodity usually brings considerable grief [spoilage].
Wed.Jan.12.	Attended a league hockey game tonight between Vernon and Armstrong.While Vernon is the better team [9 to 2], the same old spirit prevails; that is, to win at any cost, even at the expense of serious bodily harm.
Tue.Jan.18.	Went to Vernon by CP Passenger, had lunch at the National [Hotel], then put in three hours with the boys in Associated Growers' office. Green celery continues to be taboo with the trade.
Thu.Jan.27.	Wild geese have been observed going north, the earliest in fifty years.
[Jan.28/39]:	Signed CN lease for another year – my thirteenth year.

CN Railway acquired land for a turn-around on the west side of Armstrong. After CN made a deal with CP Railway for joint use of the existing CP rail line to Vernon with a CN extension to Kelowna that CP could use, CN Railway no longer needed a turn-around and leased the land to Grandpa Wilson. [See Map 5.] The lease was bounded on the west by Otter Lake Road and on the north by Wood Avenue. The eastern boundary stretched past Adair Street to include a slice of the west end of the present fairgrounds, the current sewage lagoons, and the bottomlands east of Deep Creek; and the southern boundary began just past the termination of Rosedale Avenue West and ran west. Grandpa rented to several Chinese market gardeners. Renting his CN lease guaranteed that Wilson had vegetables for shipping, as the terms of the rental agreement included shipping through his packing house.

Although vegetable production was usually hand labour, horsepower could be useful. *One of Grandpa Wilson's renters was Harry Lee. (His Chinese name was Lee Sing.) He lived near the corner of Otter Lake Road and farmed a large piece between Otter Lake Road and Deep Creek. Lee was Dad's age – a nephew of Lee Bak Bong. Harry Lee came up one time to borrow a horse to cultivate his crop, and the only one we had was Diamond – our last workhorse – lively – somewhat wild, in fact, as he'd been ridden as a cattle horse too when Ralph Flanders had him. Dad asked Harry, "You know how to drive a horse?" "Oh, yeah, yeah...," and Dad sent him off on Diamond. Dad said, "I knew when he was leavin', this didn't look too good!" Sure enough, it wasn't too long before Diamond arrived back, and that was the end of the cultivating. The horse had taken off on him.*

The Chinese renters lived in cabins on the land. Accommodation was basic. *On one of these leased lots, the house burned down. Grandpa's diary noted that carpenters had started building a new cabin for his Chinaman "today," and it should be finished "tomorrow."*

| Tue.Feb.1. | Commenced putting away our ice today [cut from Otter Lake], and it is lovely and clear, fourteen-inch-thick blocks weighing 170 to 200 lbs. [Wilson noted that produce shippers alone required several hundred tons to ice boxcars.] |
| Thu.Feb.10-12. | Almost sold out of lettuce seed today. Had to order additional seed, and many growers have not yet been supplied. The bulk of the seed |

business is coming my way. Chinese gardeners commencing to make hotbeds within the next week.

In January and February Dad would supply Harry Lee and Louie Chin with horse manure for their hotbeds. They wanted horse manure because it's hot, I guess. I remember my brother John telling a story about the time he went back east on a 4-H trip and the group visited a mushroom farm. They used horse manure to grow the mushrooms, and as the horse population decreased, they had a problem. Then they discovered that turkey manure worked well, so now they were in the mushroom and turkey business. They grew their own manure.

A well-respected Chinese market gardener, Louie Chin came to Armstrong in 1912 and grew vegetables and tended two greenhouses for W.A. Cuthbert on his Fairfield Ranch on Wood Avenue. Louie Chin remained employed at this location under two subsequent owners, Edward Poole and Vance Young, and in the 1950s he purchased land on Wood Avenue opposite City Hall. He later owned a larger acreage on Powerhouse Road and retired at eighty-eight. When he and Mrs. Chin in 1968 moved to Vancouver to be close to family, their old friends, such as, Mat. S. Hassen and Craig McKechnie, stopped to visit. Chin died at 101.

Mon.Feb.14.   Order for straight car mixed vegetables for Feb. 21 called for 12-15 tons parsnips but only 6½ tons available. May make weight with carrots. Have reshipment order for 30 crates cabbage destination Kelowna. [A reshipment order was redistributed in package sizes different from the original received, or it was an order to replace ostensibly inferior vegetables or fruit that had been shipped earlier.]

Tue.Feb.15.   Price of potatoes dropped another $3 today. Producer price is now $8 per ton. Under the auspices of the Parent Teachers' Association, Paul Lim Yuen, an educated Chinese from Vernon, addressed a large meeting in Armstrong on the Chinese/Japanese undeclared war. Silver collection in aid of Chinese war sufferers.

Fri.Feb.18. Some lettuce plants are already a good size in Comber's Greenhouses [Willowdale Avenue]. These are started extra early and transplanted into flats before being put out in the field. Maturity is reached seven to ten days ahead of seeding in hotbeds.

Sat.Feb.19. After consultation with [Interior] Vegetable Marketing Board, the price of carrots was dropped $4 per ton making the producer price $11 per ton. This was done to assist movement to Vancouver, as the [import] duty is expected to be taken off [shortly].

Tue.Feb.22. No prospect of moving the 6 tons parsnips which I have on hand.

Wed.Feb.23. The Dominion Government is now placing all un-employables on municipalities as a direct charge. Relief in general is a grave problem.

Fri.Feb.25. Ordered my first lettuce paper requirement. Have followed the plan of splitting my business among four different firms.

Mon.Feb.28. Lettuce and celery seed continues to go out.

Wed.Mar.2. At last succeeded in placing an order and will load Friday – parsnips, carrots, beets, and balance of car, apples. Found it necessary to recondition beets we have had in the [packing] house for almost three weeks. Will be glad to see the last of these vegetables.

It [diary] gives some perspective. There were problems in the business. It wasn't just make a sale and carry your money to the bank.

Tue.Mar.8. The Canadian Bag Co. representative called today. The price is very low. Delivery in July.

[Feb.4/39]: Price on bags has advanced considerably because of heavy purchases by the British government for sandbag material. [Threat of war.]

Thu.Mar.10. Wrote *History of Presbyterianism in the [Okanagan] Valley* requested by Presbytery and will show it to Dr. McKechnie to suggest changes.

Sat.Mar.12. [The minister, Mr. Barber, was ill.] Had a phone call from Vernon that the supply [substitute] had not arrived on the CN. I met the CP and spotted the young chap at the Armstrong train station and got him and his baggage back on the train [for Vernon.] It doesn't look promising.

Sun.Mar.13. The young man did remarkably well. He has studied at Knox College but is unable to [return] on account of lack of funds. He had a [field post] last year in Saskatchewan and got no salary. He is now in Vancouver selling fruit and vegetables on commission.

Mon.Mar.14. Ordered fertilizer from Canadian Industries Ltd., and Burns Co. Have also a small order with Buckerfield's. Shipment will arrive at end of month.

Tue.Mar.15. Vancouver finally came through with order for carrots and early seed potatoes. Had no difficulty getting carrots, but the potato grower was out of town. Vancouver has refused to confirm without the potatoes. The shipping game is rather exasperating at times.

Wed.Mar.16. Purchased a ton of seed potatoes from Poole and Co [competitor]. The order calls for two tons. This commodity is scarce.

[Mar.16/39]: Sawmill will be starting up for the season. Over one million feet of logs in the yard and another million hauled in the summer. Creates quite a bit of work.

Fri.Mar.18. Our 30th wedding anniversary. Bought a 1937 Ford De Luxe sedan. Made an offer [including] my old Desoto 8 car. [The newer car gave 19 miles to the gallon; his old one, 10.] *Wind continues at gale force. Hurricane proportions.*

Mon.Mar.21. [Rail]car fertilizer arrived today from Canadian Industries Ltd. in New Westminster. Most of the load will go right out to the growers and thereby save handling.

Sat.Mar.26.   350 tons of potatoes in the district but no prospect of moving them, so white farmers will [likely] buy them for feed.

I remember Dad figuring he could buy potatoes for pig feed at ten bucks a ton, and he was going down in time to get some. His brother Don was visiting and he wouldn't come. He said he wouldn't get involved in any skin game at ten dollars a ton. But that's the way it went then.

Thu.Mar.31.   *Thawing and freezing not good for tree fruits nor fall wheat.*

Fri.Apr.1.   Geo. Dunkley has purchased the Fletcher house next to ours for $1,000.

Thu.Apr.7.   A new tenant in the CN hay lands is making it a little difficult for the Chinamen in the matter of water run-off. However, we may get it straightened out satisfactorily. [Bottomland was subject to flooding.]

[April 10/39 Easter Monday]:

A holiday in town except for the sawmill. Took some flower seeds to our Chinaman [Lee Sing] to grow for us in the hot bed. We do it this way every year... we have better results. Mr. Fraser, Mr. Lancaster and myself went on a prospecting trip around St. Anne's hill and Coyote Creek – one or two leads.

Mon.Apr.25.   First delivery of asparagus. 10 days earlier than a year ago.

Thu.Apr.28.   Five new cases of scarlet fever in one family yesterday. School choirs will not go to the festival at Vernon. [Opening of Lawn Bowling season.] Supper in Foresters' Hall served by the Women's Institute.

Sat.Apr.30.   *Warm weather.* 1,000 lbs of asparagus yesterday and expect more today. Commenced grading for cannery as too much for fresh market. The Women's Institute were most reasonable in their charges. The cost for feeding 18 persons was only 20 cents each, a total of $3.60.

Mon.May 2. Asparagus is coming in quite fast and graders will have to work their full ten hours. [Vernon cannery complained of some open heads.]

Tue.May 3. Over 1,800 lbs asparagus for the cannery today. Largest delivery we ever had.

Fri.May 6. 200 lbs asparagus to Vernon cold storage, and canning begins there on Monday the 9th. [On June 1st Wilson received first returns on asparagus and wrote, "Net to grower is .622 of a cent per lb. Same as last year."]

Wed.May 18. Municipal council reduced the grant to the Fall Fair from $500 to $250. Pretty small business.

Sat.May 28. Looked over [first crop] lettuce fields. Could get 100 dozen on Tuesday or Wednesday. Another 10 days to two weeks before we can count on a carload.

Sun.May 29. *Hot and dry.* Forest fire hazard in Vancouver and Prince George.

Tue.May 31. Held another meeting of [local] shippers [as] no spread fixed between wholesaler and retailer. Cuthbert has rented his grader and warehouse space to McDonald and Co. [Packing houses kept an eye on each other's shipments and prices to growers.]

Wed.Jun.1. Outlook for lettuce sales is anything but bright.

Thu.Jun.2. Lettuce market very draggy. No dump date applied yet. American firms getting most of the business.

Fri.Jun.3. *Continued dry weather.* Repeat order on lettuce for Kamloops. Jobber [wholesaler] reports our pack much superior to other shippers. Tried to get a minimum carload of H.H.Toms [lettuce] but couldn't get enough No.1's. Meggait's house burned down this forenoon.

Sat.Jun.4. *Dry, and high winds drying crops.* Shipped set of platform scales to Vancouver for repairs. Asparagus deliveries slowing up. [Vernon] cannery may close down on June 11.

Mon.Jun.6. Held a meeting of [local] shippers in my office.

[Problem]: New line-up where one shipper becomes a jobber's agent [monopoly] has a very unsteadying effect on our future course of actions. We decided to try and ship orderly so as to at least be united against Coast competition: Poole was to try and ship a carload Wednesday while Landers and ourselves would each ship one about the end of the week.

Tue.Jun.7. *One of the longest dry spells at this time of year in a long time. High winds* played havoc with ground crops. Lettuce wilted quickly and outlook for marketing is not bright. Everything, however, usually turns out all right.

Wed.Jun.8. Shippers' meeting this forenoon at Poole's. Price of lettuce aimed at was too high. New price $1.80 a crate [gross weight is 130-140 lbs] but our information is that markets are pretty well supplied. Browne-Landers will ship tomorrow but price is open – a straight consignment deal. [Accept what the market will pay.]

Thu.Jun.9. The King's birthday is being celebrated today. Veterans holding a picnic at Kelowna. Special train from Sicamous was pretty well filled as it pulled out of Armstrong. Neither Poole nor ourselves have any suggestion of car order of lettuce. Asparagus delivery very light. At 5 p.m. received order for carload of lettuce. Loading tomorrow. Lined up help. Poole took a car also but at 20 cents a crate under our price. It was thought advisable to take the business even if it amounted to swapping nickels.

Fri.Jun.10. *Not too hot, still dry.* Lettuce showing good quality, and packing and loading proceeding nicely. Shipping 30 crates tomorrow morning to Penticton. Understand Poole is going to load again tomorrow. If he does, we will certainly be caught up with the crop.

Sat.Jun.11. Anticipate loading two cars lettuce Monday. It will mean commencing at 3 or 4 a.m. but business must be attended to when we have it. Have got all available lettuce ordered in – may have to get another shipper. Late in the afternoon the second car was cancelled so had to adjust purchases. [Some growers lost a sale.]

Mon.Jun.13. A little slime showing up in some patches of lettuce. Cuthbert loaded one car yesterday and another loading today. Poole also loading, making four cars to go out tonight all on CP passenger. Held another meeting of shippers at Poole's office. The price is to be maintained at least until another meeting on Thursday. Council meeting tonight. Lengthy agenda. Finally put the creeks under the control of the council. [Maintenance and dredging.]

Tue.Jun.14. Loading another car of lettuce. Some evidence of slime. Forced to turn down 400 dozen lettuce all from one grower. Late lettuce now maturing and fairly free from this trouble. Shipment of beets arrived at 4:30 p.m. Nothing but small express shipments in sight for tomorrow.

Wed.Jun.15. No business. *No rain.* All ground crops are suffering.

Thu.Jun.16. Shipping going to Kelowna instead of to Armstrong. Last meeting of shippers: the deal will be wide open – each shipper making the best possible deal irrespective of [other] shippers or growers. This is the result of one shipper not playing the game.

Sat.Jun.18. *Hot.* At least five or six carloads of lettuce immediately available but not much chance of moving it. [No sales.]

Mon.Jun.20. A *scorcher at 7 a.m.* Spring grain burning up. Lettuce showing slime and some evidence of caterpillar. Interviewed the Associated Growers, also Bulman's Ltd. [Vernon]. May advise my growers to sell their blackcurrant crop to Bulman's.

Wed.Jun.22. Went to Vernon re getting water rights on Deep Creek and Meighan Creek [for irrigation]. Reshipment orders on lettuce, but the lettuce is [rotting] fast and only young patches fit for shipping.

Sat.Jun.25. *Very hot again.* To date have shipped out approximately 1,800 crates of lettuce in the three weeks since shipping commenced.

Mon.Jun.27. Monday is usually a slack day. Busier toward the end of the week.

Tue.Jun.28. Business is particularly quiet today – none of the [packing] houses have any orders. Express business doing remarkably well, Kamloops being our best customer.

Thu.Jun.30. [Long weekend.] Preferred to wait until Tuesday, July 5, to ship celery.

Fri.Jul.1. Worked on the books this forenoon. Lawn Bowling Tournament in the p.m. 40 players, 1 from Kelowna, 23 from Vernon, [remainder local].

Sat.Jul.2. Our decision to refrain from shipping celery was knocked on the head when Cuthbert made ready to ship again today, so whole deal was thrown wide open and all are busy now with preparations for immediate shipping. We are loading a part-car after supper for Monday's [complete] loading at Oliver.

Mon.Jul.4. A few more celery orders received. After supper received an order to go out on the through freight for Kelowna. Got the orders placed [with growers] and [loading] gang lined up in good time.

Wed.Jul.6. Received promissory note from Bulman's Ltd. for balance of account to be paid in 60 days. Will now mail cheques to growers who have not been paid in full. Celery supply now plentiful.

Thu.Jul.7. Accompanied Mr. Locke to interview Mr. Long re blackcurrants. He contracted for 500 lbs and terms of payment were satisfactory.

Sat.Jul.9. Celery movement keeping much longer than usual. Business has been quiet today so far, although the usual time is around 4 or 5 p.m. and then work late getting the order out.

Tue.Jul.12. No business. Settling down to the "between

season slump." Poole suggested a lowering of the price [on celery] all around by 1 cent per lb. [Poole is manager of the Interior Vegetable Marketing Board as well as a shipper.] So far the large shippers in Vernon and South have not acted on it. Prairie jobbers are now being supplied locally [so] we can't compete.

Wed.Jul.13.   Ordered 1,000 lbs celery from Bill Boss. First for Bill this year and still a trifle on the green side. Orders have practically ceased, and many tons of celery have gone too far and will have to be chopped up. Five or six growers have not yet made any deliveries on account of crop being late. A carload moved out now would make the situation much easier.

Thu.Jul.14.   *Hot and dry.* Business continues dangerously slow. Celery prices dropped 1 cent per lb today.

Fri.Jul.15.   Lettuce orders are keeping up well and one grower on CN lands is kept pretty well cleaned out. [It may be Lee Sing, Wilson's largest renter.]

Sat.Jul.16.   *Sun is boiling down on the parched land.* At 3 p.m. at the station it was 99 degrees F and at 5 p.m. 106 degrees. *The hottest day in a good many years.*

Wed.Jul.20.   Visit from Prairie Exchange Inspector whose home is in Regina. He is getting a slant on inspection work at different shipping points.

Fri.Jul.22.   *Hazy and hot.* Fires are burning not so far away.

Sat.Jul.23.   Business almost non-existent, particularly in celery, only about 60 lb having gone out since Monday. Fire between here and Vernon.

Mon.Jul.25.   About 75 of the unemployed from Kamloops passed through on the CN freight today. They expect to get a few days' work in Vernon and Kelowna.

Tue.Jul.26.   Ashes from Irish Creek are falling in town and smoke obscures the sun. Business very quiet and will likely continue [so] for another month.

Thu.Jul.28.   Bill Boss is cutting out his early celery to make room for late lettuce [second crop] and feeding the celery to the cows.

Fri.Jul.29. *No rain.* Fire on Irish Creek has burned out several settlers and destroyed many tons of wheat.

Sun.Jul.31. 150 of the unemployed reached here last night and will remain 3 or 4 days. [Council's problem of food and shelter.]

Mon.Aug.1. Nothing doing in vegetables at this end of the valley. Fires under control.

Wed.Aug.3. Second crop lettuce should be ready around August 20.

Sat.Aug.6. With Bill Boss and V. Marzo went out and looked over Lee Sing's [late] lettuce fields. His earliest should be ready around 21st if weather is favourable. Boss's first cutting should be around Sept.1st.

Sun.Aug.7. *First rain since July 1 when we had a light shower.* In the memory of the oldest-timers, we have never experienced a year like this before. [Roughly three months to date without rain.]

Mon.Aug.8. Business exceptionally quiet.

Tue.Aug.9. Received new inkwell and pen ordered some time ago. [A cheerful bit of news.] It is quite an innovation and something I wanted, as the old ink bottle was somewhat out of place in the general layout of the office. The pen too writes beautifully and holds the ink for quite a long time.

Thu.Aug.11. Had some air put into my tires this morning. Have carried along for quite a long while, as W.A. Smith is building a new garage and has had no facilities in the way of air, etc., for two months.

Fri.Aug.12. Canners in the Interior will not can tomatoes unless government lowers the minimum wage for workers. Claim they can't compete with canners in Ontario and Quebec. Government reduced minimum wage by 10% so canners are willing to put up a limited quantity.

Sat.Aug.13. Looked over fairgrounds with Mat. Hassen, as some part of the CN property will have to be purchased in keeping with the extension programme now being carried on. [Wilson will lose some rental land.] Meighan Creek course may also have to be changed.

Wed.Aug.17. *Rained nearly all night and continues a steady downpour.* Business at a standstill.

Thu.Aug.18. Outlook for lettuce is fair but other vegetables including onions not so good, as Manitoba and Alberta have wonderful vegetable crops.

Fri.Aug.26. Boss is having a difficult time with his lettuce. Anticipate trouble with seed stems but slime is causing most trouble. Only 1 out of 15 fit for marketing. We anticipate culling 400 dozen.

Sat.Aug.27. First carload of late [second crop] lettuce. Boss did better than expected.

Wed.Sep.7. Poole is loading a straight car lettuce. We have an enquiry, but may be Toronto, which means 'price arrival' basis and is usually quite unsatisfactory.

Thu.Sep.8. Still no business. Vegetable shipments are behind last year's. Winnipeg is the only prospect for lettuce movement to the Prairies. Toronto is our dump or surplus market.

Mon.Sep.12. We have finally decided to load car of lettuce for shipment to Toronto. Price will probably be 25 to 50 cents a crate below BC and Prairie prices. Some Chinese growers are asking that I ship their lettuce on the same basis [consignment] as Boss and our other growers. They are afraid it may spoil, and the Prairie market is satisfied locally.

Tue.Sep.13. Visitors are in town for the Fair. A number are trying their luck at different [stalls] – just ways of separating people from their money.

Wed.Sep.14. Fred Lewis [Vernon] came with me to look at lettuce at Boss's place and at Jong Hughie's. Have an order for half a carload lettuce and am giving Boss the whole thing so he can clean up as far as he can.

Sat.Sep.17. The international scene is again tense. It was hoped that Chamberlain's visit to Hitler would ease the situation. Prepared my talk for the Bible class – the story of David and Jonathan.

Mon.Sep.19. Poole loading a car straight lettuce. *Hot weather* means lettuce is rotting fast. Marzo cut 100 dozen and claims he got only 10% of the cut. Appears to be common so serious loss inevitable. [Wilson disagrees with Chamberlain's giving a slice of Czechoslovakia to Germany.]

Tue.Sep.20. Received order for lettuce, shipping tomorrow, consignment deal for Toronto. Six growers lined up – anxious to move it before it rots.

Wed.Sep.21. Lettuce are exceptionally fine and gross weight of packed crate is 130-140 lbs. Received car order for onions at old price of $17 [per ton]. Some growers holding crop, hoping for a raise in prices. Not likely.

Thu.Sept 22. Purchased onions to make the carload. Purchased 11 tons from Louie Moon. Chamberlain is over in Germany again, the second time in 8 days.

Fri.Sep.23. Prepared my lesson for Bible class. The 23rd Psalm.

Sat.Sep.24. Poole loading a car lettuce for Toronto on consignment. Only white growers participating, the Chinese refusing to ship on this basis. Busy sorting onions all day for Brandon, Manitoba. Onion market strengthening. No business in sight for lettuce.

Mon.Sep.26. Bought 3 tons of onions. Fred Lewis and I looked over several lots and purchased 17 tons and have the promise of 28 tons more.

Sat.Oct. 1. Took in about 1,100 sax [sacks] onions. From this time on, more citizens will be applying for welfare relief. Becoming quite a problem.

Tue.Oct.4. Expect to ship four cars of onions to eastern Canada the last of the month. The buyer must have Inspection Certificate with confirmation of sale so we are sorting 70-75 sax so that Inspector can base his report on sample. Will sort whole tonnage nearer shipping date.

Wed.Oct.5.	Celery and lettuce business has again fallen off entirely. This is going to be a bad year on growers and shippers of vegetables.
Wed.Oct.12.	Jack Gaule, the Vernon inspector, arrived bright and early to inspect four carloads of onions. Completed by noon.
Fri.Oct.14.	*Ten degrees frost, the latest date for a long number of years.*
Sat.Oct.15.	Busy arranging prices with Poole to combat unfair competition.
Tue.Oct.18.	If we can guarantee against Hollowheart in potatoes, then we will get two cars for immediate shipment.
Wed.Oct.19.	Chinamen [salvaging] the best of the celery from frost-damaged crops.
Thu.Oct.20.	Price of lettuce dropped today. Reduction is 75 cents per crate on account of American imports.
Sun.Oct. 23.	[Wilson regularly notes attendance numbers in church and Sunday school; rests in the afternoon while his wife and daughters write letters, or visits friends; and listens Sunday evening to "Rev. Fuller's Old-fashioned Revival Hour" on radio.]
Tue.Oct.25.	I authorized an order for $10 of provisions for a family. Province accepts no responsibility and consequently are unable to place them on the relief rolls. 8 to 12% of Hollowheart discovered in car of potatoes shipped Saturday. After some phone calls and wires, we settled for a reduction of $3.50 per ton.
Wed.Oct.26.	Business generally very quiet and prices particularly on apples are ridiculously low. They are not expected to keep well on account of the extreme heat of the growing season.
Mon.Oct.31.	[Hallowe'en.] Cleaned up rubbish on and around the premises, as the boys would take everything that was loose including the field crates belonging to the vegetable growers.
Wed.Nov.2.	I am supplying the celery for the Old-timers Banquet tomorrow night. [200 attended.]

Thu.Nov.3.	The tips of the mountains have snow – the first this year. A sharp decline in price of onions expected, as three times as many onions in storage in BC as one year ago.
Mon.Nov.7.	Letter from CN [requesting] that I again lease land for another year. I really need the land provided our markets do not disappear entirely.
Tue.Nov.8.	Boss attended Vegetable Marketing Board in Kelowna. Same board re-elected. Poole will continue as manager of the agency. [Experience needed.]
Sat.Nov.12.	In conjunction with Poole, I am sending to the Vancouver Winter Fair six crates of celery and a few extra labels to post around. This will be the first time Armstrong puts on a celery exhibit there.
Sun.Nov.13.	World stands today in righteous indignation at the treatment of the Jews handed out by Germany.
Mon.Nov.14.	Cuthbert and Wong Chog are both loading celery today for Landers and Co. Landers has handled practically all the celery business this fall, the rest of the shippers not being able to get even an enquiry. Chas. Empey called to say he would be going back to the military hospital at Vancouver, on account [of] a return of rheumatism. I suggested he leave for good that hole in the mountain but he said the outcome was too promising.
Tue.Nov.15.	This is the payday for the Chinese gardeners, and all are agreed that this has been the poorest year for some time. Most of them are gone behind and none have made any money.
Wed.Nov.16.	Poole loading a car of celery tomorrow so he at least doing a little business while the Associated Growers are unable to get even a nibble. We never experienced a year like this before. This fall one shipper only has been doing all the business. There is something queer about the whole situation.
Thu.Nov.17.	Mr. J. Knowles, Kelowna, is going to find out, if possible, why one firm is getting all the business

	while the others quoting on the same basis are unable to get any. He arrived this afternoon and interviewed the shippers.
Sat.Nov.19.	The bottom has fallen out of the onion market – disappointing to those who preferred to store rather than sell.
Thu.Nov.24.	Have decided that a secondhand truck would be a money saver for both Lee Sing and myself in hauling produce from the field [CN land] and from warehouse to Vernon and south. Think it would pay for itself in one year. Entering into a deal with a Penticton garage for a Dodge.
[Mar.2/39]:	Purchased a truck (International). Reshipping is quite an item, and this is the first in a series of economies to enable us to continue in the business. [Lee Sing trucked produce to the south Okanagan via Kelowna ferry or Westside Road.]
Fri.Nov.25.	Wong Chog is going to load car straight celery on Monday.
Sat.Nov.26.	Poole had a car spotted at his warehouse this morning for potatoes. Wong Chog will be loading celery first of the week. No intimation of anything coming our way. Mr. McGregor of Ottawa is in the valley again making a further investigation relative to charges that a combine exists.
Mon.Nov.28.	Board of Trade Window Dressing Competition to increase sales. A "Buy at Home" campaign.
Tue.Nov.29.	Received report from Edmonton that all celery shipped from Armstrong this fall had gone into storage, and jobbers there were taking supplies as needed. The shrinkage would be heavy. One does not feel so bad to know that no direct sales were made. Will endeavour to meet this competition next year by beating them at their own game.
Wed.Nov.30.	Rain fell this afternoon. Snow practically all gone again. End of the month [and] I have to get busy on the books, but not much business so should be easy.
Thu.Dec.1.	Shipping is now practically over for the season.

Mon.Dec.5.	The streets are slush. City Christmas tree was hauled in today.
Sun.Dec.11.	Dr. McKechnie is leaving for California for his usual winter trip.
Tue.Dec.13.	Received letter today re celery situation. Some cars still unsold and [price of] others had to be adjusted, so I am decidedly better off than those who did practically all of the business. But unless there is a general pickup in our line of work, the idea of storing on the Prairies in order to get anything sold cannot continue. The loss is too heavy. The growers will just have to quit and go somewhere else.
Thu.Dec.15.	Freezing weather and no snow on the ground.
Fri.Dec.16.	Received returns from Associated Growers for all vegetables shipped to date. Business done has been paid in full.
Sat.Dec.17.	Election day in the Township and a heavy vote. Noble was elected reeve, and Biggs, Hayes, and MacDonald are councillors.
Tue.Dec.20.	Bought Christmas presents for younger folk in Sunday School. Charles Webster brought me in a box of Northern Spy apples – one of the few orchards with them. H. Ackerman got first and second in the Window Dressing Contest and Bill Harris got first in choosing the winners based on the judges' awards.
Wed.Dec.21.	Attended first hockey game of the season. Kelowna vs. Armstrong.
Thu.Dec.22.	Cars functioning without chains. Only a few inches of snow. Trainmen are buying a lot of celery these days, a parcel or a box each.
Fri.Dec.23.	Lee Sing called about 7 p.m. He brought along a great load of Christmas presents as usual. We enjoyed the visit as much as he did.
Sat.Dec.24.	People dropped in to wish me compliments of the season. We put up the Christmas tree, and Mother and the girls assisted in the decorations.
Sun.Dec.25.	Very good attendance at both Sunday school and

church. Presents for Sunday schoolers and everybody was happy.

Mon.Dec.26. Ten of us sat down to Christmas dinner, eleven counting little John: Ken, Lily, Mrs. Harvey, George Aitkin, Mrs. Beach, David Smith, Mother, Edith, Doris and myself. All had supper again at night as usual.

Tue.Dec.27. Snowed 22 inches and no sign of letting up.

Wed.Dec.28. Vancouver had a foot of snow yesterday. Snow everywhere in Canada. Edmonton is 51 degrees below zero.

In several ways 1939 was a complete contrast to 1938. Wilson noted: *Last year was the driest on record but this year promises to be the exact opposite.* On January 17th, 1939, he wrote: *As much snow now as we had altogether last year.* Snowfall to this date was 50¼ inches. On February 23rd, 1939, he recorded: *Chinese partners are commencing to make hotbeds. The snow is 2½ feet on the level, so considerable shovelling for the man with a large acreage.*

Politically, the world was drifting towards war. Wilson reported British Prime Minister Chamberlain's futile efforts to preserve peace in Europe. Finally, on September 1st, 1939, he wrote: *I got up at six o'clock to hear the fateful news. Germans bombing Warsaw. Britain and France are at war.* And two days later: *Heard news at 6 a.m. Nation is at war.* Almost immediately, Wilson lost his experienced help, as men enlisted. September 25th: *Commenced loading [rail]car at 8 a.m. Some of the help is entirely new to the job and it is impossible to make any time. We will have to put up with conditions in time of war. Poole has only two extra men and may have to get mine when we finish.*

Another change was the introduction in the valley of 'Central Selling,' or 'One Desk' marketing. Some shippers opposed the move as, under this system, produce orders were divided among them, but growers in general approved their access to wider markets. Finally, Poole approached Wilson with a proposal to reduce overhead by combining the local shipping houses and sharing profits.

Wilson needed some persuasion, but around 1940 Poole, Wilson and Cuthbert formed Armstrong Packers Ltd. *The idea at first was they would each do their own trade but have a common packing house. Then it became a completely joint operation. At that point Grandpa moved his business west to the Armstrong Packers building east of the flour mill. Cuthie owned the building. Somewhere I have the financial report for 1942. It was a good year. Grandpa and Cuthie had the first [produce] washer in town. That was something new – people wanted their potatoes cleaned – what's the world coming to! So they hunted one out and set it up on the verandah of the packing house.*

A joint packing house, however, proved only a stopgap measure. *Competition from California took out the vegetable trade here because they could grow year-round. I remember the produce section in Harrison's grocery store was quite small. But if you have to tell people that the only fresh-looking thing they're going to get is last year's cabbage, and the rest is root stuff that came out of the root cellar (which you can live on quite well, by the way), you can't compete. Nowadays the mass of produce is the gauge of a grocery store – fresh, perfect, and all coming from the south.*

Grandpa went to California once in the late forties to look at the vegetable-growing down in the Imperial Valley. He said the packing houses there shipped out more lettuce in a day than we would out of Armstrong in a year. It was mind-boggling. On another occasion he was in Vancouver and noted that the price of a crate of lettuce was a pittance. He said at that price the grower would get nothing. [Yet] some people say the packing houses didn't pay Chinese growers here enough to live on.

1952 was his worst year. The vegetable trade collapsed on its heels. He'd been in it all his life in Armstrong, and at the end of that year he wrote: "I've never seen it so bad." The prices were terrible. His was the last packing house in Armstrong. Dolph Browne ran it for a year or so after Grandpa sold in 1953, but it was petering out. My grandmother used to say that when Grandpa Wilson left, the whole business went to pieces. But Mother used to say, "No, he just got out at the right time

– the business was going to pieces anyway." At the very end Grandpa let go his lease on the CN land, and the CN sold it off. Swansons bought it for pasture. When Harry, Doug and Dolly [Swanson] sold the farm and moved to town, they kept the corner at the end of Rosedale West and built their house on it. (In days gone by, Rosedale West was called Adair Street, but it was just an extension of Rosedale Avenue, so Adair Street was relocated off Wood Avenue. Richy Landon said at the time, "I think Grandfather Adair's street was demoted!")

To celebrate the coronation in 1953 of Queen Elizabeth II, City council inaugurated the civic honour "Freeman of the City of Armstrong." John Halfpenny Wilson was the first recipient. *They gave it to him on Coronation Day [June 2nd]. David's got the scroll and had a couple of copies made for the City because they didn't have one. The calligraphy is quite fancy – except for the fact that they forgot the 'f' in Halfpenny.*

The McKechnie farm on Hullcar/Schubert Road continued to thrive. In 1935 Kenneth, Dr. McKechnie's youngest son, married Lily Wilson, the eldest of four sisters, and Dr. and Mrs. McKechnie moved out of the Schubert house into a new one they built right beside it. *Mother and Dad had gone to school together and attended the same church. She had taken up nursing in 1929 in Vernon, but the Vernon training school attached to Vernon Jubilee Hospital closed in 1931, and her class was sent to finish their final year at Royal Columbian Hospital in New Westminster. She nursed a bit as the Depression would allow. With no jobs available when she first came back to Armstrong, she helped Grandpa Wilson in the office of his packing house. However, she remembered one night getting a call that T.K. Smith was ill and needed a 'special' for a couple of weeks. As she walked over the Flats, she said it was so foggy she couldn't see a thing, but as she got closer to the house, she spotted a glimmer of light. A 'special' is a term we don't hear anymore. You could hire one at home or in the hospital. It was common if you needed a little extra care and attention.*

Lily was musical. *There was an old fellow who came to town – Jack Warburton. 'Jack the Sailor' was a fiddler and Mother and*

Dad knew him because he came to church. Three of them formed a small musical group – Jack played the violin, Marzo (I can't recall his first name) played the clarinet, and Mother, the piano. For two or three years, once a week they'd come to the [Wilson] house and play together. And it wasn't jigs and reels, it was classical music. Mother said, "You know, we never played for anybody – just ourselves." And she said it was a blank to anybody in the community that it ever happened. There's only a couple of graves over in the cemetery where the graves face west, and Jack's is one of them. His tombstone says, "Sailed the Seven Seas," and it's back to back with Oke Swenson's tombstone because his faces east, which is the general rule. Oke Swenson was an unmarried Spallumcheen farmer who died in the thirties and left his estate equally divided between the City and the Municipality, the municipal portion being a $2,000 bequest to support youth farm club activities. The Municipality invested the money in bonds, the interest from which is applied toward 4-H prizes and events. The Oke Swenson Memorial Trophy, vied for annually during the Interior Provincial Exhibition [IPE], commemorates his gift.

Lily and Kenneth had four children: John, Joan, David and Craig. *People never drove cars in the wintertime. When John was born on February 20th, 1938, Dad took Mother to the hospital in the horse and cutter. But when Joan was born on January 20th, 1940, Mother remembered all day long keeping a pot of water warm on the stove for the car when it came time for Dad to get her down to the hospital. So in 1940 they'd started to drive year round.* David arrived on May 28, 1942, and Craig on August 23, 1944. Like a prescient godmother, Annie McKechnie predicted a special relationship between Craig and his father. *Mother said that she had always taken her new babies over to Grandma for inspection, but when she brought me home from the hospital, Grandma came across to our house to see me. She insisted I resembled Dad. I think we were dead ringers. Dad was shorter than me but heavier set and stronger. We got on well. We had quieter natures – worked along beside each other and didn't need to say much.*

Although retired from medical practice, Dr. McKechnie continued to consult as needed. *When John was born, I guess Mother was overdue, and the doctor said something about hurrying things along. Grandpa was in Vancouver at the time, and he was home in a flash the next morning. He had done the first thirteen Caesarean sections in Vancouver, but a daughter-in-law on Vancouver Island had died during the procedure, so whenever anyone mentioned 'intervention,' Grandpa was on the watch.*

Dad used to tell the story about coiling hay one summer in the mid-thirties and seeing a car come into the yard and, a few minutes later, drive out of the yard into the field, and over to Grandpa. Grandpa gets in, back up into the yard, and a few minutes later, off downtown again. In the afternoon, Grandpa returns and Dad said to him, "What was that all about?" "Oh," he said, " the doctor was doing an appendectomy and things weren't lookin' quite right." He knew only one person who could help him, so he stopped the operation until Grandpa got there to finish it off. The patient lived, and he knew what had happened, and he talked about it to his dyin' day. It was 'Hank' Gamble – Everett Gamble – he lived in town here. I remember he had a son the same age as my sister, and at the reception following high school graduation, he brought his son over and introduced him to Grandpa: "Here's the man that's responsible for me bein' here and you bein' here too!!" Grandpa always said about that doctor that he knew when to quit and go for help.

He was called when a boy died in the sleigh-riding accident at the Brick School – ran his head into a tree. He couldn't do anything there. When his daughter Mar was visiting up here from Vancouver, Grandpa took her down to the hospital to have her second child and, since the doctor wasn't around, he delivered it.

I remember hearing about other incidents too. When they were putting the CN railroad through around 1925, somebody got hurt in a blasting accident – damaged the skull – and Dad said Grandpa seemed to be the one that ended up doing the fixing. He was sitting at the table holding this little metal plate and looking at it. When Dad asked about it, Grandpa said he was going to put it in the guy's head to take the pressure off the brain. Grandpa said that brains weren't difficult because

69

you could fish around in the folds. I remember him going into great detail one time about taking a .22 cartridge out of a guy's head over in Salonika [Greece]. He talked about the equipment they had there – telephone equipment – and trying to locate exactly where to bore the little hole so you could put your finger in and feel around for the bullet. But, he said, the heart you never touched. If it ran, it ran. Open-heart surgery was all after his time – those operations were just being attempted in the early '60s, and they were a total mystery to him.

Throughout his long life, Dr. McKechnie remained the linchpin of the family. *As John would always point out, Grandpa was a dominant personality – not domineering, but dominant – and Dad lived in his shadow. It was one of those situations where you were under his influence but admired him immensely – they all did.* At times John mediated between his father and grandfather. *John was more of a talker than Dad or me, so he could relate to Grandpa more easily. Grandpa told John one time about glancing through the section for readers' questions in the Winnipeg Free Press or the Western Producer, and somebody had asked how to lay the finishing on a wood project, and the one who had submitted the question was Dad!* Dr. McKechnie was astounded: *"He could have asked me!"* John explained to him that Dad had wanted to find out on his own.

In 1961 Dad had an opportunity to go east to the General Assembly of the Presbyterian Church. The opportunity only came up every six years or so and he'd never been. He really wanted to go! It was haying time – June – and, of course, Grandpa as he got older could hardly conceive of being without Dad around. If Dad wasn't here, things just weren't going to run! So Dad said to John one day, "Maybe you could talk to him and convince him." So John took on Grandpa and presented the fact that we had bought a hay baler that year and things were going to be easier than in the past, and I'd be out of school early because Recommendations would mean I wouldn't be writing exams, and I'd be available: "I think we could manage all right." So a few days later Grandpa came over to Dad: "Well, I think it will be all right – we'll make out okay without you." So Dad went. But he would never set himself against Grandpa. Dad would be away two days and Grandpa would be saying, "When is he comin' back!" He depended on him. The others were all gone. Dad was the only one around.

My grandfather called me Malcolm. The only reason Mother could think of was that before I was born, Grandma had mentioned the name as a possibility, and perhaps Grandpa had heard and liked it. Before he died, I did *hear the name Craig pass his lips, but he always called me Malcolm. In the Bible he gave to me when I was eight, he wrote my name as Kenneth C. Dad always went as KB, John as JB, but I thought KC would be too confusing and chose to run under 'Craig.'*

McKechnies lived in the Schubert house on Schubert Road until it burned on a sunny day in 1962. *September 18th. We were just using the time-honoured system of cleaning the chimney by burning it out, and the roof caught on fire.* Neighbours rushed to help. *People were packin' stuff out of the house – we didn't even know who some of them were. Young Harry Swanson must have been sixty-seven or sixty-eight at the time, and I can remember him appearing with a pile of Mother's prized dishes in his arms – you know, twelve dinner plates, twelve smaller plates – a stack about eighteen inches high – and I remember thinking, 'There's Mother's prized plates comin' out the door!' One of the castors is missing off the piano because there were two men on the front of it and Pat Hibbert alone on the back, and he had to drop it and broke the castor off. I can remember Bert Fletcher standing at the top of the stairs calling, "Anything more of value up here?" and I grabbed into the linen cupboard and shoved a stack of sheets and towels at him and off he went. David was upstairs with me and the door to the back hall was closed. I remember opening it and embers were falling down, so I said, "No!" and shut it. The house got cleaned out in jig time. When you get a whiff of smoke in your lungs, it puts a little speed into you – we got the spring house-cleaning done in twenty minutes! It was all out on the front lawn. Mrs. Dodds had gone down to their furniture store and brought back a whole bunch of boxes, and in late afternoon she and a couple of the neighbours packed everything up and labelled them. It was all very organized. And the next few days we spent time piling stuff into people's garages or wherever they had space.*

71

Afterwards, I remember we had a great debate about what to do with the front part of the [Schubert] house. The back part – the kitchen – had been added on and was sagging, and even before the fire was put out, we knew we were going to take it down. But we did a lot of thinking about the front part. Sure, looking at the way you can build or renovate today, I would have said, "Let's keep it." But at the time one of the concerns was the smell of smoke – when the house got wet in the damp weather, someone said, the smell would always be there. The house wasn't insulated either – we sawed wood every week in winter to keep warm. Grandpa and Dad had dug by hand a bit of a basement to hold a furnace, and over the years the hole had grown bigger by the same method. I can remember as kids David and I driving the tractor with a rope tied behind it to a box down in the hole, and Dad and John shovellin' in the dirt for us to drag up and dump out under the trees; you can still see it isn't level out there. Today people with bobcats dig basements and insulate.... Still, there was a history to the house and, looking back now, we'd probably have done something different and kept it. You make these decisions... you've got a house sitting there with no roof on it....

We moved in with Grandpa for about a year and a half while we constructed the new one. This house looks older than it is because forty years ago ranch-style houses were popular, and we decided we wanted two storeys. Today it wouldn't draw any note, since everyone builds colossal mansions. Grandpa brought Bill Sidney over here one day to show him the new house. Bill was a big man – the Sidneys are big people – and we didn't have the stairs in yet, just a temporary arrangement to get to the second floor, but Grandpa took him up, and we were terrified it was going to destruct under him.

In 1977 Craig met Sjoukje Egbertien Reink. *Sjoukje's aunt and uncle are Fenny and Arie (Harry) Reink, who owned the bakery in town. They were friends of the family, so we'd heard about these nieces in Holland. Sjoukje came out to visit them and stayed the winter.* Sjoukje was twenty, the eldest of three siblings, and a city girl. She laughs, *I didn't know anything about freezing and canning and baking bread.*

When we wanted a loaf of bread, we ran two or three doors down the street to the store. I still don't do much canning and I never did make bread! Instead Craig makes the bread and Sjoukje bakes it; the delicious aroma fills the kitchen. Sjoukje and Craig raised six children: Christina, Irene, Ian, William, Joanne, and Neil. She jokes, *Who would have thought it? In my family my sister was the one who loved little kids, and I was the one who didn't want anything to do with them! Babysitting was the last thing I wanted to do!* Sjoukje's talents include her cheerful adaptation to circumstances and her unfailing sense of humour.

When Sjoukje and I got married in 1978, we put up the house next door to this one – it was only one storey and classified as a mobile – but as the family grew, cheap was the order of the day and we went up – not an architectural masterpiece! After my mother died in 1992, we moved over here. Within a radius of a few hundred yards, Craig had returned to his centre.

Dr. McKechnie lived to be ninety-seven. *One person Grandpa made an acquaintance with later in life was Damian Smaha from Stepney. The Stepney Ranch was divided up about 1925 and Ukrainian people came in, like Smahas and Spelchans. Damian seemed to be a negotiator or spokesman for them. Grandpa met Damian in the hospital, which was just across Wright Street from the Presbyterian Church. We'd go to Sunday school at ten o'clock for an hour, and Grandpa would wander around the hospital and visit the patients before the church service. Damian had poor circulation in one leg and eventually lost it. He was in hospital many times. He wasn't as old as Grandpa, but they really hit it off. I don't think either of them was ever at the other's house, but they seemed to hold a great respect for each other. In a way they had similar personalities – they were both leaders. When Grandpa died, Damian couldn't come to the church service because he couldn't walk, but he got his family to drive him to the cemetery even though he couldn't get out of the car. Just as we finished at the grave, I heard my brother David say to Dad, "There's Smaha's car," and Dad and his sister went over to talk to him.*

When Grandpa died, Dad was around fifty-six. Dad died at

sixty-eight. He had Parkinson's disease, and then cancer took him. Craig lost a good friend.

Craig McKechnie still farms on Round Prairie. He grows feed for a dairy herd and with other local dairymen ships milk to Vancouver. He can appreciate his grandfather Wilson's difficulties in competing with American produce. *The problems are just as true today. Take a look at agriculture in the Okanagan Valley, and then go south into the Columbia Basin and Washington and look at it there. Huge!! We were there in 2004, as Irene had a job in a little town – and it has a McCain potato chip factory, and a French fry factory, and numerous others – not just potatoes but secondary industries.*

The amount of agricultural product is immense compared to what it used to be. Although there are fewer dairy farms around now, the amount of milk brought into the Armstrong Cheese Factory years ago on a good day can be packed around in one tanker truck. The number of chickens that go through the [Colonial Farms] chicken-killing plant in a day is astounding. And, of course, chicken farming isn't a high-labour operation. It's all automated – you see one man. But he's got all these people supplying him with machinery, feed, transport, etc. But if you go back fifty or a hundred years when a person did everything by hand, everyone did their own work. The helpers were the family and the community.

In earlier days some were making more money or less than others, and some were looking as if they were making more money but actually weren't. That goes on today too. Today the more land you farm, chances are the poorer you are compared to the person who's got a job. Sometimes I look around and think, 'Some people sure have a lot of money.' Financially, people are better off, and the farming aspect has definitely changed, but yet the economics haven't changed: you produce it and put it out on the market and you get what the market says it's worth at that time. Except for marketing boards – eggs, chickens, milk – everything else responds to supply and demand. You take what you get. You can't control the income price – you can only control the expenses, and that's where you learn to be frugal.

The economics of farming may be similar but the rhythms are different. *It used to be that farmers went to town Saturday afternoon to get groceries. That was a traditional gathering – Saturday afternoon – or, in summertime, Saturday evening. Mother would do her shopping and then walk down to her parents' house for a get-together. And it was nice in the summertime because you didn't have to rush home to milk before dark, you could sit around on the verandah in the evening and chat. I remember New Zealand stores were closed on Saturday because Saturday was sports day – all the games were on Saturday – and I remember telling a fellow that here Saturday was shopping day, and I remember him saying to me, "Can't you get your shopping done in five days a week?" Well, now they can't get it done in seven days a week. Shop all the time.*

For many years Craig has chaired the IPE's Division 17, Field and Seed, and his division report to the annual general meeting in February is handwritten and spiced with droll, off-the-cuff remarks. The meeting looks forward to hearing it. In 2006 several division reports preceding his had included numbers of entries and other data. Craig began,

> In Division 17 we don't keep statistics so we aren't able to report how many people entered how many whatnots. The grain exhibit is what stands out in our corner; it sets off our display. However, it is also the part of our entries under the most pressure. It seems that in the local farming scene, growing and showing grain is not a high priority. We appreciate very much those who show, particularly those who make sheaves….

That fall the winner of the grain sheaf competition was Jack Noble, who had gathered it beside the crop circle spotted in his field next to Brett's Road in Spallumcheen on August 2nd. *It was the first time in forty years Jack entered grain in the Fair. I remember saying to Jeanne [Noble] when she brought it in, "I hope there's no little green men in that sheaf!"*

Like others who cherish the legacy of family connection, Craig McKechnie holds two important strands: Wilson and McKechnie.

Some physical aids to memory reside 'in the basket.'

It's a big Indian [native] basket that belonged to Grandpa McKechnie. A copy of Catherine Schubert's daughter's description of their trip from Cache Creek? It's in the basket. Photos from the last 100 years that Grandpa kept? They're in the basket. He'd fish them out occasionally and we'd go through them together. Then the basket moved over to this house for a few more additions. My sister's into genealogy and people say to her, "Where did you get this picture?... Where did you find that?...." And she always says, "Well, it's in the basket."

I have a copy of Donald Graham's memories of Armstrong Spallumcheen – about fifty typewritten pages in a roll – that I think he wrote for the 50th anniversary of Spallumcheen Municipality in 1942. Donald was an early settler and the first reeve. He was living in Edmonton at the time and came back for the Jubilee and stayed at Grandpa and Grandma Wilson's place downtown. Grandpa was an alderman then and they had pictures of Donald sitting in their house. Grandpa Wilson was president of the Armstrong branch of the Okanagan Historical Society (which I just happened to get elected to last Saturday [April/06]) and he got a copy of what Donald had written. It's now in the basket.

Donald Graham is a registered owner of a piece of land in this municipality right to this day. A fellow pointed it out to me one time – just a little strip of land. He said the clerk in the Land Registry Office in Kamloops told him: "There isn't a place like Spallumcheen for little pieces of land." This one's out on Pleasant Valley Road, and I could see how it came about. Graham probably subdivided some of the farm off but wanted to keep himself an access over to Pleasant Valley Road so he didn't have to go through the dip. So this piece of property is just a path about fourteen feet wide. It's a driveway right now, and I said to the fellow who lives at the back of the property, "You can just use your neighbour's driveway." "Well, actually, I can't," he said, "it doesn't belong to me and it doesn't belong to him either." And it's not a road allowance they're both sharing – it's a separate lot. Alive or dead, Donald Graham has ensured he will never leave the community.

Donald Graham had a favourite saying: "Great events cast their shadow before them." He was heavily involved in the first flour mill in Armstrong [Okanagan Flouring Mills Company Limited], and he realized that the big mill being built in Calgary would be the end of ours. If you've got your eyes open, there's generally some foreknowledge of things coming down the line. For example, someone in business sells out and you think, 'What did they sell out for?' And then years down the road, you wonder, 'Did they see the way business was going and know this was the time to get out?' Take when Schrauwen sold the cheese factory to DairyLand in 1977 – maybe he could see how things were going. We don't even have a dairy in town anymore – all our milk goes to Vancouver.

I remember when Charlie Shepherd sold the hardware store – he was only a young man – fifty-five. In his case, of course, he didn't have any sons in the business too, and he had to face the fact that most of the Shepherds died of a heart condition before they were sixty-five, so why hang on to the store? Charlie did manage to scrape a good bit past that date just by due diligence. His older brother John Shepherd hit the sixty-five and died at eighty-three. He said when he was nearing sixty he was getting nervous – going to doctors for check-ups – but by the time he got to seventy, he quieted down a bit because he had made it over the bridge anyway! Jessie Ann (Shepherd) Gamble told him one day, "Well, I did something for my kids. I married a tough Englishman!"

The air in Armstrong Spallumcheen must contain a special ingredient, for some citizens live to an astonishing age. *When Fred Hitt celebrated his 100th birthday, the family invited people to say a few words to mark the occasion. It came up just at the spur of the moment: "Craig, you get up and say something." So I said, "Well, you know, Grandpa died when he was 97½, a pretty old person. A few years later Colin Harris made it to 98, and just after that Art Maw made it to his 99th year, so I'm glad we finally got one of the neighbours up to 100!"*

Fred Hitt died at 102. He was pretty sharp. I remember him telling about meeting somebody in the store one day when he first bought his farm back in 1930, and he asked the fellow where he was from and the guy said, "Starvation Flats." "Well," Fred says, "I come from Poverty Hill but I'm going to change the name to Prosperity Peak." Since that time there's been a lot of water under the bridge, a lot of gravel out of the pit, and a lot of turnips out of the ground. But when you can reach 100 years in good health and are still here to enjoy your neighbours and friends and have your family sitting with you, you're indeed on Prosperity Peak!

Fred's daughter, Marjorie, at his 102nd birthday party got talking about the West Country in England where Fred had come from and the place he had worked. She had visited there several years before, and she was describing the place to him, and he said, "Oh, yes, I worked there, you know; I know what it's like. Some things don't change."

Some things don't change at the McKechnie place either. *Dad always remembered this story: Gus Schubert asked Grandpa if morning glory was still growing beside the house here, and Grandpa said, yes, it was, and Gus said, "I remember my dad out there digging away trying to get rid of it," and Dad said, "Well, if Old Gus Schubert was working at it and it's still there, I think it's going to stay."* It's still *there!*

Twelve-year-old Craig McKechnie outside
his home on a sunny day

Chapter Two

Those Were the Days!

Genevieve Bernice (Becker) Culling

Krista used to say, "Tell me the same story," or else she'd like me to start a story and then add something to it. She knew them all by heart. We used to bring her out with us from Calgary. John was driving and he'd say, "Now that was a great story, Nana, a great story." Perhaps they were flowered, like all stories passed on, but they were my *stories, the way* I *remembered them.*

Genevieve's trove of stories resides in her memory and her bones. She was born in the Armstrong Spallumcheen Hospital in 1923 on April 20 – *Hitler's birthday – during the war the kids at school teased me about it.* She was raised on Becker Street, lived much of her married life in Calgary, Alberta, with her husband John, saw her son, Cameron, marry his sweetheart, Valerie, and her granddaughter, Krista, grow into a teenager. She decided to return to Armstrong and lives in Poplar Grove on Fletcher Avenue. *I'm not organized yet – things are still in boxes.* The sewing table, however, is vivid with yellow and green quilting pieces. Her tall frame stoops to touch them. *I must get this table raised. I like to work standing up.* Joey, a large, sleek, dignified, brown and white Siamese cat, shares the condo. He exits to the enclosed back garden via a neatly hemmed white cloth at the foot of a removable panel built to fit snugly between the patio doors.

Coming back to live where one grew up takes courage. *It certainly isn't like it used to be. I knew everybody – maybe not all the parents, but all the kids. In this community you could talk to everybody, and everybody said hello when they'd pass you on the street. Of course, the town was a lot smaller then.*

When I arrived back here, I had to laugh. The first time I went into Askew's [Foods], I was pushing my buggy and said good morning to somebody – I didn't know the person from a load of hay – and they gave me the dirtiest look, and I thought, 'My god, what's wrong with me?' But now I say hello to everybody, and if they don't answer, I don't give a damn! I found older men not so bad – like Mat. Hassen, for instance. Of course, when he sees my face, he knows who I am, and he says, "Oh, you're in the way again!" He has something to say back. It's wonderful!

Among her siblings Genevieve Becker enjoyed a special niche. She was the older of two girls in what amounted to her parents' second family. *Frances was fourteen years older than me, Tom was thirteen years older, and Helen was twelve years older. Then I came along and Sis [Shirley], three years after me. Sis and I were altogether different personalities – we fought like cats and dogs when we were small and disagreed when we grew up – but we were friends. The three older kids gave me my name. I don't know how they came up with it. When I was bad, Mom used to say I was named after a saint and why didn't I act like one!*

Like her name, the Becker ancestry is a mixture of substance and romance. The Becker forebears were millers and fought in several of the wars that forged the American nation. Genevieve and Shirley traced the genealogy from 1635. *Johannes Becker was a sailor with the East India Company out of Holland. His third trip out he remained in Albany, New York, and three generations – grandfather, father, and son – fought in the American War of Independence [1776-83]. They weren't on the shooting line – they were carrying supplies and guarding prisoners. One of them fought in the War of 1812 [against Canada]. Grandpa Becker fought in the American Civil War [1861-65]. He lied about his age. He was born in 1849 but said he was born in 1847, so he was only sixteen when he put in his term. Cameron has Grandpa's discharge certificate signed by Abraham Lincoln. (I think Mr. B.F. Young had one too.) Grandpa died in 1914 before I was born, and Grandma was the 'first but one' of all the widows to receive the Civil War pension. I have no idea how much the pension was. I always wanted to ask, but in those days you did not ask those kind of questions.*

Charles Jay Becker came to Armstrong by happenstance. *The story goes that Grandpa sold milling equipment out of Chicago and travelled all along the US/Canada border from east to west. The border wasn't like it is today – you could cross easily back and forth. He used to come to Vancouver and travel up into the little bits and pieces of towns, and when he got to Armstrong, he decided this was his country. He and Grandma Becker had married in Deseronto, Ontario, and Dad and Uncle Jay and Aunty Prudence were all born there. Dad – Francis Jones Becker – was nine years old when Grandpa moved the family here in 1895. They lived in a house beside Clayton's machine shop [Brown Derby Café] 'til Grandpa Charles bought land and built their house on top of the hill on Becker Street, which was later named after him. The house is still there [2940]. They [owners] haven't changed the windows, but they've added a double garage – we used to walk right through there – and they've taken down the big trees in the front and planted others. Grey Avenue wasn't there either – Grandpa's place went from Clayton's [at Douglas Street intersection] to the manse [3010] – and the back of it went through to Moray Street. It was really a whole block, but everybody had a big acreage then.*

Dad told us how he and Uncle Jay would take their lard pails after school, on Saturdays, and during summer holidays and pick berries – wild strawberries, raspberries and huckleberries – in what they called 'the jungle' – the lowlands or Flats around south Okanagan Street. (After this land was cleared, the Chinese had their market gardens there.) Grandma Becker canned all this fruit, as it was the only preserves they had for some years until Grandpa cleared land around the new house for a garden of their own. Dad always claimed the berries he and Uncle Jay picked tasted better than any he had eaten since.

Mother's family, the Clintons, had a farm at Larkin X-Road. Grandma Clinton had thirteen children, and Mother – Lille [Lil]

– was the eldest. Lille Clinton's mother, Anna Haack, was born in Germany and came to Armstrong Spallumcheen to join her married sister, Helena Ehmke. *Aunty Ehmke and Uncle Herman were really my great-aunt and -uncle.* Apparently, a group had welcomed the Ehmkes and other immigrants on their arrival in Vancouver. *They took them off the ship and fed and toadied to them before they went on their way. Aunty Ehmke had her eldest baby, Henry, in her arms. The story goes that a native woman took the baby to look after it, and Aunty Ehmke went hysterical – she thought she was going to keep it! Aunty Ehmke's house is still there on Patterson Avenue [2775]. Of course, it had a picket fence all around it. And it seems like they've shoved the sidewalk right up against the front of the house. But the house wasn't on the street – you had to walk up to the house. Patterson Avenue was much narrower then.*

Grandma Clinton followed her sister to Armstrong a year or two later – I think she was sixteen – and she brought her sampler with her. She made it when she was thirteen years old. Anna Haack's sampler is a miracle of understated excellence. It is a white linen rectangle twenty inches long and sixteen inches wide. The tiny handstitching is mainly white; rare sections contrast in red. It is a precious possession. *Mom had it for ages, but after she died, my two older sisters cleaned house – started sorting things out and burning them. When I came home from work one afternoon, the bonfire was going. My Ayaitchess [Armstrong High School] annuals – my song-books – were all up in smoke. I guess they lit the fire with them. The only thing I could save was the sampler. It has two burn holes in it where I put out the flames.* Genevieve's care has removed the char.

The sampler is unusual. *In Calgary I belonged to the Bow River Quilters. They were making samplers [and embroidering] trees and houses on them, and I say, "Next meeting I'll bring you my grand-mother's sampler. It's nothing like yours." And when they saw it, they were amazed.* This sampler is, in fact, a sample of all the different kinds of sewing that a woman at that time needed to know how to do. *It started out one whole piece, and then she cut it to show hem-ming styles and different patches. Here she weaves for the different tweeds.* The tweed samples are sewn in red. *This one's the chevron – you see, they patched men's pants and had to match the pattern. This piece was all corset stitches – these are the holes for the straps in the corsets – all the hemstitching joining seams. See the different kinds and sizes of buttonholes – lace on some of them. Remember they wore chemises [undershirts, or camisoles]. These stitches were all on chemises. See her name here?* A.H. Haack, along with the name of her town, Heide, and the year, 1879, are also embroidered in red. The sampler contains at least twenty-four different kinds of stitching, patching and embroidery. *The back is just as pretty as the front.*

Anna Haack's voyage as a teenager from Germany to Armstrong Spallumcheen was an adventure. Another was a period as a single parent. *My mom never told me until I was getting married and had to fill out a marriage certificate that her maiden name was not Clinton. Both she and Uncle Otto were Unterbrinks. Grandma first married a local man named Henry Unterbrink – I don't know what he did here. He was one of three brothers – the other two stayed in the United States. When Mom was born, Grandma was seventeen. We do not know exactly what happened because nobody ever said, but Henry Unterbrink went to Victoria and ran a carriage company, like a taxi, or jitney, and built carriages. Then he came back and wanted Grandma to go with him to the States because he was lonely for his brothers. And Grandma wouldn't – she wanted to stay here with her sister, Aunty Ehmke. So she was left here with the children and they never saw him again.*

In her second marriage Anna Haack laid down her roots. *Grandpa Clinton – Thomas Clinton – was a sailor and had gone around the Horn of South America several times. This time he de-cided not to get back on the ship and came up the Fraser to the Thompson in a canoe. He landed in Kamloops – this part of the story is foggy – and rode to the Okanagan where he met and married Grandma and bought the farm at the top of the hill on Larkin X-Road. It starts at that line of old trees and joins onto O'Keefe Ranch.* Clinton Road commemorates the family's presence. The acreage is extensive, productive and flat. *On the flats Grandpa either owned it or farmed it. He grew wheat and hay – had a foreman, Robert Main, and a threshing crew of twenty-five. (Bob Main himself owned land on both sides of Larkin X-Road – people along here were big ranchers and they worked for one another.) Grandpa owned Larkin train depot too because it was on his property. They'd load their grain and other produce there. See the little house with the red barn behind it? [4433]. Well, the barn is still standing, but the house used to be a beautiful two-storey, and that's where Grandpa and Grandma Clinton lived.*

Grandpa and Grandma were great friends with the O'Keefes, and the children went to school and church together on O'Keefe Ranch. The Clinton kids rode horseback down the hill to get there. You must remember the land wasn't cleared – it was bushy – and there'd be bears, and the horses would smell one and zoom! – they were gone! Mom said she doesn't know why the branches didn't cut their heads off!

Being the eldest Clinton child in a large family, Mom said she did a lot of the milking, and this particular evening there was a bad thunderstorm. Mom had just milked a cow and lifted her stool away to let the calf finish off the udder when a bolt of lightning struck it. The calf tore 'round and 'round in circles with its tongue hanging out – she couldn't stop it – and she ran for her dad. Grandpa Clinton had to kill it next day, as it couldn't eat. Mom couldn't finish the milking. She kept thinking that if she hadn't moved at that particular moment, the lightning would have struck her instead.

In the small community of Armstrong Spallumcheen, Lille Mae Clinton and Francis Jones Becker became better acquainted. *When Dad and Mom were courting, they would take the democrat and a horse called Nellie – a native cayuse – and go for a drive along the old Otter Lake Road. But Dad said they always had to take along some of Mom's younger brothers and sisters as chaperones, which spoiled any ideas he might have had for wooing or even a kiss. One time they managed to get away in the horse and buggy by themselves.*

Well, I guess whenever some wooing and kissing took place Dad dropped the reins, but each time he did, Old Nellie would stop and look around at them! Dad said it was disconcerting and they'd burst out laughing. Old Nellie was a better chaperone than the kids!

Francis Jones Becker had earned his miller's certificate in Chicago and found a job at the flour mill in Pawha near Wenatchee in Washington state. There he took his new wife. *Uncle Otto worked at the mill too and boarded with them. In the summer the water wasn't fit to drink (no filter systems in those days) and people drank beer instead. On their way home from work, Dad and Uncle would stop at the tavern and pick up a bucket of cool beer. Mom said she wasn't keen on it but always had a glass as, being pregnant with Frances, she needed some liquid. And when callers came to tea, women served beer with their cookies and cake. Since Mom was having guests this particular afternoon, Dad had brought home an extra bucket of beer the night before. Mom entertained royally (she always did!) but when her guests got up to leave, she couldn't get out of her chair – she was drunk! The ladies put her to bed, and Aunt Grace [Unterbrink] – Mom's half-sister who lived nearby – stayed with her until Dad got home. She found out the hard way that you didn't drink beer like tea!*

The Beckers stayed only a year and a half in Washington. *Dad had caught malaria. He took quinine all his life, and every time the malaria flared up again, he was sicker than a dog. He also seemed to be allergic to flour because whenever he got a cut or abrasion at the mill, it festered.* Infections from unimportant wounds continued to plague him. *He couldn't take out a sliver but it festered, and he'd sit soaking his hand in Epsom salts.*

Around 1910 Armstrong became the Beckers' permanent home. *Mom was carrying Tom at the time. They moved into a little, four-room house on Moray Street that Dad built in a hurry because they'd decided they weren't going to live with either set of parents. It had two bedrooms (one for them and one for the kids), a living and dining room, a kitchen, and a back porch. It's still there [2970], and so are the two fir trees beside it – they are real old.*

Francis Jones decided to turn his woodworking hobby into a business. *Dad started up his Sash and Door factory on Wood Avenue – if somebody constructed a new house, he made all the doors and windows for it, and he built furniture. I have a picture of Dad in front of the shop. He used to hire three men. One was Mr. Ernie [Ernest] Mason, who lived on the corner of Rosedale and Jarvis [2810]; he had the most beautiful garden and we used to come and pick his sweetpeas. Another was Mr. Simington, who lived on Wood Avenue in a house that's now the Brown Derby Café.*

The years went by and the three Becker children grew into teenagers. Genevieve's advent took them by surprise. *When I was expected, the little house was too small, so Dad secretly bought the Schneider house.* Just down the hill from his parents' home, it had five bedrooms and sat on three-quarters of an acre of orchard and hay. It was to be a coming home surprise for Lille. While she was in hospital for the customary fortnight giving birth and resting, he moved the three older children from the 'little house' on Moray Street to the 'big house' on Becker [3070]. *They hated it 'cause there was no furniture in it yet – just the beds and the kitchen table – it was empty and hollow and it echoed. And after school, they would sit out on the back steps and wait for Dad to come home from work. On the day he picked Mom up in the horse and buggy from the hospital, she couldn't understand why he was taking the long way 'round – she's tired, holding a new baby, can't figure this out – but Dad had the route all planned. Of course, because they knew he was coming with me and Mom, the three kids were all out in the front and came running. Dad said to Mom, "This is your surprise. I bought Schneider's house."*

They needed furniture to fill it, and Dad made it all. For the front [guest] bedroom downstairs Dad made the bed, the dresser, the little vanity table with wings and its little stool, and a hope chest. The parents had the middle bedroom off the living room. *Dad built the dresser and the chest of drawers, but Mom wanted an iron bed*

90

– they were the style – and an iron headboard with big brass knobs. Tom had the room off the kitchen – the back bedroom. Dad built a huge buffet to fit the dining room, but they ordered the table – walnut with leather seats. Upstairs were the two bedrooms for Helen and Frances, and later for Sis and me. I had a boudoir that had doors and reached the ceiling, a bed with a canopy, a three-drawer dresser with a mirror that tilted, a vanity table and a vanity chair with a cane bottom. A cane seat was an exotic touch. *The Christmas of my first year in high school, he made me a desk with a stool. My room had dormer windows that faced north over the orchard, and in spring instead of doing my homework I just gazed and sniffed – the apple blossoms were out and it was beautiful. And in summertime the apples were ripening and you could see the one at the top of the tree: 'Now, how do I get that apple!' I wish I could sit up there again.*

The place was idyllic, and childhood in the twenties, a time of modest plenty. Two-year-old Genevieve had her portrait taken by the local photographer, Mr. C.W. Holliday. The style is classical, and the cherub is artfully swathed in white tulle. *I wasn't too happy because I had been wearing a really pretty dress Mom made, and I had to take it off.*

One misadventure around this age almost cost her life. *I used to play with my cousin Bobby Beatty – Aunt Annie's youngest boy – when she'd come up to visit Mom and have tea. Because he was a bit older, we'd play outside. Tom's bicycle had a little piece of wire holding his chain together, and for some reason I pulled it off and swallowed it. I told Bobby not to tell Tom or Mother and he didn't. And, of course, I got ptomaine poisoning. Dr. Van Kleeck made house calls every day and brought me a cute, little, hot water bottle to cheer me up. But he couldn't figure out what was wrong with me. I wasn't eating – I wasn't doing anything – and I was getting weaker and weaker. So Mother was feeding me bread with lots of sugar in warm skim milk. (Even to this day I only like cream if it's whipped.) I had to use the potty, not the flush toilet, and Mom put my crib at the foot of her bed and watched me like a hawk. Finally,*

Aunt Annie and Bobby came again, and when Bobby saw me, he was really upset. They went out to the kitchen to have their tea and Bobby was crying. "What's the matter?" And he told them what had happened ''cause he didn't want Genevieve to be sick!' Eventually I passed the wire, but what I remember most is the warm bread and milk and Mother feeding me.

Genevieve's father was not so fortunate as his daughter. When she was going on two years, he lost much of his left hand in an industrial accident. *In Dad's shop the tools were antiquated compared to today. I remember watching him use them when he babysat Sis and I, and we had to sit and play with the putty. The electric sander made a heck of a noise.*

He was holding a board with his left hand on the worktable and making this big, circular movement with the sander in his right. And he made the circle too big and the sander went diagonally over his left hand. His little finger was whole, but he cut off the three middle fingers and took a piece out of the side of his thumb. Martha Pehota lived across from the shop and Dad ran to her – he was a sissy when it came to blood or somebody hurt. She probably saved his life. She more or less stopped the bleeding and wrapped his hand up and took him to the doctor. Re-attaching fingers was not then a medical option and the digits went into the rubbish.

It was a real major catastrophe. It took him years to learn to use half his thumb and his little finger. I can remember Mom having to tie his shoes... do up his buttons... attach his cufflinks... knot his tie. For photos he used to put his hands either in his pockets or behind his back. But he conquered it! He wouldn't let Mom dress him after a while, and he used that left hand like you wouldn't believe. He could hold his fork to cut his meat, or steady a nail or a tack to hammer it in. He didn't like mitts, and when you knit him a pair of gloves, you had to remember on the left hand to knit the thumb and the little finger and cast off at the base of the other three. And even when he bought leather gloves, he went to Adair the tailor and had him remove three fingers because he didn't like them dangling. And, of course, by this time everyone knew about the hand, so it wasn't embarrassing – it was part of him. He was a great dancer, and when he partnered you, he held your elbow. The only thing he didn't accomplish was to tie his bowtie when he wore tails. I can remember them getting all dressed up to go to a Masonic ball or the New Year's dance, and the last thing he'd need was to put on his bowtie: "Mom!" *And Mom would do up his tie.*

Francis Jones regularly spent time with his daughters, since at the Becker house, every Sunday was Mother's day. *Dad worked on Saturday so Sunday was his day with us kids. Mom stayed in bed Sunday mornings and Dad made pancakes. Mom had a special mixing bowl. Saturday night she put in the flour, baking powder, salt, and sugar, and stuck an egg in the middle of the pile. He did the rest.*

Sometimes we'd go down to Old Mr. Sawyer's who ran the candy and ice cream shop. Dad would walk in and say, "A couple of cones, please, Tom." Then out would come one for Sis and one for me. And I'd think: 'What is a couple? How come Mr. Sawyer knows what a couple is?' I never asked, of course, because in those days children were seen and not heard. Mr. and Mrs. Sawyer made their own chocolates and Mom loved coconut chocolates. They were coconut centres dipped in chocolate and rolled in coconut. And Dad would always buy a few to take home to her.

Some Sundays in the fall, particularly, we'd take our little pails and go with Dad over to Rosedale Avenue to gather mushrooms on the golf course. They put sheep on it to keep the grass mowed, and of course you know sheep manure makes the most beautiful mushrooms! They were the little pink ones that you peel. Another place we used to pick them was the fairgrounds because they put sheep out there for the same reason. I had some mushrooms on the lawn here and I wanted to eat them in the worst way, but I wasn't too sure because I hadn't unpacked my mushroom book.

Sunday's schedule came to include two constants: Sunday

school, and a visit to the girls' paternal grandmother. *I was brought up Anglican. When Sis was a baby, Mom used to take me to Sunday school, and then either Mom or Dad would come later for church and collect me. When Sis was three or four, Dad would take us up afterwards to see Grandma Becker. The first place Dad would head was her pantry. He loved leftovers, and Grandma used to keep in little dishes whatever they had had the day before. (Nobody ever threw anything out – if there was a spoonful, you saved it.) Grandma knew we were coming and always had a plate of cookies on the kitchen table, and Sis and I would sit there eating cookies like little angels.*

House plans were different then. There was a parlour and a great big dining room, and half the dining room was usually living room – the radio was there, and the lounge. We were never in the parlour. Sometimes, though, we'd go into the living room and Grandma would lay on the lounge in front of the bay window that faced south and read us a story. Most of them were by Thornton W. Burgess. The one I liked best and gave to Cameron was about Happy Jack, the squirrel. Dad read us bedtime stories out of the ten volumes of My Book House. It started with the nursery rhymes and went on to Aesop's fables and fairy tales. He had made himself a walnut rocking chair with wide armrests, and Sis would sit on one side and I'd sit on the other in our nighties to listen. I guess it really all started with Grandma Becker because she read her children stories when they were little, and Dad carried on the tradition. I loved him.

When Genevieve was growing up, children related to adults in ways that implied both respect and a community network. *Sometimes we called older people 'Mr.' or 'Mrs.', but most of the time if they were friends of Mom and Dad, we called them 'uncle' and 'aunt.' Mr. Abbott was the druggist, and all the businessmen were friends, so to us they [Abbotts] were 'Uncle' Edgar and 'Aunt' Irene. The Jamiesons were 'aunt' and 'uncle.' Mom's cousins were 'aunt' and 'uncle' because they were as old as she was. You never called a grown-up by a first name.*

Some aspects of this relationship ran counter to Genevieve's temperament, which was demonstrative rather than restrained. *Now we give everybody a hug. In those days it was taboo to touch anybody. Dad was more affectionate than Mother. Before he went off to work in the morning, we all had breakfast together and he kissed us goodbye on the forehead: "Goodbye, be good girls." And if they were going to a party or a dance, he kissed us on the forehead: "Goodnight, see you in the morning." And he usually brought us home a souvenir of some kind from the party. But to go in the door and greet your grandmother, you didn't hug her. Instead, "Hi, Grandma, how are you today?" And she always had a smile.*

Nobody ever said they loved you. I can remember telling my parents I loved them, *but they never reciprocated. I had my tonsils out in the hospital when I was six. In those days they used ether, and when I came out of the anaesthetic I was hemorrhaging, and I went berserk. I was so relieved to see Mother I can remember jumping up on the bed and hugging her and telling her how much I loved her. But I can't remember her saying it back.* If self-restraint was a womanly virtue, self-effacement was its complement. Genevieve, however, had a forceful personality. *Lots of times my older sisters and brother used to put me down, and I didn't know why. The girls treated me like aunts. I can remember sitting in the corner where the telephone was because I had done something wrong. What – I didn't know.*

Genevieve's sixth birthday, however, was a milestone: she was the star and her father lost his teeth. *I remember my sixth birthday as if it was yesterday. I think every kid in town was asked! I had ice cream and presents! I always treasured the cups and saucers from the Ledoux girls. One was a miniature – blue-grey with fluted edges – and the other was white with a nursery rhyme printed along the edge.*

Dad loved ice cream, so we had saved some. When he came home, Mother was busy entertaining, as the mothers came too, and I ran out to the kitchen to get him his ice cream, and he wasn't talking very well. "Daddy, what's wrong?" "Don't tell Mom!" He'd had all his teeth pulled!! He had come straight home from the hospital, and he wanted that ice cream in the worst way. I didn't tell, and I guess this was how much attention Mom paid to Dad because it wasn't 'til the next day that she noticed! Not long after, Mom bet she could have the same thing done as quickly as Dad, but she ended up in hospital with an infected ear. Dentures were the in-thing – your teeth always looked nice. No cavities, no pain, no upkeep. *Even my sisters had their teeth pulled. After seeing them, I vowed I would keep every one of mine. What really cured me, though, was having my six-year molars extracted because my other ones were coming in behind them.*

When Genevieve began school in 1929, there were three schools in town. *We called them the 'little school,' which was in the park; the 'big school,' which was the consolidated elementary school that had opened in 1921; and the 'high school,' which was at the corner of Bridge Street and Pleasant Valley Road. I started grade 1 at the little school, and when I got to grade 2, I went to the big school. High school started in grade 9. The little school was originally built as a high school, and the elementary school was on Bridge Street. That was my dad's first school when he came to town. I have a picture of Aunty Prudy, Alta Hassard and Fay Armstrong in front of that school. It didn't have the second floor on it – they had to add it to get more room. You must remember that there was an awful lot of young people in town then.*

School chums became lifelong friends. *I put together an album for the Year 2000 Homecoming... pictures of my friends... like Thup Marshall. Her real name was Louise, but when she was tiny, she heard her older sisters say "Shut up!" when their boyfriends teased them, so she repeated "Thup!!" and carried that name from then on. Her father, Art Marshall, ran the Co-op store. Betty Garner was another friend. I still call her Garner and she still calls me Becker. Both her parents were teachers at the big school and R.J. Garner was the vice-principal for years – he was my teacher – he was a great guy.*

We were taught to read phonetically. Genevieve practised by deciphering building signs. *Usually, when it came to buying meat in the summertime, Mom would send Sis and I down to Dad's shop for money. (We didn't have a fridge – Mom used to keep things cool in the basement.) The police station on Patterson Avenue had two domed windows with a bar down the middle of each one, and as we passed by it, I would see the words POL and ICE written on either side of the bar on one window, and OFF and ICE on the other window. So I would say out loud to myself, "POL...ICE...OFF... ICE." One night at the table I chirped up, "Oh, that's right near the POL...ICE...OFF...ICE." Dad just howled. "Now," he said, "put them together."* What a revelation!

Musical herself, Lille wished her daughters to enjoy the benefits of graceful living. *When they were in the 'little house,' Mom bought a piano for the older kids. It was one of her first purchases. Dad lugged that piano to the 'big house.' We all took lessons – even Tom. 'Aunty' Jean Phillips lived across the street and had a beautiful alto voice. She'd come over and Mom would blow on the mouth organ – she had a neck brace for it – and play the piano, and Jean would sing. I began piano lessons around age six and I had three teachers: Mrs. Chamberlain, Miss Gordon, and Mrs. Knight-Harris. I took dancing lessons too because I was tall and Mother thought I was getting awkward. I took slipper dancing, tap dancing, ballroom dancing, and ballet dancing until I grew out of my shoes. Jack Linus and Betty Whitworth taught us gymnastics. I could do back flips – anything. (Maybe that's what's wrong with my back!) We took classes in the Rec. [Recreation] Hall after school and in the evening. I enjoyed it all.*

The passing of time altered Sunday's routine. *When Sis was old enough, we walked to Sunday school by ourselves, and on the way we'd stop at 'Uncle' Harry Hope's, the blacksmith. (When Mom and Dad lived in the 'little house,' he lived right behind us on Jarvis Street.) He worked on Sundays. I remember the big plough horses he'd be shoeing. He'd warn, "You girls stay back!" because he wasn't sure what they might do, and then he'd come to the door and talk to us. He made Sis and I each a ring out of a shoe nail. He kept the square head on it – a little knob for decoration – and twisted the shank around. I've kept mine all these years.*

Activities associated with St. James Church were an important part of Genevieve's youth. *Religion was all we had in the '30s. The church was our social outlet too, no matter which one you attended.* The church's calendar of fasts and feasts moved the year along. *We celebrated Christmases together – everybody at the house. Easter was wonderful because Uncle Tommy's four would come along with Aunt Lena's three and we'd hunt Easter eggs in the barn. Mother usually cooked a ham and the aunts brought jellies or other delicacies, and there was a feast. If it was a nice day and a little cold, we kids wore our jackets and ate outside.*

Families had more children then and we had a big Sunday school. Mrs. Tom Thomas was our Sunday school teacher, and our leader for the Junior W.A. [Women's Auxiliary] – we held our meetings at her house. She was also our church's bazaar convenor, and she used to make trays of the most gorgeous two-layer candy for us to sell there – a white layer and a pink layer. I've never been able to replicate it and I've never seen a recipe for it. As I recall, it was a combination of icing sugar and coconut, and she must have boiled it to a certain degree, but it wasn't fudge. Remember the cookie sheets my mother used had high sides – and she'd cut it up in bars four inches long, two inches wide, and an inch and a half thick, and they'd be a nickel. Kids just went crazy over it.

In Sunday school I played the tinkly piano for our hymns. My favourites to this day are "All things bright and beautiful" and "Little drops of water." They don't play these hymns any more. She recalls other titles that have been displaced: "Now the day is over," "Jesus loves me," "God sees the little sparrow fall," and "Gentle Jesus, meek and mild." *Mr. Pellett played the organ in church, and he taught me to play it for Children's Day. We were never allowed into church unless it was a special day like that one, or you at-*

tended the service with your parents. I can only remember going to church regularly when I was around ten years old and about to be confirmed.

After we were confirmed, we didn't go to Sunday school any more and Mrs. Pellett started a choir. That's when I stopped going to church. Some of the kids thought that Mrs. Pellett should supply cookies and candy at choir practice. I came home and said to Mother, "I'm not going to sing in the choir or go to church any more. I don't have to be paid *to go to church. If I go, I'm going on my own!" Mom was really upset. She could see I was serious – I can just imagine what was going through her mind. In the end she had a talk with Mrs. Pellett and found out there were certain kids she* did *have to bribe. I thought it was despicable, but Mother finally got me to go back, and by this time I was confirmed and a little older and had a bit more sense.*

St. James felt like home to Genevieve for another reason. *You must remember that Dad made nearly everything in that church – lectern, pews, altar, pulpit... you name it. He did not pay for them all himself, but he always donated his labour because* that's *the way it went. One thing Mr. Groves made was the Rook, or Litany Arch, that stands above the first step to the altar. I can remember Sis and I sitting in the front pew while he and Dad put that thing up. Mr. and Mrs. Groves were Mrs. [Doctor] Van Kleeck's parents, and they lived in the little brick house down on Fletcher Avenue [2375]. Mr. Groves was the magistrate at one time.*

Remember, the town was small then, and everybody seemed to take part. Things today have changed so much. People aren't as religious as they used to be. I think the war had a lot to do with it – the fathers almost didn't believe in God as a result of what they'd been through. John fought in Italy, and he wouldn't talk about his experiences. When it came to religion, sometimes he was okay with it and he'd come to church. Another time: "Don't mention it!" He wasn't the only one who felt this way.

Living in town, the Becker girls had playmates close at hand, and summertime brought endless days of fun. *The Phillips lived across from us – Ross and Stewart, and the twins Beverley and Duff. South of them was the Crozier family – Dorothy and Kathleen, Dan, Jamie and Joyce. North of us were the Ledoux family – Gwen and Isabel and Violet – and behind us on Moray were the Dick Thomas girls – seven of them – Agnes, Annie, Eva, Mabel, Elsie, Marjorie, and Betty. We played with them all the time – we used to cut through a hole in the hedge and then across the orchard instead of using the street – but we had to make sure we never left our place without asking first. It was the same for them.* The hole in the hedge was man-made. *Somebody threw a cigarette – in the old days, a roller. The story goes that Tom was sitting in the bathroom 'concentrating,' as Mother called it, and somebody yelled "Fire!!" She said she never saw that boy move so fast. The thing was to get the hose attached to one of the outside taps to put the fire out. It burnt a hole, so we could go through the hedge instead of our front gate.*

The other day in the Morning Star [Oct.21/05], I read Mabel Thomas's obituary. It doesn't mention any of her sisters except Elsie so they must all be gone too. You don't hear about people and all of a sudden you read an obit. It hit me with a wallop. Their mother we called 'Aunt' Liz. She was deaf – you really had to holler at her – but she got to a point where she could read your lips and know what you were saying. In my mind, it was only weeks after her husband passed away, she could hear. Isn't that amazing? There were a lot of Thomases in town then – three brothers from England – Spark, Dick, and Tom. Spark was a great birder. He kept canaries, doves, budgies – you name it. And now there doesn't seem to be one Thomas in town, not even the kids.

Because of the proliferation of barns, outbuildings, trees, and hedges, adaptations of Hide and Seek were popular games. *We played Kick the Can – just bang… bang… bang… and run like heck! First you drew a big circle on the ground and put a can in the centre. Whoever was 'It' counted on the tree and everybody ran and hid. Then the person had to find the kids who were hiding but also had to guard the can. If a kid made it into the circle and kicked the can, he was home free.* Another variation was called Run, Sheep, Run. *You started from a certain spot but you went in two gangs, one gang hiding from the other, and the Shepherd watched to see which came back first without being caught.*

The Becker barn supplied a stage. *In the spring when the hay was all out of the loft, it left the floor shiny and you could dance on it. We'd produce concerts and charge a safety pin – this is the '30s – you didn't ask for money. We'd dress up in our mothers' clothes: "Could we have this?" "Could we have that?" The parents would come – mostly the moms – and crawl up into the loft and sit around while we performed. We'd dance and do tricks and sing comic songs. We were really silly but they laughed.*

Mom sewed gunny sacks together to make us a tent to play in. Sis and I loved it and tried sleeping in it – we never lasted the night. In the crabapple tree next to the back door, we had a tree house. It had no roof, but shelves laid across branches held all the playthings we could lug into it. It was lovely when the tree was in bloom and bees flying around – a great place to read.

In summer children could leave off wearing shoes. *Sis went barefoot and I tried, but I hated the feel. Then I went out in the orchard to get an apple, and of course the bees are around and I step on one! So Genevieve never went without a pair of old shoes – no way!* There was, however, something worse than a bee sting. *Mom hated running shoes – but I wanted to be in track [and field] so she bought me the running shoes, and naturally I wore them around. When we were kids, it was wooden sidewalks and gravel roads, but they were building forms on Becker Street for cement sidewalks, and I had to go and step on a board with a nail in it. I come hopping into the house with the board nailed to my foot, and Mom was so mad: "If you'd had your leather shoes on...!!" She pulls off the board and my shoes and socks, and fills a beer bottle with coal oil.* Lille always had coal oil and beer bottles on hand. The coal oil was to medicate the cow. *She asked everyone to save beer bottles for her tomato juice. And she holds my foot up and puts the mouth of the bottle against the nail hole, and you could see the coal oil drawing the poison out – a stream of blood going into the bottle.*

Medicating the cow happened fairly frequently. *We had a milk cow named Pansy – a beautiful little Jersey. In the spring when the grass was fresh and green, Mom would tether her out with a steel stake and chain in the vacant lots on either side of our property. But Pansy bloated very easily. At such times Mom would fill a long-necked liquor bottle with coal oil and milk and empty it down her throat to get rid of the gas. One day Mom was at a W.A. meeting, and when Sis and I came home from school and checked on Pansy, she was bloated. We didn't know what to do 'cept walk her up and down the alley as we used to do while Mom fixed the liquor bottle. But Pansy went down on her front knees and wouldn't get up! I was hauling on her chain from the front and yelling at Sis to hit her in the rear with a switch, and we were both bawling from fright, and screaming at one another, so I gave up and ran into the house to try to fix the bottle. I was in the middle of it when Mom came home.* She rescued all three.

Another time Pansy was bloated so bad Mom had to call the vet. Lille anticipated extreme measures. *She put the cow in the chicken run and ordered Sis and me up to the house, but we were so curious we sneaked down to the old smokehouse at the bottom of the chicken run and climbed up on the roof to watch. Dr. Keevil punctured Pansy's stomach, and the gas and green grass flew into the air like a geyser. We both let out a screech and, of course, Mom saw us: "Well, I guess it was an education."*

The return to school in the fall brought a different set of games. *At elementary school the boys shot marbles all the time and the girls skipped and played jacks. I liked skipping best. Recess was at least fifteen minutes and lunch, always an hour. If it rained, the girls had a little playroom down in the basement on the east side – the home ec. [economics] room – and the boys used the manual training room on the west side. There were two lunchrooms, one for boys and the other for girls – we were all segregated.*

Any chance to visit Aunt Helena and Uncle Floyd Hunter and their cousins in Knob Hill, however, was Genevieve's favourite time of all. *When Mom was sick, Aunt Lena took care of Sis and I, and when Lena was sick, Bernie and Nonie came down to our place. I used to just* love *to go up to Aunt Lena's because we'd have to heat water and take a bath in the old tin tub in front of the stove, and we had to run to the outhouse and use the slippery catalogue, and squat on the chamber pot at night, but the* best *thing was being able to take my lunch to school and eat in the lunchroom! And Bernie and Nonie loved to stay with us for the opposite reasons – the bathtub, the in-side toilet, and coming home for lunch, as Mom always provided a good meal. Our house had all the amenities and I didn't appreciate them at all. And now I wouldn't bath in a tin tub for anybody!*

In comparison to summer's emancipation, dressing for winter was a penance, especially for the girls. *Everybody wore long winter underwear called 'combinations,' which meant an undershirt with leggings attached. But instead of a slit back and front on the leggings as the boys had, the girls had a flap on the back that buttoned up – and to try to do up those silly buttons!! Over the underwear girls wore a waist with long garters attached to hold up their ribbed cotton stockings. Next came fleece-lined bloomers that reached their knees. The top layer was a skirt attached to another waist like a jumper and covered by a sweater. Outside leggings were usu-ally khaki coloured and had to be taken off at school because girls weren't allowed to wear pants. To keep our ankles thin – you had to have thin ankles – we wore boots laced tight. (I had them until I was in grade 8, for god's sake, and hated them. I was so glad when I could wear oxfords!) And if the weather was bad, you pulled on a pair of your dad's wool work socks over your boots and covered them with mud rubbers. A toque or a tam on your head. We could hardly walk – and we must have looked awful – but so did everybody else.*

(The first pants girls ever wore – beach pyjamas – came in when

we were about ten years old. Frances sent Shirley and I each a pair, and Mrs. Thomas ['Aunt' Liz] made Betty and Marjorie each a pair, and we had our pictures taken. We felt very mod.)

Hallowe'en was a bright spot in the cold days. *The kids travelled in gangs. You didn't knock on doors and ask for treats – you played tricks – something stupid like soaping windows. I still blame Dan and Jamie Crozier for puttin' a big bag of dead worms at the front door.* With so many youth in the neighbourhood, adults were unlikely to escape attention. *Dad's shop on Wood Avenue had a two-by-four outhouse over a hole in the yard. On November 1st he could find his outhouse* anywhere *in the city (even on the high school roof before they added the second storey!) It was usually the Fisher boys, the Watt boys and the Mills boys that did it. This particular year they put it on a flat car on a standing train. Well, guess what! It was hauled to Sicamous! Uncle Jay – Dad's brother – was the stationmaster for both the Canadian National and the Canadian Pacific Railway in Sicamous, and when this silly outhouse arrived, he knew it was Dad's. So he wired stationmaster Gullivan in Armstrong – in those days you didn't telephone, you wired – and Dad had to pay for the shipment back, since Uncle Jay didn't know what to do with it!* Brotherly love? *Dad said it would have been cheaper to build another one.*

Another time they put the outhouse on the high school steps. I've never forgotten it because I was going to high school at the time. J.M. Murray was the principal, and of course he knew it was Dad's, and he also knew who had done it! So he made them carry it right down the main street – the Fisher boys and the Watt boys and the Mills boys – with himself marching behind them – and made them set it back over the hole. And Dad stood there and laughed. He probably looked forward every year to seeing where it would end up.

The location of the Becker house gave an excellent view of fires in downtown Armstrong. *We used to watch the fires upstairs from my bedroom dormer window. The town didn't have a siren then – just*

*the old dingdong – and when that bell was tolled at the fire station
in the night, it made the weirdest sound. Dad would jump out of bed
and get dressed and go in spite of his hand because he always said,
"I may not be able to hold a hose but there must be* something *I can
do. If somebody's in there, I can carry them out." (Actually, he did
learn to hold things in the crook of his elbow.) The fire in 1933 destroyed several businesses including the Okanagan Hotel. It was a
beautiful hotel – I can remember being in the rotunda with Dad. The
fire that burnt the Co-op happened in February during the cold winter of 1950. By this time we had a siren. In the morning Helen said,
"Let's go down and see what happened" because Dad had come
home and gone to bed. The damage was horrible, and, of course, it's
never been built up the same.*

When Genevieve was ten, the Depression was in full spate and
money was tight. *Parents never gave allowances – you earned them.
I remember earning a penny raking the lawn, bringing in the wood,
throwing the wood into the woodshed. A* big *penny was worth a heck
of a lot more to us than a little one! And that's what I'd get from
Mom and Dad for some small chore they might have hired somebody
else to do. I also started babysitting. I always got a nickel. First I
babysat my nieces, and I think eventually I babysat every kid in town
at the time. I loved babies. I took care of Art and Daphne Hope's
kids, Carolyn Hoover, Betty Brown.... In high school I paid for my
perms. I'd have my ten cents to go to the Saturday afternoon movie
matinee at the Star Theatre, since I'd be babysitting at night.*

One babysitting job at Mara Lake lasted a summer. *'Uncle'
Edgar Abbott had ten acres on Mara Lake... it was beautiful. But
'Aunt' Irene didn't like going to their cabin because they were the
only ones on the property and [adjacent to] one of the two Relief
Camps on the lake. (Relief gangs came from anywhere in the valley.
The men had to work for $10 a month to feed their family – it wasn't
much but in those days you could manage.)* Edgar Abbott solved
his wife's problem. *He asked Dad to build a cabin on the acreage
and gave him the choice of location, along with 'Uncle' Steele and
'Aunt' Agnes Fisher. So there were three cabins instead of one.* One

summer Genevieve babysat Teddy and Barbara Woodland, Edgar Abbott's grandchildren. *I was fifteen or so at the time. After Teddy was born, Kathleen got felons [inflammatory sores] in her hands – she couldn't hold Teddy let alone bath him, so I went over. After Kathleen got better, they'd go off to a show and I got two bits until midnight. Anything after that was fifty cents!*

Genevieve's small regular income helped Lille clothe her. *I was always tall – a head taller than any of my friends from the time I started school. But I'm long-waisted, not long-legged. On a dress the waist was too high; if I got a shirt or a blouse, I had to put a tail on it. So Mom made all my clothes. She had an old White that she sold a cow for – I learned to sew on that machine. Frances and Helen would send home their castoffs and Mother would rip them apart and make something for Sis and I – we never wore them as they were. The only exception was a yellow pleated skirt that fitted me perfectly. And from a green dress Frances had sent, Mom made a lovely blouse to go with it.*

One sewing project was uniquely memorable. *Mom always made us a special Easter outfit, but the one I remember was an ensemble! – a dress with its own little jacket.* In a photo taken on Easter morning, eight-year-old Genevieve poses under a garden arch in her many-coloured costume. *The print was lilac and orange, and Mother had trimmed the cuffs in orange and I had an orange straw hat. And, of course, white gloves and black patent shoes. We always had black patents for Sunday. Sis's little outfit was the same pattern in blue and yellow, and Mother had trimmed hers with blue to go with her blue hat. We always got our new hats at Chapman's.*

Genevieve had chosen the dress material at Piggott's. *In the spring Mrs. Piggott would get in nice dresses and new bolts of cloth, and cotton cost only two bits or so a yard. Mother didn't like shopping unless it was absolutely necessary, and you must remember, in those days you could buy something and take it back if you changed your mind. So she would send us down with my babysitting money, and if we saw a bolt we liked, we bought some. Either Freda or Rose*

Piggott waited on us – Mrs. Piggott was the boss.

I always had to wear homemade clothes. Not that Mother didn't make them perfectly – they were wonderful – but I wanted a boughten dress like everybody else. I'd try on all the dresses at Piggott's and they'd never fit – except once. This one had a white background with horizontal orange stripes and brown horses on it, and the horizontal stripes made me look fatter because I was always skinny. The ties were up under my arms, but all I had to do was resew them at my waist. It was my first boughten dress – $1.98. It represented approximately forty babysitting jobs at a nickel a time.

On one occasion Genevieve lost her cherished black patent shoes. *We had had a lot of snow one winter, and that spring we had water, water, everywhere. The neighbour boys and older kids had made rafts, and after school they were floating them in their backyards.* Naturally, Genevieve wanted a ride. *Our house was on a terrace, and our vegetable garden, to the north of it. I decided to cut through the garden, but I'd only got a few feet when I started to sink! Oh, how I screamed! I was petrified of the Chinese who gardened in the Flats, and I thought I was going to China!! Luckily, Tom was coming home and ran and rescued me, but to reach me he had to lay down planks. I lost my shoes and socks and was stricken that I was wearing my black patents. When Dad ploughed the garden later, he found them, but they were ruined and I never had another pair as nice. Always it seems bad things happen to favourites.* Why was Genevieve wearing her black patents on a weekday? *It was a case of wearing things out. I was growing, and the black patents were usually bought a bit larger than my school shoes, so when my oxfords got too small, I could wear my old patents to school. After all, this was the thirties.* Parents planned ahead.

Over the years Genevieve developed a special relationship with Grandmother Becker, who had not paid much attention to Genevieve's three older siblings. *Grandma was very tall and thin, very stern, prim and proper, yet very down to earth. I figured in my mind that earlier she wasn't ready to be a grandma. Even today some people don't want to be grandmas because it makes them feel old. But when Sis and I came along, it was another story – she was ready.* Mrs. Becker may also have recognized something of herself in her lanky granddaughter and cemented that bond in a singular rite of passage. *I remember going up once by myself to see her, and she said, "How old are you!" I thought this was odd. "I'm twelve." "Good," she says, "you can have a glass of wine." Now this wine was either dandelion wine, beet wine, or rhubarb wine – she made them all. She went into the pantry and brought out a little, stemmed wine glass and put it beside a cookie on a side plate covered with a handmade doily. And we sat at the table and she had a glass too. I've never forgot that day – I was so pleased.*

From time to time Genevieve stayed overnight with her grandmother. *Aunty Prudy lived with Grandma and took care of her, and when she was away, I'd take her place. We always had porridge, toast, and Postum in the morning – she never would let us drink coffee. Sometimes if it was Saturday or Sunday morning, we'd have an egg from one of her chickens. And she loved to do jigsaw puzzles, and we'd sit and work on them together. I had the feeling that she liked having me around.*

She was so thin but she loved to cook. She made delicious angel food cakes and beat the whites for ages. She had a favourite utensil that she mixed things with – an old dinner knife. She made pie dough with her hands, and then she'd use the knife to scrape the dough off them. I'd get goosebumps watching her because on the backs of her hands all the veins were sticking up, and I was sure she was going to puncture one. "Grandma, don't do that!!" And she'd laugh and say, "I won't cut myself. I promise."

She had a chopping bowl – a shallow, wooden bowl about eight or ten inches across – and a knife rounded to fit it. The blade looked like a stationary guillotine with the handle placed over the top of the blade instead of on the end of it, and one pushed downward to chop. *If she was making stew, she chopped the onion and meat, or if she was making fruit cake, she'd chop up the fruit, because you didn't get it precut as you do today – you had to buy your pineapple and the whole lemon or lime and chop the rind yourself.*

Mrs. Becker passed on to Genevieve her skill in needlework. *I'd go up after school, and maybe she was sewing. I helped her make a white and blue 'basket' quilt out of broadcloth – the basket was in tiny triangles and she was sewing it all by hand, and she showed me how. I remember making quilt squares with her. I used a machine to baste-sew, but [I learned] you don't baste-sew when you're sewing pieces together – you backstitch. Then she showed me how to do roll-hemming, and I helped her roll-hem damask napkins. (When you bought a damask tablecloth, you also bought the napkins, but they were on a roll and had raw edges.) That's when I noticed Grandma was using both her hands.*

Grandma was left-handed, but she was always made to use her right. One day I showed her the apron I had made in home ec. She said I had done a good job, and she wouldn't tell me to rip it out and redo it! Then she told me about the first apron she had made. Her mother had given her material and a pattern, and she finished it all by hand. Her mother said she had done a beautiful job, but she must take it apart without damaging the material and resew it correctly with her right hand. Her mother had spotted her using her left.

Genevieve motions to a large linen doily centering a bowl of flowers. *This is my grandmother's work – it's a hundred years old.* The article is pristine; *when something is* made *by hand, you* wash *it by hand. It's satin stitch cutwork – the stitch is padded. You draw one thread through and then you go over it again to raise it – the same with these little dots – and that's why the design stands up. I'd watch Grandma Becker crochet or sew. She'd be using her right hand and switch to her left – she said her right hand got tired.*

Sometimes when I arrived at the house, she didn't have the ironing done. She had the old cast irons that you heated on top of the stove and tested with your finger for temperature. The irons were heavy and her arms so skinny – she'd ask me to iron. She showed

109

me how to fold a tablecloth without ironing a 'tent' into the middle. (When you fold something in four and iron it, the creases intersect in the centre of the cloth.) Instead she'd fold the tablecloth longways in half so it wouldn't drag on the floor, and iron it on both sides. Then without ironing it further, she'd fold it in thirds, and fold it again from the bottom in thirds and lay it in the drawer. Smaller linens could be ironed out flat and then folded in thirds twice. And I still do it today. My mother probably did the same thing, but she didn't get a chance to show me because Grandma showed me first. I wish I'd not been taught to listen and not be heard – I wish I'd asked her more questions.

Genevieve's maternal grandmother was less of an influence in her life. *Grandma Becker had only three children. With thirteen children Grandma Clinton had umpteen grandchildren, so she didn't bother with us so much. She did her rounds once a week on a Wednesday. She'd visit her friends in the morning, see Uncle Tommy and Aunt Aggie, and then come and see Mom and Dad and have tea. She didn't have rubber on the end of her cane, and I can hear her yet tapping up our cement walk. "Here comes Grandma!" She hated cats. And of course we always had a kitty of some kind and, wouldn't you know, the first place that cat landed would be in Grandma's lap. I can still hear her screaming, "Lille, Lille, get this cat* **off** *me!!" and her hands are fluttering in the air so she doesn't touch it. But Mom was always busy making tea, so Sis or I would run and grab it.*

I also have only one memory of Grandpa Clinton. I must have been three or so when somebody passed away, and we were up at the big farmhouse on Larkin. Sis was a baby because she was lying on the floor on a mat, and it was dinnertime. There was a great big stove, and I was sitting at the table that fed a threshing crew, and I remember Grandpa coming over – I can see it yet – he comes and sits beside me on the bench. In those days you put your teaspoons on the table in a bowl – usually a cut-glass bowl. And he picks it up and jingles it in front of me and says to Grandma, "How come you're not feedin' this kid!" And he bent over and kissed me on top of the head. He passed away in 1926. Grandma sold the farm to their fore-

man, Bob Main, and moved into town with Uncle Arthur and Aunt Mary in the house on Pleasant Valley Road that my niece Phyllis Brett lives in now [3245] beside the old cheese factory. Anna Haack Clinton lived into her late eighties. *When my brother Tom's oldest girl, Sharon, had her twenty-first birthday, she proudly had her picture taken with her father, my mom, and Grandma Clinton. She said, "Nobody at the age of twenty-one has a great-grandmother!" Mom passed away before Grandma did, which really upset her.*

Grandmother Becker's sharing of a glass of wine recognized Genevieve's advent to womanhood. Her parents celebrated in a similar way. *At my twelfth birthday there were twelve girls: the two Ledoux girls, two Thomas girls, Betty Renault, Elizabeth Smith, Patsy Hobson, Helen Watson, Pat Warner.... I have a photo taken of us all.*

Today everybody is so open. When it came to sexual information, my mother never told me anything – she passed me books. To find out about my monthly period, I received a little book called Marjorie May's Twelfth Birthday put out by Kotex. It was about four inches square – cute as heck. I kept it all these years and gave it to Krista. We didn't learn completely *on our own. By this time we were having sex education in high school – only it was in the science room and it was about pigs! How pigs procreated! I can remember the slides yet!!*

Mom herself was naïve and most of the time did not catch a mildly off-colour story or joke. She only ever had one drink, as she swore it always went to her head. I have a hunch she feigned it – I think she didn't really like the taste, but she didn't want to be left out. Her favourite was a type of liqueur called Bonne Santé [Good Health]. One time after Sis and I were married, she was having a Bonne Santé with all of us and out came this story. Her children had never heard it before:

When Mom and Dad moved to Pawha, Washington, she was soon pregnant with Frances. Mom didn't know many people and kept herself busy taking care of Dad and Uncle Otto – cooking, washing clothes, starching hard collars, and pressing suits. Dad had cut his thumb, and since infection always set in quickly, he had to keep it well bandaged and protected with a thumbstall. One evening at supper Dad complained to Mom that his thumbstall was not staying on at work and wanted her to make some stronger ones. "Oh," she said, "I found the best thumbstall in Otto's jacket today when I was pressing his suit." She was starting to get up from the table to get it when they both stopped her with odd looks on their faces and told her to sit down. Dad was waiting for Uncle Otto to explain, and Otto was waiting for Dad to say something, and Mom was getting more and more irate! Finally, Dad said he would talk about it when they were alone. It was then she found out that the thumbstall she had found was a slipper, the name for a French safe, or condom!

I can see her leaning up against the cupboard with her little glass of Bonne Santé, laughing like heck. Now *it was funny, but at the time she was furious. She said, "I didn't speak to them for weeks!" Dad was grinning. My dad never laughed out loud. He just put his hand to his face and shook all over.*

Mother was inclined to be a bit stuck up – a very proud person – and for her to tell that story! – I don't think people who knew her would believe it. In my own mind I'm positive my mother was not drunk... never... in any way, shape or form. I've seen Dad three sheets to the wind, but that was the time he was sick and shouldn't have been drinking at all. He had rheumatic fever around Christmastime in the '30s, just before the war, and one thing led to another and he wasn't improving. Finally, Frances, my oldest sister, said, "The only way you're going to get over this is to think about something else. Let's go out for a walk. Let's go and see Mr. Mason." So that's where they went, and of course, Ernie offered him a Christmas drink. I suppose Dad only had one drink... but he couldn't walk... and Frances was half-carrying him home down the hill. And we're watching this spectacle out the dining-room window! So were the neighbours, presumably. *Mother was livid! And of course, Frances was trying to explain: "He only had one drink!"* "Well, one too many!!" *Listening to the three of them was laugh-*

able. Oh, boy, those were the days!

Genevieve and Shirley were both introduced to 'a little glass of something' within the family. *In January business was slow, and that's when Dad made furniture. The weather was terrible too – in earlier times we had a lot more snow. He always saved a bottle of rum from Christmas, or bought another if he could, and we had it in January.* Here is what would happen: *Dad would come in the door and wash up, and Mother would put out a water glass, a juice glass, and two little shot glasses. The kettle was boiling and a lemon ready. Dad would pour rum into the big glass and fill it with hot water, squeeze the lemon, add a bit of sugar and nutmeg and stir. He'd pour first into Mom's glass, and then into Sis's and mine, and we'd sit and drink it.* This little ritual helped the dark days pass.

Lille Becker loved entertaining and used any excuse to camouflage the effects of the Depression. *In the '30s you listened to the radio, and you played a lot of cards. Auction bridge came in first and then contract bridge. Come Lent [the forty days prior to Easter], Mom and Dad always hosted two evenings of what she called Lenten bridge. She would have twelve to thirteen tables – she had to borrow the tables and chairs, but she always had enough dishes. She served food, and people put in a donation – a dime or so. It was a lot of fun. One of the guests who always came to the second evening was the Roman Catholic padre, who loved to play cards. In those days the division between Protestants and Catholics was strict, but he attended Mother's funeral – I've never forgotten that kindness.*

One year somebody didn't show up, and Mother and Dad said to me, "You have to play. There's nobody else, and we can't sit in." (They went around helping people who didn't know how to bid.) I was twelve or thirteen and they'd been teaching me the game, but this would be my first real sit! I remember I was playing in the parlour! The location alone was heady. *I don't remember the other two, but the man beside me was Jim Lancaster. (Jim and his father ran a men's store.) I sorted out my cards and couldn't believe it – I had twelve hearts and a low spade. I looked at the others and thought, 'Is this a joke? They're playing a trick on a kid!' "Mother!!" She came and looked over my shoulder and said, "Hmmm, my goodness" – she didn't want to give it away – then she said, "Bid six hearts." Jim doubled me, which is normal, but my partner said, "Seven hearts" because she had a couple of aces. Then the third person redoubled and Mother redoubled again. So what does Jim Lancaster lead? The Ace of Spades! Jim only had one ace so he was going to play it! That was it!! I went down, and I've never had a hand like that again.*

Another opportunity for a good time was a wedding shower. *Mother gave everybody showers. Evelyn Patten was Great-aunt Sophie [Ehmke] Patten's daughter, and in the '30s was to marry Young Jim Jamieson. (Jim and Barbara Jamieson lived next door to Grandma Becker in what used to be the United Church rectory.) Mom had what she called 'A Poor Man's Shower' for Evelyn.* Her inspiration was the comic strip "Maggie and Jiggs." *'Aunty' Jean Phillips dressed up as Maggie; and Mom, with a stocking over her head to make her look bald, was Jiggs. There were sixty or more guests. Refreshments were hardboiled eggs in the shell – shells ended up all over the place. Sis and I wheeled in first the presents, and later the eggs, in an old galvanized washtub sitting in a wheelbarrow. The barrow needed painting and was darn near falling apart.* The idea was a hit. *Evelyn was opening her presents – there weren't that many – and she got this package of three wooden spoons, and on the end of one of them was a little kewpie doll tied with a big ribbon, and on the spoon handle was written: 'At the end of a long spoon.' Everybody was laughing – they thought it was really funny – and I wondered what it meant. Of course, you never asked. Innocent old Genevieve – it'd take me years to find out.*

Lille had more surprises on the programme. *In our house two closets, one in the guest bedroom and the other in Mom and Dad's room, joined together as one. This closet made a right-angled corner under the stairs and had no lighting, particularly as one of my sisters made sure on that occasion that the closet door stayed shut.* The setting was perfect for mystery and mayhem. *'Aunty' Jean Phillips sat on Mom and Dad's bed under a funny bed light and told for-*

tunes, and in order to get to her from the guest room, the women had to pass through the closet. It was blacker than pitch, and they were fumbling their way among the clothes hanging up. To make it worse, Mom hid in the angle of the closet, and as they went by, she pinched the ones she knew and scared the daylights out of the ones she didn't know by whirling a New Year's rattler at them. She had the women screaming and everybody else wondering what was going on! That party was the talk of the town.

Nobody went home early that night. Sis and I were allowed to stay up. 'Aunty' Jean was reading cards and making the fortunes up, but I can remember Mrs. Crozier loved to read teacups. She and Mom used to visit back and forth all the time. Mom read cards too but she wouldn't read ours, so we'd get Mrs. Crozier to read our teacups. They had a garden on the north side of their property, and in the wintertime old Roddy Crozier, who ran the City waterworks, would flood the garden, and I learned to skate on Mother's old brown blades. We had a lot of fun on that rink. All the neighbourhood kids came, and if they didn't own skates, they slid in their boots. And we used to sleighride down the big hill on Dad's property onto the Dick Thomas property on Moray – the one with the seven girls.

Always looking to add sizzle to her days, Lille decided to learn to drive a car. In 1929 her husband had bought a new Chevrolet, and one day she ventured forth. *My sister Frances was teaching her, and Sis and I were sitting in the back because we were too young to leave at home. Besides, Mom was fun and there was bound to be something going on.* They were right. *In those days there wasn't power steering – she didn't even know how to shift gears – and she went too fast down the Dip on Pleasant Valley Road and darn near hit a telephone pole! I can hear Frances screaming yet! She took over the wheel and declared that Mother would* never *make a driver. When I think about it now, it's really funny, but it was almost a disaster at the time.*

The Dirty Thirties gave grief to many neighbours, and Lille made an attempt to share. *Mother was like a matriarch – people would run to her when they were in trouble – so whatever happened,*

115

Mom knew about it. In our orchard we had Yellow Transparent apples, Duchess – which Mom loved to use in applesauce and pies – Wealthy, a Snow Apple, and a Delicious; and sometimes in the fall we had a heck of a lot of apples stored in wooden boxes. Mom hated to see them go to waste. One year she got Dad to load the car and deliver them to people she knew would appreciate them. Next thing she knew, some of the boxes reappeared on the front porch. She was taken aback. Dad, of course, didn't know which boxes he'd dropped off at which house, and Mom at first couldn't figure out why the people didn't want them. Then she realized that if she charged a little something, people would come and get them. So she put out a little sign: '5 cents a box.' And people picked them up. They needed to preserve their self-respect.

The Beckers were also feeling the pinch. *Mother and Dad had to mortgage the house to save the shop. Mom said, "I'll live in a tent to save the business!" Sometime during the '40s they burnt the mortgage. We lit it on top of the kitchen range and celebrated!*

Genevieve was always on the lookout for more work. *Once Dad built the cabin at Mara Lake, we had to earn money to buy a new sundress or bathing suit. So for several summers for two weeks, Sis and I got up at 5 a.m. and walked the three miles out to Mr. Thomas Cary's on Otter Lake Road [1510] to pick currants. It was all gravel but in those days you never thought anything of walking – you walked everywhere – that's the way it was! I like driving that road now. So many corners keep you alert. And in spring you see the green and growing things. Otter Lake Road has hardly changed from the time Dad was courting Mom in the democrat.*

To pick currants Sis and I wore big straw hats and long sleeves. We always quit at noon because Mr. Cary didn't want us working out there longer, and if it got too hot, we'd quit at ten. He had made stools for us to sit on, and we stripped the blackcurrant branches into boxes. Redcurrants were softer, so you picked them by the stem. We always took our lunch and sometimes 'Grandma' Cary made lemonade. We had to clean the currants before we went home – the place was covered in fir trees, and we'd sit where it was shady and cool. We'd love it when there was a breeze so we could hold up the box to the wind and blow the leaves away – otherwise, we had to ferret them out one by one. We earned a nickel a pound.

At the end of the two weeks, we'd pack up the car and away we'd go to the lake. Mom hated the lake – it didn't have the amenities – it was too much like livin' in the old days... carrying water in two lard pails... Coleman gas lamps (I kept one)... an outhouse. But it was fun! My arthritic toe reminds me of Bill and Frank Fisher, Jim and Ken Watt, and Peter Poole. They loved to tease the girls, and one time they were after us to dunk us and we're running down the beach, and I tripped and sprained my big toe. OHHHH, it was sore for so darn long. It still bugs me.

One summer Genevieve worked at the Armstrong Pea Factory. She needed good eyesight and quick reflexes. *Farmers grew peas, dried and harvested them, and brought them into the factory by the sack or the ton. Some of them were infected with weevil; the outer layer of the pea hid the worm but it left a little hole. The girls sat on both sides of a conveyor belt, and as it carried the peas along, we'd snatch the infected ones and throw them in our sacks. Sometimes we'd have to check the same peas two or three times because they were re-examined at the other end of the belt. We didn't get paid by the hour – would you believe, we got paid by the number of weevil peas in our sacks! I have a photo of the girls sitting in front of the Pea Factory.*

One year, summer's end sent Genevieve to high school. Her feelings were mixed. *I just loved basketball. We played Salmon Arm, Vernon, Lumby and Enderby. We didn't need the bus for a game in Enderby; we'd go in cars and usually Mr. Linfield [principal] or Mr. Snowsell [vice-principal] drove. But I was **always** the tallest in school, and some of the kids weren't very nice about it – they could be little shits. I was never called Genevieve, always Becker or Becky – the men teachers, especially, called me Becker. And of course when we played basketball, it was always "Becky! Becky! Becky!" when the kids wanted me to pass the ball.*

In grade 10, however, two serendipitous events removed the stigma from her height: Mr. Bill Plummer returned to Armstrong to teach and coach, and the Ireland girls appeared in class.

During the 1920s and '30s there was a lot of men teachers and no place for them to board. Bill Plummer and Wilf Willander came to live at our house because my sisters and Tom were gone; I was three and Mom was expecting Sis. Easter was spring-cleaning time and the men washed windows and shook out the mats and toadied to me. They were like family. I can remember Plummer taking me for walks and an ice cream cone. He had big feet – I guess he took a size 12 – and my feet were big for my age but a lot smaller than his. I have the photo Mom took of our mud rubbers. Eventually, of course, the fellows moved on.

When we heard we were having a new teacher, Bill Plummer, I recognized the name, and I thought, 'I'm not going to say I know him – I'll just pretend I'm somebody else.' But when I walked into the class, he said, "Genevieve!" And I sort of looked up and said, "Yessir?" And he said, "I'm not 'sir.' You must remember me!" I did remember him – he looked exactly the same. And of course he was our basketball coach and it worked out wonderfully.

The appearance of the Ireland teenagers, however, was a delightful shock. *Mr. Cecil Ireland was the new stationmaster. Mrs. Ireland's maiden name was May Lingings – she had grown up in Armstrong – and they had a boy – Young Jim – and three girls. Lulla (whose real name was Aldyth) and Dinty (whose real name was Edyth) were twins; Rinky (Eileen) was younger. Lulla was about the same height as me and Rinky was taller! And Lulla and Rinky played basketball! We were friends right from the word go! And, of course, we never mentioned the word 'height!' Oh, what a **relief** to have somebody as tall as me! You have no idea what that meant! My whole life seemed to change.*

I always remember Mrs. Purslow. She taught algebra, geometry and etiquette, and when she called me Becker or Becky periodically, she'd apologize and correct herself: "Genevieve." Each class had five rows of seats. When we moved from room to room, I always [opted for] the front seat in the middle row because I realized that if you sat in the back, the teachers picked on you for answers. The boys usually sat on one side of the room and the girls on the other. Across from me in Mrs. Purslow's class sat David Smith, Bruce Van Kleeck, and Art Johnson, and one day they were raising heck. Mrs. Purslow was a very calm person, the nicest teacher you could ever wish for, but this time she got on her high horse and went after them.

I'm sprawled out in my desk at the front because I wanted to get on with it – I loved math and they were disturbing the whole class. She finished with them and snapped, "And Becker! You haul in a couple of yards of legs!!" So Genevieve pulled up straight in a hurry! When the bell rang, we stood and picked up our books. "Genevieve, will you stay." And she apologized, and I remember I started to cry because I felt bad – I didn't have *to stick my long legs out in front of her.*

Mrs. Purslow had smallpox when she was young and her face was pitted. Her students were oblivious to the imperfection. *She was a beautiful lady – she had what I can only describe as an aura about her. She was our chaperone one time we played basketball in Vernon. Instead of going to the dance, four or five of us girls wanted to go to a show, so she took us. It was during the war, and lots of militiamen from the army camp in Vernon were in the audience. We were sitting in a row, and one soldier turned around to look at us, spotted Mrs. Purslow, and said, "That's a face only a mother could love!" I wanted to get up and* wham *that guy, and in unison the bunch of us told him to "Shut up and turn around!!"*

But her hands were exquisite. She had to have some *part of her that didn't get marked up. They were the smallest, neatest little hands and, of course, her handwriting was beautiful.*

Vern Flatekval [local archivist] is trying his darndest to find out more about Mrs. Purslow because he thinks she should be down in writ-

ing and remembered. Like a lot of the boys who went to the high school, he thought the world of her. She was most understanding – the motherly type – and I know they went to her with all their young troubles.

During the fall of 1938, one of the infectious diseases that periodically sickened, maimed or killed the youth surfaced in the community. *I can't remember if it was scarlet fever or polio. I was staying in Vernon with my friend Violet Sparks, who used to live along Patterson Avenue, and Mom made me come home. Everybody was to stay away from school and in quarantine. Mom had a heck of a time keeping us busy.*

Lille's solution was needlework. *That's when I did the needlepoint for this chair – when I got to Calgary and saw this Duncan Fife, I was determined to buy it and put my needlepoint on the seat, and I did!* The piece is a complex arrangement of small posies flanking a large, central bouquet. The hues are natural. *I did a lot of petit point too – so tiny.* She pulls from a drawer two glass-framed ovals, the petit point flowers only an inch in diameter. Rifling through again, she finds a large, framed piece. *This parrot was my first needlepoint of a pair – the other was a canary. Another thing I sure did a lot of was embroidery. We embroidered on flour sacks because when you opened out all the seams, they just fitted a card table.*

In those sequestered weeks Genevieve also learned to knit and honed her sewing skills. She used them later to please her little granddaughter. *I used to make Krista's clothes before she started school. (After that, she was always in jeans.) I smocked her six dresses.* A photo shows the child in a peach dress with puffed sleeves, the collar embroidered with flowers, and diagonal smocking to the waist. *I knitted her a blue suit that the knit and purl made into pleats. For her sixth birthday I made her a green velvet dress with wide, white, lace-edged collar and cuffs that you could take off and wash. Krista was always so proud of her dresses. When we went out to dinner, she always wanted to wear them, and she* strutted.

Once during the period of quarantine Genevieve found herself in trouble with the law. *Mom always phoned her grocery orders to Phillips and Whitehouse, and they were delivered either by Warner's or Blackburn's Transfer. (The two other grocery stores, the Co-op and Overwaitea, had the same service.) Helen was home with her new baby, David – he'd been born on September 23rd – and she had quite a time with him. Milk formulas didn't agree with him – he was fussing and crying and spitting up all the time, and Helen was so worried. One day Mom sent her to bed to get her out of the way, and put me to rocking David and walking the floor with him.*

Finally, Mom took him and said, "You have to go up to Phillips and Whitehouse and get some canned milk and we'll try him on that." "But, Mom, I'm in quarantine! The cop will catch me!" The cop was Old Mr. Elliott and everybody was scared of him. Mother said, "Well, I can't go and they won't deliver it right away. You have to go, but you come right back." "But I'll have to pass the police office!" The station was on Patterson Avenue across from a vacant lot [Nelson's Glass], and Phillips and Whitehouse was on Okanagan Street. There was little chance she might escape notice. *I didn't want to go but the baby is crying, and I go. And Mr. Elliott caught me!*

*"**That Becker child!! What are you doing out here??**" And I'm shaking in my timbers. So I said my nephew was sick and I had to get milk from Phillips and Whitehouse. "**Get in the car!!**" I get in and he drives me home and practically drags me up the walk. He rings the doorbell and Mother appears with David screaming in her arms. Elliott's yelling over him at Mother, "**What do you mean sending this kid out! Why didn't you phone me!!**" And she's yelling right back at him: "You are **not** the delivery man, and she never greeted **anybody**! I phoned and told them to give it to her at the door and she was to run home!"* Three caterwaulers against one was an uneven scrap. *Elliott says, "I'll get it for you. How many d'ya want?" And of course after he left, I'm still sniffling. "I told ya so!"*

Polio attacked again in 1941. *My first high school principal was J.M. Murray; the Murrays lost their only son, Young John.* The *Armstrong Advertiser* reported that the iron lung requisitioned from Penticton did not arrive in time. *The Henley girl died. Norman MacDonald and Daphne Vickers recovered.*

More mundane illnesses took the wind out of Genevieve's sails. *I repeated grade 10 because I missed so much school. We couldn't change out of our basketball strip in Salmon Arm because the room was so small. You couldn't get two teams in it, and there were ten of us and ten of them. Coming home in the bus, I'd sit with Betty Garner, but as she got bus-sick, she sat by the window and kept it open. It was winter and I got lumbago [rheumatism]. Then in the spring I got appendicitis.*

I had felt sick and didn't go to a track meet with the kids – usually we went as a roaring team. The next day at recess we're sittin' in the sunshine and leanin' against the school fence. All of a sudden I fall over the fence into the bridal wreath! Some of the boys pick me up, and Mr. Snowsell comes running and takes me home. I have this big lump on my side. Mom takes me into Dr. Haugen's office and says, "I'm sure she's pregnant." Gawd almighty! I just about died! And the thing is I was ignorant – I didn't even know how to get pregnant – Mother told me nothing. Dr. Haugen examined me and told mother I had an absessed appendix. He was really scared it was going to break, and he didn't want me to go back to school, play basketball or do anything physical. "And don't ever say that in front of her again!" He was Icelandic – he spoke with an accent, and you listened!

Throughout high school Lille and Francis Becker kept a friendly eye on their daughters and made their friends feel welcome. *My sixteenth birthday was a whopper – we had a dinner party and dance – and I had boys! (Ninety percent of them were killed in the war.) We cleared the dining-room table to the side and put on the gramophone. It was wonderful! My mother went to a lot of trouble – she cooked everything – she was great.* The menu was extensive. *We had 'poached eggs on toast' – a piece of cake with peaches and whipped cream, and my birthday cake, of course. I don't know what we drank – since we were sixteen, probably tea and coffee, but Mom used to make ginger ale and put it in beer bottles.*

We'd come home from a school dance, and if Mom and Dad were in bed they would get up, and she would make pancakes or waffles for the whole gang. Mom and Dad were friends with Bill and Mrs. Sidney, Chip's parents. Sometimes Chip [Gordon] would go home and get a steak and bring it over for Mom to fry, or he'd have the steak in the back of a car when he left for the dance. We didn't drink at dances – going outside to drink was a bad *thing. Instead, when we were in our twenties, we brought it home. (You couldn't buy alcohol until you were twenty-one.) Dad didn't like beer, so we'd buy a bottle of rye or scotch and add mixers, and everybody had some, and of course Mom would always have a little.*

Until the Second World War came along, Christmas at the Becker house was thrilling. *There were no houses up behind the big school – it was forest – and Dad would chop down a forty-foot tree. (It was City land, I guess – nobody gave a rip.) The ceilings in the old house were eleven foot, so he always made sure he got a tall one. He'd saw off the top, and we'd haul it home on the sleigh. In high school we had our friends come the Sunday before Christmas and help us decorate. It was a* big *do. Mother always made doughnuts for us all. She was a superb cook – she could feed six people on two pork chops. And she fried in lard, of course – everybody did. She would stand over the old cast iron pan on the stove, just frying away. I don't know why we didn't get sick.*

Mom always made a three-tier Christmas cake and we helped ice it, and of course when we were small, Dad was Santa Claus and took a piece out of the bottom layer. He always made us sleighs for Christmas. Mom made all the cookies and the candy – divinity fudge, chocolate fudge, French creams, stuffed dates. There used to be at least twenty people for Christmas dinner as the family grew – Tom had four girls and a boy – Helen and Frances each had a boy. Come New Year's, we used to go 'round from house to house and ask for a piece of Christmas cake – every piece you got gave you a good month in the new year, so you had to collect twelve pieces. You'd be surprised how many ladies had it ready and waiting for us – little

123

slivers wrapped in waxed paper. I can remember Thup Marshall and I going up and down our street, and up and down her street until we reached our quota and then we'd sit down and eat it. I don't know when that custom went out – maybe when I got too old for it.

The war changed everything. The boys enlisted and most of them didn't come home. Bert Schubert, the two Murray boys – Jack and Bill; the two Fisher boys – Bill and Frank; Hollingsworth, the Southam boys – oh, gosh, so many. I remember one time in the '40s when the war was on and Christmas was so horrible – none of the family came home. Frances was living in Calgary, Helen was married and nursing in Penticton, and Tom was in St. Thomas, Ontario, in the air force. Dad loved Christmas. If he didn't have a gang around, forget it! He loved the noise. That year he wished [Armstrong Spallumcheen] had an orphanage so he could invite them all. The only person we had for Christmas was 'Silent' Warner. He was older than Dad and used to do odd jobs for us. 'Silent' Warner was deaf. He didn't wear a horn like 'Uncle' Harry Hope – you had to write what you wanted to say – but he could read lips too.

One wartime Christmas, however, was almost like old times. *After church on Christmas Eve, the house was full! Everybody including Tom came home. The Thornton boys were there – Jim and Jack – and some of the boys on embarkation leave before going overseas. One of them was Tommy Thomas, one of the sons of Tom Thomas. We had a whoopee cushion. The rocking chair had a bevel in the seat, and the cushion just fit beautifully. And Tommy Thomas was just having a ball with it. He started mimicking people in church – just the women, not the men. He'd sit on this darn cushion and it would go off, and this time it was Mrs. Smith, and the next time it was Mrs. Young. Honestly! Helen and Frances had put it in their Christmas parcel, and Mother said she wished she'd never left it out! I can see Tommy Thomas yet!*

Everybody did something for the war effort. Mother would come home from Red Cross meetings with boxes of socks and mitts and helmets [balaclavas], and some knitters hadn't cast off properly and she would have to refinish them. And, of course, she said to me, "It's time you learned to do these things." And the wool was terrible, you know – all that khaki, re-dyed, itchy – I don't know how the boys ever wore them – but I guess if they were freezing to death, they put them on.

During the war a full page in each *Ayaitchess* annual records its effect on the student body. The page is designated **Honor Roll**, and subsumes columns of names of both boys and girls under such headings as Killed in Action, Prisoner of War, On Active Service, On Call. *They graduated and joined up. I counted close to 300 kids that left here.*

Betty Garner, Roy Pearson, Frank Gates, the Students' Council – we were all involved in putting out the first high school annual in 1941. Genevieve lays out copies from 1941, 1942 and 1943. *These annuals all belong to Betty Garner. She is giving them to the [Armstrong Spallumcheen] Museum because they don't have these particular issues. Of course, my sisters burnt all mine.*

Just look at the printing. Know how it was done? First of all, each page was typed with special ink on special paper. Then they melted a jelly. Did you ever see a jelly pad? The apparatus had a tray that the jelly fitted in. With a roller you pressed the sheet that you had just typed onto the set jelly. Then you took a sheet of blank paper and rolled each one onto the master sheet and hoped the printing came off right. And you could only use the master for so many copies, and then you had to type a new master. Eventually we got a Gestetner, but you can see in these first annuals how some of the printing is very poor.

Betty Armstrong drew all the illustrations. Each is signed BMA. *She never went by 'Elizabeth.' She loved to draw and she copied Varga and Petty, artists who did a lot of calendars for different stores. I wish I had kept one. The 'Petty girls' were famous in the '30s and '40s.*

Betty Garner named the annual the Ayaitchess and wrote the School Song. We sang it all the time.

The tune Betty chose was called "The Empire March of Freedom" and her words were these:

Throughout the Okanagan Valley
In any field you care to name,
In basketball, or track, or hockey,
In any other sport or game;
The red-and-white, our High School colors
Are a sign of victory.
We're all for one, one for all together,
It's the A.H.S. for me!

Chorus:
So clear the way for the teams
Of the good old A.H.S.
The red-and-white in any fight
Does very well, we must confess.
We're out to win against all odds,
We never fear the stiffest fray;
We're all for one, one for all,
We're proud of the A.H.S. today!

See my ring finger? The knuckle is enlarged. *In 1942 Armstrong High School defeated Vernon in Kamloops and won the North Okanagan High School Basketball Championship. I played centre, and Rinky and Lulla played right and left forward.* The girls were a formidable trio. *I remember all the kids who were on the team. We stayed with the Tennant family, as Dr. Tennant had left Armstrong and gone to Kamloops to treat the natives.*

The rivalry between Armstrong and Vernon was intense. *A girl called Blackburn – no relation to the family in town – played centre and was my guard, and she knocked me over whenever she could. That's exactly what she did, and I fell on my left side with my hand underneath me and the fingers bent backwards and the fourth finger was broken. It was black and blue and all my fingers were sausages, but Dr. Tennant wasn't allowed to treat me. He said, "I'm sorry, Genevieve, I can't do a thing for you. When you go home, ask your doctor to x-ray it and see what's wrong. Make sure the school pays for it." When I got home and Mother saw my hand, she said, "Oh, my goodness..." and as an afterthought, "Thank heaven it wasn't your right hand!" I went to Dr. Haugen, and although I hadn't asked, he sent the bill to the school, but they didn't pay it. That finger never healed properly, but we won the tournament and Vernon was mad.*

I have school photos of the kids – some of the boys were interested in photography so, of course, some cameras weren't focused properly or there was a bit of movement. One photo has '1942' written on the basketball. In 1942 Thup Marshall, Betty Garner and I graduated together. Betty Garner gave the valedictory.

In elementary school Genevieve thought she'd like to become a teacher. *Principal T.A. Aldworth taught me in grade 8. Miss Adair got real sick – her married name was Landon – and T.A. asked me if I would take her grade 6 class: "And here's what she wants you to do." I enjoyed it! I had to send one little boy out in the hall lots of times, but T.A. would come and check on me regularly to see things were going all right. So I wanted to go to Normal School. Then the war came along. All the boys left, and there's no money to send me to Vancouver. So after I graduated in 1942, I married Ian Macpherson from Enderby. We had gone together in high school, and he was unable to enlist because he was classified 4F.* The caption under Genevieve's name in the 1942 *Ayaitchess* foretells the nuptials:

Genevieve's slim,
Genevieve's tall,
And there's only one guy
Dates this beautiful doll.

After I was married, I worked with my aunt Mrs. Etter in the office at the sawmill for W.J. Smith, 'Sawdust' Billy. I used the four-foot-long Remington adding machine – it was huge! – and a technician from Kelowna came up to service it. The numbers were in the thousands, so I didn't have to press each key a dozen times as you might on a calculator. The job was interesting. I wish I had taken my scaler test. The boys used to come into the office and ask me to add up the numbers in their scaling logs, but to get their certificate, they were supposed to be able to do it in their heads. When Aunty retired, I worked with Nadine, Bert Fletcher's wife. She was a sister-in-law to Joe Mullen that ran the Armstrong Cheese Factory.

Her marriage lasted three years, and Genevieve returned to the Becker home to await the arrival of their son. *When Cameron was a few months old, I worked briefly at the FM shop – Faber and Macdonald – women's wear. Faber was the woman and Macdonald was the man. They had one store in Vernon and opened another here. It was located east of Clarke's Jewellery on Railway Avenue.* A better position, that of office secretary, presented itself with the opening of a gypsum mine, Gypsum, Lime and Alabastine, in Falkland in 1947. *I travelled to work by train and stayed for the week.* Two-year old Cameron accompanied her. *I had a babysitter for him in Falkland, Mr. and Mrs. Ben Munsell. We called them 'Grandpa' and 'Grandma' Munsell, and Ben insisted we were related. When some of the boys from Armstrong started to work there, they all had cars and on weekends I'd get a ride home and back. When I didn't get a ride, I came home on the train Saturday morning at 8:30 and returned to Falkland Saturday night. Then the company built a new bunkhouse and included an apartment for me.* During this period she met her husband John Culling, who worked at the mine too. *I was there until the mine closed in 1956. We married when Cameron was eleven and moved to Alberta. I had no more children.*

Mother died in 1950. She wasn't well for several years. After an operation she had an aneurysm in her groin, and in those days nothing could be done to dissolve it. The clot broke and reached her heart. In 1985 I had a blood clot in my left leg from crossing them, but I lived because they put me on medication right off the bat: Warfarin, which is rat poison – it thins the blood. Science is really booming these days. There are so many cures for this and that but so many more diseases. We had never heard of Alzheimer's.

In 1952 Dad sold our place on Becker for $8,000 and moved into the Armstrong Hotel. Today the house is nothing like it was. So many people lived in it and everybody changed it, so it isn't even an-

tique anymore. The spruce hedge that flanked Becker Street is gone. Only the towering maples remain. *Dad died in 1964. His malaria was always a problem.*

Genevieve and Shirley continued to share their interest in genealogy and were eligible to belong to the National Society of Daughters of the American Revolution [NSDAR]. *To be a member of NSDAR, you had an ancestor that had participated in the War of Independence; in our case, Pieter Becker. Shirley became regent of the New Caledonia chapter in Kelowna, and I spent time as regent of the Heritage chapter in Calgary. This is a piece of original flooring of a building in Washington, DC, from the revolutionary period.* It is a two-inch section of varnished tongue-and-groove wood stamped "Certified piece Constitutional Hall stage floor." *They took up the best parts of the floor and sold them to raise money for renovations at historic sites.*

When Lille Becker revealed the family's Unterbrink connection, Shirley began to track that branch of the family. *Grandpa Henry Unterbrink had remarried. Sis found the Unterbrink relations in the States, and in 1985 we went down to Fort Wayne, Indiana, and met them. We found our shirt-tail relations, but I never visited so many graveyards in all my life!*

Once again Genevieve has taken up residence in Armstrong Spallumcheen. Earlier for a brief time she herself owned property on Becker Street. *There was a piece beside Dad's place that was a vacant lot [2980]. He said to me, "Have you got some money? It's up for taxes. Buy it." So I did and sold it two months later for twice the price.* Genevieve has some opinions about her community: *I could never understand why they split Armstrong Spallumcheen into two jurisdictions. It should never have been sanctioned.*

She flips through an album of projects she sewed and quilted over the years. The photographs merge her past and present. *This is my first quilt, made from all the dresses I sewed for Krista. I gave it to her – it's the only one I have registered... This one depicts the rose window Dad had put in above the altar in St. James church for*

Mom... A yellow and green reversible tablecloth in log cabin pattern... Shirt and vest... Quillow... Dresden plate quilt... Daisy quilt made by hand – no two petals the same... Costume for Krista and her horse, Viking – she's a senorita, and the horse wears a tuxedo – she won the Canadian Equestrian Championship... Every fall the Quilters had a retreat where we each made a square on a certain theme and then raffled the bunch – this time I happened to get it and made this Christmas quilt. They were the nicest women you could wish for, generous and kind. I'll be damned if I'm going to give up the club. I send in my dues and tell them to mail me the newsletter... When Sis married Art Danallanko in 1946, her sister-in-law Mamie gave her fourteen squares for a wedding present. Mamie had made them in the '30s or during the war because they are all featherstitched and embroidered and the material is old. Sis didn't do anything with them, and after she died, my niece Wendy asked me if I'd like to have them. There were eleven large butterflies and three smaller ones. The quilt in question uses only twelve squares. *If you notice, this butterfly is smaller than the others. They say you have to have a mistake – something irregular – in each quilt to show it was handmade.* That criterion may be a metaphor for living.

Genevieve is struck by a sudden recollection. *Ohhhh... remember they replaced the wooden sidewalks on Becker? Well, the cement was still wet and Benny Sugden wrote his initials in it...* B.S. *(Of course, he always said it stood for* Brown Sugar!*) I'm on my way to school and catch him... and I tell him you aren't supposed to... his initials aren't very nice... and he says, "Oh, that's all right, Genevieve," and he adds* + G.B. *So Benny Sugden's and my name are still in that cement.*

I wanted to see if I could find the place. I thought I'd better pick my time or people would wonder what I was up to: "Why's that old lady trompin' up and down Becker Street?" So not long ago I parked the car – there wasn't much traffic – put the blinkers on – got out and walked up to the house. Then I walked from the house down the street and tried to gauge where our hedge had ended, and to visualize where those initials might be. I couldn't find them. All those new driveways have likely knocked them out!

130

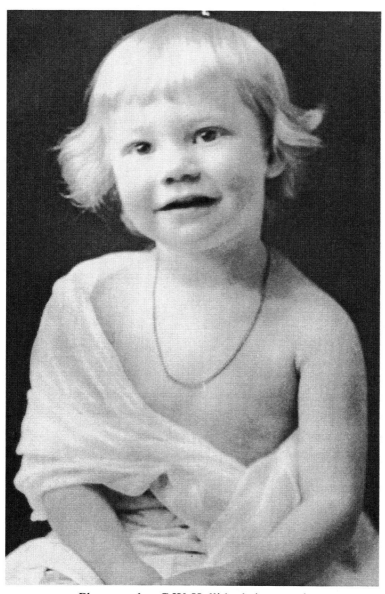

Photographer C.W. Holliday's image of
two-year-old Genevieve Becker

Chapter Three

Anvils, Archives, and Art

William Earl 'Bill' Clayton

My father came here in 1905, you see, and he kind of liked the town. He was an American and walked from Vernon to Armstrong down the railroad tracks, so the story goes, and there was a blacksmith shop right where the museum is now. And he thought he'd better go in and try and find a job.

Bill Clayton is speaking about the family business, a smithy and machine shop that for seven decades was a landmark on Pleasant Valley Road just east of Bridge Street and is now the Armstrong Spallumcheen Museum and Art Gallery. Bill, born on December 17, 1924, worked on the site first with his father, then with his brother, and finally on his own.

Dad was born in 1876 in Wisconsin – twelve kids in the family – so he left home early. He migrated westward and took the first job that he could find – working in a smithy. There he learned the trade. *He did try to get into the Spanish-American War [1898 in Cuba] but he was too thin. [Besides] he didn't like Americans – he said they talked too much and he preferred to stay in the background – so in 1903 or '04 he crossed into Canada roughly at Calgary and went to work for the CPR.*

However, Frank Albert Clayton was looking for a place in which to settle down. *I know he didn't come through to the Okanagan by train – he'd have told me all about that. He must have gone along the border because he came up through Penticton – he was not enthused about Kelowna, I remember – it didn't turn his crank – and he liked Armstrong better than any town he had seen in the valley.* Better still, it supported two blacksmith shops.

There was a fellow in the smithy [on Railway Avenue] by the name of Heinzie (Dad always called him Heinzie), who was renting the shop from a Mrs. Wallace, who lived next door where the Brown Derby Café is now. Mr. Wallace had been a blacksmith but he had died. Dad worked for Heinzie for a while, and then Heinzie decided to pull out and went over to the other shop to work for Daniels – Blackburn's livery barn was just opposite [2545 Patterson Avenue]. My dad ended up renting the shop from Mrs. Wallace and then he bought it. I don't think he had to pay too much for it – she was only too glad to be rid of it.

Bill retrieves an old photograph. *That's a picture of the original building. It was taken about 1906 or '07, shortly after Dad came.*

Frank Albert Clayton already owns the smithy. A black signboard above the open double doors fronting the street proclaims in meticulous white print:

Horse	**F.A. Clayton**	*Wagon*
Shoeing		*Repairing*

GENERAL   BLACKSMITH.

You'll notice the inside of the doors is all white. Fastened back, they highlight the exterior of the clapboard building. *There was a glanders scare here – it's a contagious disease to do with horses – and they had to disinfect everything. They put whitewash [lime and water] on the doors to supposedly kill all the germs. I'm sure it didn't but that's beside the point.* Horses walked inside the smithy to be shoed. *The building was set back from the street – in this photo you can still see the rear of Mrs. Wallace's house.*

The camera has caught five men. Three of them dressed in suits, vests, ties and hats are facing front, and the third has positioned his good-looking riding horse sideways for a full view of the animal. *I asked my dad once what breed it was, but he said it was just something that needed shoeing. I haven't got a clue – horse – that's all I know.* Bill has no interest in four-legged machines.

Second from the left, the only one seated, is a slight young man wearing suspenders over long-sleeved white underwear, and work-pants. He looks like an apprentice but is, in fact, the owner, Frank Clayton. *He was a very fast worker – he was perspiring all the time. A blacksmith has to be fast. When you heat up a piece of iron, you don't want to be thinking... 'What am I going to do?... Shall I hit it here... or there?... Maybe I'll hit it there....' Well, the damn iron would be cooled off! When you take the iron out of the forge, you got to start hittin' it right away – you want to do as much work in a 'heat' as possible before you have to stick it back in the fire.*

Dad's sitting on a horseshoe keg. They were round, about ten inches in diameter and eighteen inches high – not very big – because they'd have about 100 pounds of horseshoes in them and were heavy. The sturdy workman standing to his right is his hired man. *That's Art Kaiser. He was Mrs. Charlie Hoover's brother. Charlie Hoover owned the [Inland] Flour Mill. Dad told me the names of the other three but I've forgotten – just roustabouts, he said.*

As you can see, the building wasn't big – about thirty feet wide and forty feet long. It came down from Lansdowne about the same time, I presume, as [St. James] Anglican Church [1892]. (Of course, the west end of the church has since been added on – if you go inside, you can plainly see a seam on the floor where the boards joined up.)

Sometime around 1915 my dad built an addition to the smithy right to the sidewalk. He added a piece forty-eight feet square, and this is the part that still exists today. In Bill's second photograph the front of the building is wider and has the familiar museum silhouette. *You can see the original doors were much smaller – they just had to be big enough for a horse to walk through, or maybe a wagon – they were enlarged several times over the years to allow bigger equipment inside.*

Then in the mid-1950s my brother and I tore off the back of the building – the original smithy – and extended from Dad's 1915 addition north about sixty-four feet toward Slab Alley [Wood Avenue]. If you measured the length of the building now, it would be around 112 feet. And there's a definite hump in the museum floor where we added on – a miscalculation, plain and simple.

I had that first picture of the old smithy in our [business] cal-endar one year when I was at the machine shop after Dad died, and everybody that came along congratulated me. I was sorry I hadn't done it before he died, but I was a little leery. He didn't like attention – he certainly didn't like crowds – he just stood back and observed because he was quite shy.

Bill Clayton isn't shy. A tall, lanky, outgoing man with a warm personality and a ready smile, he lives at 2930 Becker Street just two doors north of the house in which he grew up. *You can see the house from here – it's got a tin roof on it now. It didn't have a tin roof years ago and it wasn't purple either – it was white and looked altogether different. 1907 or '08 was when that house was built.*

Frank Clayton needed to build a house because he had found a wife. *He met my mother – Maude Billson – there's a big pic-ture in the museum – a beautiful picture. She came from England in 1906 to visit her uncle. He said she could get a job down at Greenhow's at O'Keefe Ranch, but by the time my mother got there, the position was filled. So she took a job serving table in the Armstrong Hotel. My father had a room at the hotel. She probably served him his breakfast and supper, and maybe he hopped over the tracks for lunch too. They got married in 1907 and Mabel was born in 1908.*

Of their six children, the first five were born in their new house. *After Mabel there was Eva, and then John came along. Then we had a little gap, and then Art came along, then Frank, and seven years later I was the last. Dr. Van Kleeck delivered me. He died before I was old enough to remember him but he was well respected. He ran for political office one time, but the voters decided he could serve the community better by being a doctor.*

When I was born, Mother was forty-three, and Dr. Van Kleeck thought she should go to the Armstrong Hospital on account of her

age. She said she had to take three doses of castor oil to get *me out –
it was a long delivery – it took all day. I was a long baby, she said.*

*I was taller than all my brothers and very thin. People that were
garden variety could get pants made to measure. Years ago, that used to
be the rage. The Co-op was on the corner of [the present] Rose Valley
Square – half of it was a grocery store and the other half, gents' furnish-
ings. Mr. Youngblood ran the suit department, and you could get quite a
nice suit there for thirty dollars made to measure out of Montreal.*

It was a two-trip suit. *Actually, it was a two-trip, three-piece
suit: jacket, vest, and pants. There'd be a bunch of samples and
you'd pick out the material, and Mr. Youngblood would measure you
up and send the numbers away and after a while they sent the suit
back to him, and you'd try it on for a fitting. Then back again to
Montreal it would go for adjustments. The name of the tailors in
Montreal was 'The House of Stone.' It was a masculine name, and
I remember I used to feel quite honoured to be wearing a suit made
by 'The House of Stone.'*

*You had one good suit supposedly for Sunday best, and maybe a
sports jacket and casual pants for going to a movie or something less for-
mal. That's when you got 'unfinished' pants – you'd hem them up yourself.*

*They had shoes in the Co-op too – maybe not the greatest selec-
tion, but we were easily satisfied, you know. Mine were about size
10½, so I could buy them there. There used to be a fella that made
shoes – a Mr. Tyler – where the Brown Derby Café is. My brothers
didn't like his shoes because the leather was stiff and had fuzzy stuff
on it – it wasn't nice and shiny. I never had a pair made because by
my time there were more shoes comin' in.*

*When I went to high school, I wore a tie every day. Most of the
boys did – pants and a shirt and tie. Some didn't, I grant you, because they didn't have ties – some wore an imitation tie on an elastic
that went around your neck underneath your collar. But that wasn't
considered very good because the knot was too perfect and people*

could tell you hadn't tied it yourself.

Years ago people dressed up more than they do now. It shakes me to see it – especially the boys – baggy pants – the crotch down to their knees – it's such a shame. You see pictures of earlier days – women with their big fancy hats on – and gloves – you don't see gloves anymore, do you? Today nobody dresses up – we used to put on our best clothes to go to a funeral – show respect. Now people go in jeans! It's a different world.

The world was changing too around Frank Albert Clayton's smithy. In the early years of the twentieth century, Henry Ford's motorcar appeared on the roads. At first the new machines were rare and didn't cause a ripple at the forge. *It depended where you lived and how much money you had. There were still plenty of horses and wagons around in the 1930s and '40s.*

Horsepower and human ingenuity often worked in tandem. *For people in early days, necessity was the mother of invention. An emery stone, for instance, was heavy – thirty or forty pounds – they used it to sharpen ploughshares, mattocks, axes, crowbars, rock drills, cold chisels.... Dad said on the Prairies they used windmills to turn it because the wind blew all the time. Sometimes the smithy was built beside a creek to use waterpower. But the easiest way was to put a horse on a treadmill. Drive him onto it – lock the front and put a board across his rear. When he felt it move under him, he would lurch back and hit the board, and then step ahead to get away from it – and he would keep this up and power the emery stone. Dad used a little stationary gas engine to power his equipment.*

Seeing Dad was a blacksmith, he liked welding, so in time he got more into the welding end of it. At first he had three shops, shall we say – three departments. Closest to the street in his addition was the Blacksmith Shop and the forge where he shoed the horses. The room behind it in the original old smithy he called the Wagon Shop – where he repaired wagons – and behind that again was the Welding Shop. Don't get too excited about the size of these rooms!

140

But in the late 1920s, horses were kind of passin' by the wayside, you know, and those 'infernal automobiles' were more prevalent. My father thought we'd better modernize – keep up with the times. So by 1930 he had shoved the Blacksmith Shop back into the Wagon Shop to make a large area out front for repairin' cars, and he run it as a garage for a few years. That was a <u>disaster</u>*. One, he wasn't a very good mechanic so he didn't make any money at it; two, he wasn't a talker and he couldn't meet the public; and three, the Depression came along, and what cars were around were converted into 'Bennett buggies' and pulled by a horse because people couldn't afford repairs or gasoline. So Dad could look ahead pretty good, but he got a little too carried away. He got a little too progressive, theoretically.*

But he was still a blacksmith, so he kept on welding up farm implements and all that jazz, and he made more money in the back part with his welding than he did in the front part fixin' cars. So he was actually able to figure out that "this car business wasn't going anyplace with me," and he rented the garage for a couple of years and that was <u>another</u> *disaster. Renting is always a bugbear. He'd see things they were doing wrong – like giving credit to bad customers, so they didn't have enough money to pay the rent. He'd let it go for a while and then he'd blow up. He wasn't a very successful landlord. But renting is a pesky job. I rented a house once and it drove me insane... bad tenants... phone you up anytime... heating bills sky high... whatever.*

At that point Frank Albert gave up on cars. *He decided the Wagon Shop was too small, and he moved back into the front addition as well, which gave him a lot more room. Then he modernized into a machine shop. We had a metal lathe, and a drill press, a hydraulic press, welding machines. If people had a bent plough or broke a piece off a binder, they'd bring it in, and he would straighten up the plough or fix the break. He repaired threshing machines and well pumps, then branched into sawmill components, and logging equipment, and any machines allied with these industries.*

It was a two-man shop, shall we say. He had various different men – usually just one at a time – a handyman to hold something for him, or drill the holes in the metal. Someone to take something apart for him to straighten a piece, and then to put it back together again after he'd finished working on it. Somebody to help him lift things – somebody on the other end.

Seven years younger than his nearest sibling, Bill migrated through elementary school on his own. *I was nearly fifteen when World War Two was declared – I was just goin' into grade eight – I'd missed a year or two.* In truth, elementary school was something of a bad memory. *One of the men teachers was something else. He'd pick up a book and fire it. "Ya chump! Ya doughhead!" He would get right after you – come up behind where you were sittin' and box your ears. The kids' ears were as red as beets.*

I don't remember much about high school other than pickin' up scrap iron one summer. The Powers That Be thought we should send it off to the war effort. How are we going to get it there? Get the Municipality to donate a truck and a driver, and three or four of us school kids to ride in the back! And we went around to all the farmers and picked up anything metal that the farmers didn't use any more – parts off a plough or a binder – a set of harrows – a hay rake that had rusted out – old machinery that was just hangin' around – an eyesore. Then we brought it down to town and loaded it into boxcars here, and it was hauled off to a smelter someplace. Of course, we thought it was great fun. Ridin' on a truck and goin' out to all these places. Throwin' the stuff into the truck – throwin' it into the boxcars. It's a wonder we didn't get hurt! Perish the thought! And it was all volunteer – no one got paid for nothin'!

Bill was also ready to hand as his father's helper in the machine shop. *After school and Saturdays – he didn't usually work on Sunday – he invariably needed help. I'm eating, so I need to pay my way – like a farm boy who has to milk the cow. Actually my father and I – we didn't always get along because we had quite an age difference. He was forty-eight years old when I was born, and when I was a teenager, he was in his sixties. We got along pretty good at*

142

home about the time I got ready to go away – when I was eighteen or nineteen years old. But in my earlier teens we didn't get along too well. He was getting' up in years and workin' hard, and he didn't have time for me – let's be honest here!

Mom used to go to bat for me because I was the baby – she never said much. But my father was a very gruff man, and I used to have to work with him, you see, and you had to know exactly *what he was thinking. He didn't say, "Bring me that chisel." You were supposed to be watchin' him and* know *that he wants a chisel. And don't fool around. You had to be very observant of what he was doin' – keep your mind on your job – you can't be lookin' out the window – that tool had to be right beside him – you had to be thinking ahead all the time. There used to be a dentist here that reminded me so much of my father. He went through assistants like you change your socks. They had to know what tool he wanted next. My father was the same way. It was good training though. You turned out to be a real good employee, I'll tell you!*

When Bill was partway through grade twelve, his father found him an apprenticeship. *I didn't particularly like school – I wasn't a student – mediocre. This chance come up and my dad thought I'd better get in there. To be absolutely honest with you, I often wondered how he found out about it. He never said much, but I always figured it happened this way:*

There was a salesman used to come up from Vancouver selling hardware, and I think Dad was talking to him about how he wished he could get me into a machine shop – he knew I was interested. And as far as I can tell, this salesman must have said, "Well, I know of Laurie Lobb in Rosedale." He had about six men workin' for him – fairly big – about the right size for me to go in as an apprentice. Rosedale is about seven miles out of Chilliwack up the Fraser Canyon. I went down there as an apprentice for four years.

I lived in different boarding houses – there were lots of boarding houses years ago. People making a little extra money serving

*breakfast and supper, putting up lunches. I had to walk about a mile
and a half to work, or ride a bicycle, but that was all right. And I
never really got homesick – my brothers when they left home got
homesick – but I was able to take it in my stride for some reason.
I used to come up about three times a year by train – it cost only
about fifteen dollars from Chilliwack return. So I could get on the
train down there at 9 p.m. and be here at 8:30 the next morning, so
what more could I ask? We usually worked Saturday down there, but
sometimes I got Saturday off and could leave Friday night. There
was no trains out of Armstrong on Sunday, so I wouldn't get back
until Monday night – I got an extra day. The reason the train didn't
run on Sunday had something to do with the Lord's Day Act, I'm
told. It even extended to freight trains. The only time a freight train
went through here on Sunday was in the fall when the fruit and vegetables were being shipped.*

Laurie Lobb's Rosedale Machine Shop was a happy choice.
*Laurie Lobb was a wonderful employer – wonderful mannerisms
– very polite – very religious – no smokin' or swearin' – oh, no, he
toed the line – he went to church every Sunday. Oh boy, a wonderful man. Couldn't be better.* In fact, Lobb was like a father to young
Bill. *Just about! Just about! I was very fortunate.*

So was his new employer. Bill brought with him his father's
hard-taught training. *Oh, yes, Laurie Lobb was watching all the
time too. He was very, very conscientious. Nothin' went by him.
But he wasn't as tough – altogether different. [Instead] he was kind
of a penny pincher, you know, watched his expenses carefully. He
wouldn't want to give nothin' away.*

*Everything had to be marked down – all the materials we used
– all the welding rods, cotter pins, nuts and bolts, washers.... If [the
job] needed a little piece of iron, he'd charge fifteen or twenty cents
for it. If the bookkeeper phoned Vancouver for some part, he marked
it down in a book: 'One phone call to So-and-so in Vancouver regarding....' Then that phone call was charged up to the customer. He
was frugal, that would be the word.*

He did well too. He made money. And I learned a lot from that – I sure did – I brought back that frugalness with me when I left there. A key to any business is to be frugal. You can't (pardon the expression) be slack-assed. It doesn't matter if you're a farmer or what you are – you have to be frugal. I was very, very fortunate to work for him. It was a wonderful experience – the best thing that ever happened to me.

By the time Bill finished his apprenticeship and returned to Armstrong, Frank Albert was seventy-two years old and toying with the idea of retirement. *My dad was gettin' tired because he worked six days a week, and he wanted to sell the shop. He wanted a rest. But he couldn't find anybody to buy it – of course, he didn't advertise it either! He didn't want anybody to know! Perish the thought!! People would be coming around with all the questions: "How much do you want for it?... Why do you want to sell it?... What are you going to do with all your extra time, Frank?" It would drive him nuts!*

That's the sort of man he was – very bashful, and very, very proud. At the end of his life he needed to use a cane. So when he got to the shop, he'd leave the cane here because he didn't want anybody uptown to see him with it. He'd do his business, come back down to the shop, pick up the cane and go home. I remember when the old age pension cheques came out. Having to take money from the government was like accepting charity. He'd never cash the cheque at the bank himself – no way! He'd send my mother in with it. Maude could have charged a commission.

So my brother Art and I thought maybe we should take over the shop. We made a pretty good deal with my dad – he was only too happy to let us have it. No fuss, no muss. *He wanted to get the hell out! It was 1948 – he'd been in the business for forty-three years.*

The partnership with his brother had its natural ups and downs. *I know a fella once told me, "Partnership is a poor ship to sail in!" It's true too. It can be very good if you have the right partner, but heaven help you if you have the wrong one! Brothers are too critical of each other – we don't talk enough. One of the keys to success in anything is communication. And when you're in partnership with somebody, you have to work at it – trust me! [But] very often brothers don't get along for many years, and then when they get older, they start to get together – bury the hatchet.*

A sudden and devastating illness complicated the relationship. *My brother and I were in business about fifteen years together, and then he got spinal meningitis. It was like an old person suffering a stroke – he walked with a pronounced limp and one arm wasn't any good. He had a complete change of personality – a hundred miles from his normal self – very hard to live with. He lost all zest for work – he didn't have the heart for it. He used to go to the Legion to escape – to spear the odd drink and some conversation. After Art died, I was able to buy out his wife, Caroline. I got rid of the business in 1988. I went forty years.*

His brother's disease was Bill's second encounter with a fateful malady. *One of the greatest discoveries I ever seen in my life was the discovery of the Salk vaccine for infantile paralysis. We had those terrible epidemics years ago. One started out down in Penticton with a case there, and then it moved to Kelowna, then one or two cases in Vernon, and the schools didn't open at all – [the kids] were quarantined. With it you had two choices – you either died or you were a cripple. It used to scare the pants off the authorities. And it always came in the latter part of August after a long, hot, dry summer. It was called 'infantile' paralysis but teenagers would get it too. It always stuck in my throat that one chap, a school friend of mine, died – his name was John Murray. Then along came that Salk vaccine [1954] and it stopped that damn disease just like that! It was unbelievable! What a blessing!*

And the worst discovery was the atom bomb.

When he wasn't working, Bill enjoyed dancing. *People went to dances more than they do now – we used to have dances every Friday or Saturday night. We'd go up to Hullcar or Knob Hill or*

146

Salmon River – there was a school out there. Always somebody play-ing a fiddle or a piano. They wrapped up before midnight because a lot of people went to church on Sunday and didn't stay out too late.

It was the same thing in town. During the week bars used to close at 10:30 or 11 o'clock at night – people had to work the next day. But I always remember a fellow who lived over on Rosedale. He was a World War One veteran and got a pension once a month. He'd pick up his cheque downtown and cash it and, of course, he'd stop at the Legion to treat himself and his buddies. And of course he'd stay too long. He had a little dog that was always with him – a Springer spaniel – and sometimes the dog would come home by himself after supper. And the missus knew what had happened, and she'd take the wheelbarrow and go down the street until she found her man in the ditch. I don't know how she ever got him loaded into the damn wheelbarrow – he wouldn't be able to cooperate very much! And it must have been a job wheeling him home.

In 1951 at the age of twenty-six, Bill married. *Her name was Ethel Cederlund. She lived in Stepney. There were about four girls in her family, and her parents were Swedish. Her mother was an Olson. Her parents didn't know each other in Sweden, but it just so happened they both moved to Enderby about 1915 and they got acquainted there.*

Ethel and I met at a dance at Grindrod. It was a thriving little community years ago – they had a hall. Ethel had a daughter from a previous marriage, Carol Swift, who lives in Vernon. Ethel and I had a girl, Linda. She married Harry Bongers, a dairyman, and they live out in Sleepy Hollow. They have three kids.

With the passage of time, the old smithy was feeling its age, and Bill was having reservations about the location. *I felt I was in the wrong place. I'd rented from the CPR quite a piece of land across from me on Pleasant Valley Road where we parked large equipment – tractors and loggin' trucks that had come in for repairs. To fix them, we had to cross the street, and the traffic drove us crazy – the high school was there, and the City Hall just down the street – it*

147

was a very busy corner of town. And besides the rent to the CPR, we had to pay the taxes on it – I got choked up with that. So I bought the property beside me from Andy Kineshanko – the current museum parking lot – it was a BA service station at one time – and I parked some machinery there. But I felt that the place was unsightly for people coming into town – so much junk around made it look like a scrapyard. Nobody asked me to move, but I just felt I should *move.*

Then the sawmill relocated out of town [Otter Lake X-Road and Highway 97A]. Suddenly land was available around Wood Avenue East and Mill Street. *I thought if I moved down there, I'd be out of everybody's road – 100 times better for me. So in 1977 I bought the lot down on Kirton Avenue and put up the Armstrong Machine Shop that is there now. I moved into it, and the silly smithy stayed empty for over a year. I was gettin' panicky because I was wantin' the money and I needed to sell it to somebody! And then a man came along and run for mayor – his name was Marve Kirton – and he offered me a price – he was going to turn it into some sort of civic complex. I wanted $100,000 but it ended up at $80,000 – we split the difference. That $80,000 came in very handy.*

The first months at the new shop weren't all roses. *We used to get a lot of walk-in traffic at the old location, but when I went down to the new place, I never got any walk-in traffic – we were too far away. Actually, my business went downhill for a few months. I hadn't even put a sign on the old place to tell anybody where I had moved – that's how stupid I was – I just thought everybody would know!* With a little thought, that initial blip was rectified. *Bill Danal was a sign painter. He painted the sign and we put it up – it worked out fine.*

Having been an apprentice himself, Bill Clayton had a good eye for choosing his workers. *I had three or four helpers at the old location and five or six at the new shop – they all moved down there with me. I wanted welders or machinists – you had to know how to weld and run a lathe. Sometimes I took an apprentice, but my business was a little too small. One disadvantage is that you can take an apprentice and teach him the trade for four or five years, and then off he goes someplace else – you can't hang onto him. Of course, you don't have to pay him much.*

148

It's better to have an experienced person and then you don't have to explain the job to them all the time. I had a chap working for me once – his name was Percy Peerless and he learnt his trade in England. When he was fourteen or fifteen years old, his mother said, "Well, you should be a machinist, Percy." And she went to a machine shop and made a deal with the owner, and Mrs. Peerless paid him so much a week to teach Percy the trade. After a year she didn't have to pay him quite so much because Percy was gettin' a little smarter, and after three or four years it was just about a saw-off – Percy was workin' for nothin', shall we say. And then the next year Percy made a little bit of money. Eventually after about six or seven years, Percy was makin' a journeyman's wages. It worked out pretty good. Percy brought his training to the Clayton machine shop. *He was a real good machinist – a fine old Englishman.*

Another person who worked for me was Ernie Heighton. He was a very loyal employee – a very good employee – and he's still there. He owns it – he bought it off me in 1988. The Clayton family had owned the same business in Armstrong for over eighty years. *It made me feel real good that he bought it and made a good success of it. I am very proud of what he has done.*

In the 1970s and '80s, both Bill Clayton and the old smithy on Railway Avenue were caught up in the process of change. Bill and Ethel bought their lot on Becker Street in 1971, built their new home and moved from 2925 Rosedale Avenue – *Barry Gagnon lives there now.* And in 1978 an enthusiastic group of local residents formed the Armstrong Spallumcheen Museum and Archives Society, the goal of which was to secure a permanent building for the preservation of local history and artifacts while old-timers and their legacy of treasures and memories were still at hand.

Ever since Mayor Marvin Kirton had acquired the smithy for the City's use, the addition north of the 'hump' had been a storage shed for equipment, such as, the street sweeper. The ugly duckling, however, was about to become a swan. In December, 1982, the *Armstrong Advertiser* reported that City Council led by Mayor John Ross had agreed to lease the front part of the building – Frank Clayton's 1915 addition – to the Museum and Archives Society for one dollar per year for the next five years. Beginning in June, 1983, with leverage from government grants, citizen donations, and volunteer enthusiasm, the accumulated grime from sixty-eight years of honest labour was scrubbed off and carted away. The official opening of the Armstrong Spallumcheen Museum at 2 p.m. on October 29th, 1983, highlighted a log-cutting ceremony using a crosscut saw, and the music of the Old Time Fiddlers. *I was very pleased the machine shop turned into a museum. It was a wonderful idea.*

More was to come. On July 15, 1987, the *Armstrong Advertiser* reported that Russell (Rusty) Freeze had spearheaded a plan to turn the rear of the building into an art gallery to encourage and showcase local artists as well as their more well-known colleagues. Again residents flew into action, and the first show opened on April 8, 1988. At the annual general meeting that May, the enlarged mandate was recognized by the society's new name: The Armstrong Spallumcheen Museum and Arts Society.

Bill has adapted to a life outside the machine shop. *Ethel and I did a little bit of travellin' to begin with, and now I'm busy around the yard – this lot is 150 feet square. I do a fair amount of cooking too. I don't go to church as often as I should. My mother was a great Anglican and it's been kind of instilled into me, [but] I have a hard job gettin' enthused now, to be honest. I find the service long – an hour and a quarter – the hard pew.... It's too much for me.*

Bill, however, is an excellent walker. *Walking is cheap exercise. I picked it up shortly after I retired. I walk to different places every day – take different routes – see something different every time. And I see people to talk to. I think it will take me half an hour and it ends up being two hours – I keep running into people.*

Bill's friends are important to him. *Tom LeDuc and I go for coffee a couple of times a week. I have a job sometimes to hear what he says – he has a quiet voice, and my hearing isn't the best. I never say anything though.* Tom is in his nineties – he has seniority.

Bill Clayton, aged fourteen, on the front step of his home

Chapter Four

A Hitt-Price Medley

Raymond Harry Hitt

My name is Hitt, and you remember Hitler. I can remember three or four round-faced Poles [eastern Europeans] coming up here in the '60s asking for raspberries. I picked about seven crates and they come to get them. "Hitt..." they said, "what nationality is that?" "Oh," I said, "it's English." "Well, if you were German, we wouldn't deal with you." These guys would have been around fifty, and had been invaded by Germany in the Second War.

Aged seven in 1939, Raymond was old enough to soak up the debates and speculations that swirled about the kitchen table when Canada became involved in World War Two. *Even as a kid I knew the war was key – everybody was talking about the war. You probably heard about how the Germans went into Russia. They didn't count on it turning cold. That was one of the things that beat them – the machinery froze up on them. Your antifreeze wasn't readily available like it is today.*

Some table talk was controversial. *The Germans were trying to beat Russia but some said the British were behind it as well... that some of them were pro-Nazi. Then, of course, you had the two things that start with c – communists and the catholic church – the church was scared of communists. Winston Churchill on a visit to Italy during the war [August, 1944] went to see the pope. As a kid I can remember my uncle – he was a [staunch] Orangeman – smoking a pipe and saying, "I don't know why Churchill has to go and see the pope"; he thought they might have had it all arranged to beat Russia to protect the church.*

Lord knows what kind of information we were getting – it wasn't the gospel truth by any means. I don't think people were too suspi-

155

cious then. Grown-ups thought whatever the government said was the truth – they really had that idea – you weren't supposed to question anything. We sure as heck know different nowadays.

Even at school the war intruded. *I chummed with a German kid, and I was told by one of my fellow classmates not to hang around with him anymore. The present generation don't realize the feeling there was against the Germans. And it was the* second *war after having a go at one another in the first one! There was all kinds of stuff you couldn't buy. You couldn't get much sweets. Lots of times you couldn't even get a chocolate bar. We had ration books – I've still got some of them.* Sugar was rationed and highly coveted. *The neighbours had bees and, of course, they could get sugar to feed the bees.... Anyway... Mom used to make that puffed wheat cookie. She'd put some in my sister's lunch and all the kids would bug her for them, so Mother had to quit doing it. You know how kids are – if you had something that they hadn't got. Some people will go nuts if they have candy or cookies and eat them all at once. I have a tendency to eat just a bit and save it, and I think that's bred into me from the war.*

I don't turn lights on as much as others either because, you see, if you had to light a goldarn coal oil lamp every time, you didn't do it – you'd get by. I think there's a change in attitude now on things like that.

Prudence was a useful, often necessary, trait, as Raymond's mother and father had left a settled home to build a life in a new country. *Both parents came from England. Mom was a Price.* Nora Margaret Beatrice Price was born on August 31, 1898, and for most of her early life lived in Stroud, Gloucestershire, with her father and mother, Henry (Harry) and Margaret, and her older brothers Ewart, Stan, and Heygate, above a pub, the Greyhound, which her parents operated. The pub was located on Lansdowne Street, a main thoroughfare in the bustling village. *I remember hearing the pub had a dog, and one guy used to throw copper pennies to it, and it would catch and eat them. Of course, it died.* When the family decided in

1906 to immigrate to Canada, at a farewell dinner the community presented her father with two guns – one for killing game to put on the table and the other for protection. They said he would need them in the wild West.

A second gift to the family, a liquor cabinet, became the property of the female descendants. *It had drawers and a place for three bottles. I don't know for sure, but it was probably a gift from the brewers because Granny Price did most of the buying for the pub. So after Granny died, Mother got it, and it sat in the middle of that sideboard for years. It blocked the mirror behind it, and I never realized how discoloured the mirror had got until [sister] Marjorie, the only girl, took the cabinet. And her daughter, Dixie, is the only girl in the next generation, so she'll get it.*

After a lengthy sea voyage, the family arrived in Montreal and caught the train to Winnipeg. It was a forlorn and unhappy move.

Mom was nearly eight. Her brother Ewart was still back in England then. He was married at nineteen and a widower at twenty-one – his wife Kate had TB [tuberculosis]. She wasn't doing worth a darn, apparently, in England, and the doctor told her, "You might as well go to Canada and take a chance on it. You ain't going to make it here, anyway." They'd never let her in today, would they! She died in Winnipeg. They lost Heygate in Winnipeg too. Before they emigrated, while training as an ironworker's apprentice, Heygate had hurt his leg. In Winnipeg it grew steadily worse, and he died of gangrene at the age of nineteen. *Today they'd have done something – operated.*

The Prices discovered that job opportunities for British immigrants were limited. Advertisements might declare outright: "No Englishman need apply!" In some cases they were perceived to hold higher expectations for wages and working conditions than other nationalities. *Besides that, a lot of them were 'gentlemen' – absolutely useless for farm work – they'd come from a city and didn't have a clue. Half of them wouldn't know how to harness a horse!* After many rebuffs Henry Price found a job as a night watchman;

and Stan, at a meat plant – *he said if you knew what went on, you wouldn't eat it.* Nora herself survived a freak accident at school. A team of horses pulling a sleigh bolted into the schoolyard, the horses knocked her down, and the sleigh ran over her. Thereafter large animals terrified her. *For the first year after it was built, Mom went to Lord Selkirk School in Winnipeg. Then the family left. They had read all these pamphlets about BC:* "Green acreage in beautiful Deer Park." *Of course, they gave a line of bullshit that you could make a living on ten acres of orchard.*

My grandfather Price knew cloth (before operating the Greyhound pub, he had repaired weaving looms), but he didn't know a thing about farming. They get into Enderby [August 1, 1911] and go into a café. I can remember Mother saying the goldarn flies were all over everything. Before they brought out DDT, good lord! The flies in the summer! I remember as a little kid, we were buying some wheat from the Hallers – Albert Haller's parents were German and into the sauerkraut. I can remember going to their screen door – and the outside of the screen was just plastered *with flies – they could smell it. The younger generation don't realize – they worry about a few flies – well!!*

And then the [horse and buggy] trek from Enderby up the old Canyon Road – a desolate place – bush on both sides. Stan said, *I hope we'll never be any worse off than we have been.* "Green acreage" turned out to be spindly pine scrub on sand – *a godforsaken place – it must have been a shock.* Henry decided to look farther in Hullcar district and found some better farmland.

They had to build a house for the winter, you see. For a while they lived in a tent. People told them they could live in a tent all winter here! You remember those snake fences? Well, the snow the following spring was up to the top of those fences – it was unreal! [Luckily] they'd got a bit of the house built that first summer and finished it over the winter. Hoover had a sawmill in Hullcar, so that's probably where they bought the lumber. People didn't worry about having as much [living] space as you do nowadays – and you didn't have your electrical appliances – just the basics. They had a well down below near where Len Price is now [4389 Hullcar Road].

They planted apple trees. The brochures had promised success. *In February we'd get nice sunny days and colder than a son of a gun at night. I can remember Stan and Grandpa planted some on a southeast slope [double trouble], and it would get so blessed hot in the daytime the sap would rise, and the sun would just cook them. Then it would drop down to zero [Fahrenheit] at night. The combination of these two extremes broke the bark on the trees and weakened them. It must have been pretty tough sledding for a while.*

Mother never went to school afterwards. There was a school along there towards Hullcar Hall, but there was horses and cows running free all over the place – and she had to walk – so there was no way *she was going to school. She was thirteen or fourteen at the time.* Nora would, however, collect the mail, as the Hullcar post office was close by. *For a few years after Mom and her family came, there was a postal outlet in the Crane house [4342 Hullcar Road]. They'd bring the mail out to Crane's from the Armstrong or Enderby post office. Some of the letters were addressed to Deer Park – it was another name for Hullcar.*

Deer Park was aptly named. *There were oodles of deer up there, I believe, though there are more around here now than forty or fifty years ago. They were wilder then – wouldn't let you get near them. [Also] people used to shoot deer in the summertime – they'd probably have four or five kids to feed – shoot a deer, dress it, divide it with a few others, and you'd have it used up in no time. There were no deep-freezes or anything like that. There'd be a certain number of [beef] cattle, but deer was free and cheap. The natives were using them too. (Today deer are safer in town than in the wild where there's cougar and coyote.)*

There were also lots of rabbits out Hullcar way. Dad used to shoot them with a shotgun, skin and eat them. Then they got a disease that killed them off. In my real young days we'd see lots of rab-

bits when we used to fish up Deep Creek. I can remember coming back with twenty or thirty little brook trout and Mom would fry 'em up. There's not a heck of a lot of water in the creek now. I was talking to Harold Shrock – he's lived in Deep Creek for fifty years and he's never seen it like this.

Nora lost contact with her school friends in Winnipeg. *After the First War broke out, some of the boys would have been old enough to enlist. Mother often used to say, "I don't know what happened to a lot of them." She never heard of them again.* She did, however, make a new acquaintance. Driving to Armstrong one day, she and her mother passed by another buggy containing two young strangers. *She asked her mother who they were. "I think they're the Hitt boys."* Nora thought it was the funniest name she had ever heard. *Of course, there were not that many people around here then, so you'd get to know everybody.* Ten years later Nora Price and Frederick Charles Hitt were married.

The eighth of nine children, Frederick Charles was born on June 11, 1893, on a mixed farm at Cullompton, Devonshire; therefore, unlike the Prices, he had some previous experience with the vagaries of agriculture. In 1911 he and his brother Jim, two years his senior, along with four schoolmates immigrated to Canada. One got off the train in Saskatchewan, four including Frederick Charles and Jim disembarked at Calgary, and the sixth went on to Vancouver. *It's a big move when you're barely eighteen – literally on your own. His dad thought he might never see [his boys] again. I wonder how the kids of today would manage if you shipped them out.*

There were places you could go to get a job – a private deal. In an interview in the early 1990s with local archivist Patricia Brinnen, Frederick Charles recalled that Calgary real estate agents posted job opportunities in their storefront windows: *"There was so much work in them days, you didn't have to look for work – work was looking for you!"* Jim found employment at a dairy farm near Banff. *Dad and another fellow went down to High River. Dad was applying for the job, but the boss wanted to take the other fellow because Dad was only eighteen and a little, short, five-foot-three.* His companion honourably declined the offer: *"No, you've got arrangements with him!"* The boss played his last card. *He wanted to know if Dad could harness a horse.* No problem.

Next he got on the crew that was building irrigation ditches at Bassano, Alberta. The Bow River runs nearby. *He was given a three-horse team on a wagon, and he goes out the first day on the job and things go good. He gets back to the bunkhouse to eat supper – and the boys ask, "How did you and Old Doctor get along?"* Frederick Charles didn't get the joke. *He didn't know Old Doctor was the name of his sorrel horse. The team would get out in the irrigation ditch and the sorrel would lay down. So they'd had quite a time with him – whenever he took the notion, he lay down – he was useless. Apparently, the horse lay down for the guy that Dad replaced, and the fellow goes to the supply wagon and gets a chunk of chain, and when the horse went down the next time, he laid it to him! The boss got mad, but the guy just handed him the reins: "If you don't think what I did was right, then I quit." But he knew what he was doin' – he'd cured that horse. Dad's [bunkmates], though, had expected a young kid like him to have the same trouble. But the credit should have gone to the other guy – it was one case where beatin' the horse was the only way to straighten him out.*

Building an irrigation ditch was an assembly line project – teams of horses and wagons circling around an elevated grader that was cutting the ditch and accumulating the dirt. *It was 'cut' and 'fill,' cutting someplace and filling someplace else. An open flume ran along a ditch, and even on the level they'd have to cut to make banks for the ditch. They'd have to fill in other places, and a horse on each end of a section of iron rail would drag it along to smoothe the banks. Pretty steep cuts in some places – the team would have to hold the wagon back going down the slope to the grader.*

The grader would be digging the 'cut,' and a belt would pull the dirt high enough so that a wagon could get underneath it – and then the belt would drop the dirt into the wagon. A three-horse team was necessary to haul the weight up- and downhill. *He'd drive off to where*

161

the fill was needed and the next team would come in right behind him. The foreman would tell the [teamster] where to put the dirt. He'd pull a lever, the floor of the wagon would drop, and the dirt would fall out. Then he'd crank it up again, turn around and go back to the grader for another load. It was an awful job – dirty and repetitious. It was also dangerous. *The driver sat over the front wheels of the wagon, and he could [detach] the piece that held the dirt in case the wagon slipped off the bank somewhere and the horses fell on him....*

Dad put in a claim on a homestead at Coronation, [Alberta] – never even went there – worked on another farm for quite a while. The people were Mennonites, and the fellow had three or four girls and he asked Dad if he'd like to come to church – I think they were looking for new blood! It had been dryer than heck in 1910 and then it was wetter than a son of a gun in 1911, and they never even got some of the threshing done until the spring of 1912. Apparently it was in the stooks all winter. (When it froze up there, it froze once and for all, so the grain was okay.) So they were threshing on Easter Sunday, which was a real no-no back in those days, but they had to get the blessed stuff off the field in order to work it – put in the new crop.

By this time Frederick Charles had weathered two years on his own, as Jim had early given up on Alberta and moved to Armstrong. Frederick Charles joined him in 1913. *Jim wrote to Dad telling him what a nice place this was – it was like Devon – and that's why he came. He and Jim bought that place on Hallam Road where Art Cayford lives [4377]. 1913 was the year that Armstrong was incorporated as a city. Dad told me that when they bought the place [in Spallumcheen], their taxes were paying for wooden side-walks in Armstrong. And Armstrong didn't like paying for roads in Spallumcheen, so they had a little squabble and separated.*

Dad and Jim had a bit of an orchard. Their neighbours were Docksteader, Maw, Chapple, Swanson, and LeDuc. *They farmed for a year, then Jim [enlisted] for the First War. In Kamloops he was just about ready to be shipped out when he stopped a runaway team – hurt his shoulder – and he couldn't go. Know what they did with him? Put him up on the railway in Rogers Pass to guard the bridges against the Germans who were in Canada. If countries were at war with you, you never knew if the guy livin' next door to you was [sympathetic] to their cause. The railway was the link across Canada. Blowing the bridges would be like cutting the western provinces off. So Jim spent the war years there.* Several of Raymond's photographs record Jim's service: "Wartime guarding the bridges." In one, five uniformed men and a black Labrador dog stand next to a rock-lettered icon on the ground:

102nd Rocky Mountain Rangers
Canada

In another, an iron trestle bridge cuts the sky behind the group, their combined rifles forming an upright pyramid beside them.

Dad was left on the farm – he had been classified 4F – Fail, I suppose – he hadn't got good feet. One day this guy comes to him and said, "If we got somebody to run the place for you, would you enlist?" Dad said, " Why don't you get him to go?" This fellow was trying to keep somebody's kid out of the war. Some people don't realize this kind of thing went on, [but] it's a plain, cold fact.

The weather hurt Frederick Charles's farming prospects. His small orchard suffered in the bitter winter of 1915-16. *There was all kinds of orchard then out at Hullcar and along Pleasant Valley Road, but that winter just wiped them out – so cold – just like 1949-50 – six weeks of zero F. and below. What it didn't kill, it damaged. It was a disaster. They're bitching about this and that in the fruit industry now, but the major problem back then was freezing. The varieties weren't standing up to it.*

The end of the war brought a sense of restlessness and unease. Both boys were homesick and fed up with Canada. In the fall of 1919 they found a prospective buyer for their property, Floyd Hunter on Crawford Road acting for them as agent, and they returned to England. *They really intended to stay. I think Dad may have been interested in some girl back there, possibly a sister of Aunt Diana's, [Sid Hitt's wife], but I never really dug into that. And him being out here for those first few years, she may have got married. Then, of course, the war came along, and there was no way he could get back then.*

But Dad knew [immediately] he wasn't going to stay: He said, "I hadn't been back in England <u>no time</u> and I knew I was in the wrong place! There was no chance of advancement. Here, you could go ahead and buy something and get going!" Rather ironic – Floyd writes him and tells him the deal fell through. Dad didn't give a darn because he wanted to come back anyway!

No sooner was he here and working outside one day when a realtor come along and said, "I've got somebody looking at the place." "It's off the market." "Do you mind if I show him around anyway?" And when the guy asked him what he wanted for it, Dad jacked up the price. The buyer lived with him for a week or so because he wanted to move in right away. Then Dad used the money to buy a bigger property – the Ives farm on Parkinson Road [5162] right next to the original Stan Parkinson place in Hullcar – eighty acres – cows – mixed farming – a lot of bush, of course. You'd cut logs in the winter and haul them by sleigh to the sawmill in town. And Mother was in Hullcar District, you see, and they met at dances at Hullcar Hall. They were married on March 14, 1923. *He'd have been getting darn close to the thirty mark. Mother was twenty-four.*

Frederick Charles decided that he "was going to *sell* farm produce instead of growing it." He sold his land to Sid, who had first immigrated in 1904, returned to England in 1910 and married, and with Diana and their children had made a second attempt in 1922. Sid had called his son Frederick James, a fond reminder of his younger brother Frederick Charles. *One was in England and one was in Canada so it didn't matter. It was a mix-up when they moved back here – 'Old Fred' and 'Young Fred' they used to call them. You notice now there's darn few boys called after their fathers. When I was a kid, there was always a 'John Junior' or a 'Jim Junior.'* A year or so before Frederick

Charles died in 1995, Herbert Hitt, a descendant of Harry, the oldest Hitt boy, came to Canada expressly to see him. It was Frederick Charles' first contact since 1920 with his Devonshire relations.

Freed of their farm, the newlyweds Frederick Charles and Nora Hitt moved to Calgary. *Dad run a fruit and vegetable stall in what was called 'The Market.'* He told some good stories about the place. *A customer who had bought a pound of butter at one stall heard talk that a mouse had got into the cream. She brought the butter back and said she was sure it wouldn't hurt anything, but the thought of the mouse bothered her... would he exchange it? "Oh, sure," the guy says, and he goes to the back and takes the wrapper off another pound and puts it on hers and brings the same butter out to her. Of course, she thought it was just beautiful butter then!*

The Market had a cement floor and it was a bugger on Dad's bad feet. He couldn't stand it. He found a better job at Lindsay MacMaster's farm outside Calgary near Airdrie. *He needed a man and his wife, a farm worker and a housekeeper. The MacMasters had a meat market, and I can remember Dad saying they had to eat so many damn wieners!*

The Hitts returned to Armstrong in 1926 and Frederick Charles found employment as Edwin Chapple's farm manager. *Chapple owned a drugstore in town and a big farm [120 acres] on Knob Hill Road, and Dad was running it for him – there was fruit trees on the place. Mom and Dad lived in a cabin on the property to start with, and when Chapples [relocated] to Vernon, they moved into his house [4341 Salmon River Road.]* With its white lower storey and red upper storey, the house was striking. Built on a hill facing east, it was visible from Armstrong. The wooden doorframes were an inch thick and a foot wide, and wood predominated throughout the ten-roomed interior. Sliding doors linked the dining room and the living room on the main floor, and an elaborate staircase climbed from the foyer to four bedrooms, which included a nursery off the master bedroom. 'Below stairs' were the kitchen, a small bathroom, the maid's room, and, a rarity, a second, steeper staircase for the servants' use. A large cistern in the basement trapped rainwater that was periodically pumped by hand into a smaller cistern in the attic, from which gravity supplied running water. Ewart Price built the kitchen cupboards, which bear his name.

Despite its grandeur, however, Frederick Charles and Nora Hitt needed a permanent home. In 1930, just as the Depression was underway, opportunity knocked. *This farm went up for auction at a tax sale.* The farm was a sixty-acre parcel (six ten-acre lots, 27-32) with a three-roomed house against a hillside along Schubert Road [4537]. Less than one-third was cleared, and pieces of the Old Kamloops Road wandered through it. Steele Springs supplied the water. *A fellow called Everett or Everard owned it first and built his house on top of the hill. It burned. Rawlings bought the place next and started this house – I think he was a tobacco salesman – but he didn't keep it up.* In fact, by bidding on the property, Frederick Charles was taking a chance, as some disappointed farmers had dubbed the neighbourhood 'Poverty Hill.'

Frederick Charles weighed the pros and cons; the pros were more compelling: *There was some awful dry years in the '20s, but this place wasn't as dry as some of 'em was. Land clearing would be simpler in sandy soil because in clay the stumps were harder to pull out. A previous owner had started an apple orchard; yet on other places without irrigation [like this one], the soil was too sandy to hold the water, even for apples.* A towering Anjou pear dominates a piece of the ground above the house – *it was just a whip when we came. Besides, Dad wasn't that concerned about makin' a livin' off the land.* He had a back-up scheme in mind.

Dad was going to go into chickens. He had had a chicken house at Chapple's, you see, and apparently the Co-op used to phone up all the time for eggs, so Dad could see there was a good market. In the wintertime you couldn't even buy eggs – crazy as it sounds today – they just run the chickens around the farm in summer and never looked after them in winter, so the beggars didn't lay.

Mat. Hassen, Senior was the auctioneer. Dad knew him quite well and had been talking to him about the place. Donovan Clemson was bidding on it too, but Dad nodded to increase the bid, and he got it.

Frederick Charles kept his chickens warm and well fed at every stage throughout the year. He added laying mash to the traditional diet of grain. He had incubators, a brooder house for the hatched chicks, a chicken house, and finally quarters for adult birds. *The brooder house was a bowling alley that he got moved out of town. It was sixty-four feet long, and he put an old coal stove at each end for heat.* His production peaked one year at 1600 birds. *He usually had 300-400 laying hens.*

Every day on the train, express went out of Armstrong under his Valley Vista [Farm] brand – I think I still have some labels. He used to ship eggs to Bob Hume in Revelstoke two or three times a week. You see, Revelstoke was a railway town, and even in the Depression there was still a lot of money there. Humes were old-timers who had a second store down in the Kootenays. They used those eggs as a drawing card because you could crack open other eggs and there'd be a chicken in the darn thing! So if you went to a store and got good eggs, you'd go back for that brand – and that's how Dad built up his business.

I think he was shipping minimum four or five 30-dozen cases a week. He would ship at least two cases at a time and, of course, the [Hume] stores were running them close to a 'loss leader,' holding the price down to attract business. You know the story – people don't just buy what they come in for. The stores knew they had a good thing.

The family remembers Bob Hume's inspection of the Hitt poultry prior to placing his first order. That year Frederick Charles had some nervous Leghorns that panic at the presence of strangers in the chicken house and then refuse to lay. When he and Hume arrived at the door, he raised his hand and knocked. Hume, of course, didn't realize the sound was a warning to the birds and exclaimed, "God, Fred, you're polite!"

Routine, consistent candling maintained the quality of Hitt eggs.

Dad candled his eggs every evening down in the basement here. He put a naptha gas lamp inside an old, metal mailbox and he looked though a hole in the mailbox at the egg. You could look right through the egg and you could spot anything inside it – blood... cracks... a little chicken.... Raymond has custody of a naptha gas lamp that used to hang in Knob Hill Hall. It is about twenty inches tall with a round base that holds about a litre of gas. *Some lamps had a pump hanging on it; others had the pump as an accessory. You pumped the gas up into the two mantles and lit it with a match. You turned this little spigot on the side to adjust the flow.* The mantles were narrow, white sacks suspended from the top of the lamp. *When they began to dull down a bit, you pumped the gas up again. It gave a heck of a light.*

Another essential gadget in the Hitt production line was the egg grader, a dainty and ingenious contraption about nine inches long attached to a narrow board grooved to fit snugly over an egg crate. *Dad bought the equipment and [assembled] it on the board. It graded small, medium, large, and extra large eggs – there were no jumbo eggs then.* At the rear of the grader a balance beam rests on a tiny sawhorse-shaped stand. The front of the balance beam is a hollow ring in which the egg sits. Two small weights of differing lengths are mounted one in front of the other on the beam and flip toward or away from the hollow ring. A third weight that sits in a hole in the board may be removed and hooked on the underside of the balance beam to provide extra ballast.

A small egg sitting in the ring may require the two weights flipped toward it in order to force the beam down to register the weight. *They were called pullet or peewee eggs.* A medium egg may need only the longer one flipped toward the ring. A large egg was heavy enough to balance both weights flipped toward the rear of the beam while the extra-large egg required the addition of the third weight. *You wouldn't have to weigh every one – you'd get used to the weight of an egg. Large sizes don't have as much weight as back in them days. Sometimes I test the store-bought eggs on the grader and they're a bit light!*

Dad had chickens right into the '40s. When the Humes closed their stores, Dad shipped to the Egg Pool run by Howard and Maude Spears on Okanagan Street just north of the Armstrong Advertiser. In the same building behind the Egg Pool they had a killing plant – the old hens, stewing birds, and broilers. You couldn't buy your chickens sexed, you see – you had to raise 500 to get 250 pullets, so you'd kill off the roosters as soon as you could. During the Second War, Slade and Stewart Produce hauled groceries – mostly vegetables – from Penticton to all the little stores up the valley and picked up eggs and chicken from the Egg Pool on the way back. They had refrigeration. They had a big place in Vancouver as well so they could sell them there.

There was a canteen at the Vernon army camp. Some of the boys were going overseas, and they'd thrown in a bunch of money for a chicken supper. So they come up to place the order, and we killed some chickens for them. My sister and I went with Dad when he delivered the birds and they give us Jello. You couldn't buy Jello during the war – it all went overseas – some of it may have been used in making armaments.

Two other family stories commemorate Raymond's advent on July 1, 1932, at the height of haying season. *Max Clemson was helping Dad get his first crop into the barn. Mom went out to tell him she had to go to the hospital. He said he'd take her as soon as they got the load into the loft.* First things first. He achieved both objectives.

The second story places Raymond firmly in the male camp. Nora belonged to the Knob Hill Ladies' Aid, a social and charitable organization that held meetings in members' homes. Men called these get-togethers 'hen parties.' One day little Raymond announced to his father's friends that he was going to the Ladies' Aid at Caswell's. *I was just learning to talk. I said we were going to the Ladies' Aid and cackle.*

Raymond's sister, Marjorie, was born on June 30th in 1934, and living space was cramped. *The upstairs in the original house wasn't finished.* Nora's brother Ewart built an addition in the late '30s that included the luxury of indoor plumbing, and her nephew Ron finished the upstairs bedrooms around 1950. *Sixteen feet was added to the kitchen, but the verandah was built first. Everybody wondered about this goldarned house with a verandah that stuck out sixteen feet and nothing built behind it! Of course, it wasn't that way long. In summer people spent time on the verandah because they cooked inside and the house would get so hot.*

Frederick Charles increased his arable land by logging trees in the mid-west of the property. A stand of tall fir remains. To loosen the stumps of the felled trees, he detonated stumping powder. It was a dangerous product. In the 1930s in a quarry north of the Hitt house, Spallumcheen municipality also used stumping powder to loosen rock for gravel roads. *They drilled into the bank – it was hard as cement – and after they put in the stumping powder, the fools filled in the hole with rocks. The hole acted like a bloody cannon.* Nora recalled a thunderous detonation hurling a flight of good-sized missiles past her kitchen window.

During quieter moments Frederick Charles planted three shade trees that today dwarf the house: *That's a golden willow – willows like water – Dad started it with a little stick in the ground. The other old one is an acacia – thorny beggars – that cold winter never fizzed on them. You see all kinds of them around here – they have the big white flowers and seed pods. The third one is a horse chestnut –* the flowers sit erectly on the branches like miniature, lighted Christmas trees – *lots of little seedlings growing up underneath it.* A large water tank for Raymond's small cow-calf operation floods underneath the willow. *I let the tank overflow to give Reg Kienast's bees a drink. With the mites and diseases I'm afraid the wild ones aren't going to survive – we'll have to depend on these [domestic] bees.*

Frederick Charles decided to branch out. *On the west side of Lot 28, I've got about three acres of orchard. Dad started it in 1937. He bought 200 Italian prunes – I think Art Williamson got six of them – otherwise, the whole shootin' match was planted back there – 22 by 22 feet apart. But he run into problems with them dying back. boron deficiency – a trace element missing in the soil – that, and the cold winters, created dieback. So once he changed soil composition it was okay. (I don't know if you've seen alfalfa fields that sometimes look very pale. Lack of boron there too.)*

Then Dad added peach plums. He had some over on the Cayford place. They are a peach colour, and when they're ripe they pick like a peach. If a tree died, he often filled [the space] with a Bradshaw plum or a Maglio. Back in the '50s there were some Maglios showin' at the IPE. They were quite a popular plum. But you couldn't grow them as a large tree like the regular plums because they used to take a beatin' in the cold weather. They come in blossom early in the spring and are prone to frost.

Raymond has increased the size of the orchard. *The outside row of trees didn't exist in the beginning because that land was left for road allowance on an extension of Round Prairie Road that never happened – they figured it would go all the way up behind Fred Mitchell's [4863 Schubert Road; currently Tillaart] and hook some-where into the north end of Schubert Road.* He has also planted both early and late varieties to improve his sales capacity at the local farmers' markets three days a week – Monday and Thursday mornings in Vernon and Saturday morning in Armstrong. In 2005 the trees were loaded to the ground. *We were pickin' all the time and couldn't hardly keep up to the demand – you wanted enough there to last you at least 'til eleven or better in the morning. We'd take twelve to fifteen of those asparagus lugs [crates] filled with prunes, and then we'd have to come back and pick some more for the next market. We were sellin' them for two dollars an ice cream pail – about six pounds – or three pails for five dollars. We had so darn many of them, and I knew it was better to give people a decent price than to keep bringin' 'em back. We'd have had a lot of sortin' to do.* Raymond's nephew Rae Gordon helped with the crop. Rae re-members, *We'd be trying to load them into containers at the market, and no sooner were they out than we'd sell them and have to put out more. We couldn't keep up!* Both the pickers and Raymond's heavy yellow truck got a workout. ·

We shipped prunes to the Prairies, you know, back in the late

'50s and the '60s – strictly illegal because Tree Fruits [Marketing Board] had complete control of sales in those days. So we put an ad in the Free Press Prairie Farmer and shipped C.O.D. We'd charge $1.10 for a 20-pound lug, and we'd have to buy the lug out of that. We shipped 200-300 lugs for a few years. I can remember one time the station agent said, "You'd better watch out – there's been a Tree Fruits guy snoopin' around!"

Remember the old postal money orders? Here's one from a lady we sent the prunes to and didn't even cash. It was overlooked, so we figured we'd just hold on to it.

The Canadian Postal Money Order is dated September 25th, 1968. The accompanying letter in clear, cursive penmanship reads:

Dear Mr. Hitt,

According to our neighbour James Purves, you will again be able to supply us with plums @$1.10. These plums are always so appreciated, especially for flavor sakes. Have noticed too that they freeze very well.

Could you please send 5 boxes to: Gordon Porter, Bredenbury, Sask.

You will find enclosed a money order for five dollars and fifty cents ($5.50).

Thank you kindly.

Yours truly,
Mrs. Gordon Porter

It cost a whole five cents to send that letter. The stamp on the envelope commemorates the life of the Honourable George Brown, 1818-1880, editor of the *Globe* newspaper in Toronto, parliamentarian, and a member of the Charlottetown Conference in 1864 that preceded Canadian Confederation.

In addition to prunes, Raymond's second major crop is turnips and squash that he plants east and west of the timber on land that his father cleared. He still uses the tractor his family bought in 1951 along with two newer models for preparing the ground and moving the crop from the field. *You have to rotate [the plots] for good results. I plant Hubbard or Sweetmeat squash, mainly. They get crossed sometimes. You plant them in hills 10 feet by 12 feet apart, six or seven seeds in a hill. I use my own seeds quite a bit. The turnips are Swedes.* Since both these vegetables keep well, Raymond sells and gives them away once a month over the winter at the Odd Fellows' Saturday morning Pancake Breakfast and Flea Market. *I had Dad's egg grader at the Flea Market yesterday – I was sizing some of Shannon's eggs for sale – and a couple of different people wanted to buy it!* Among the artifacts in the building is a large, colourful print titled "Our Talisman or Emblematic Fellowship" that consists of symbols having to do with the fraternity. *Frank Becker had the Sash and Door [business], and they bought a whole bunch of these prints and he framed them. I have one too – Dad belonged for years.*

Between 2001 and 2006 an addition to the Hitt farm was Shannon Gates's herd of purebred Nubian and La Mancha goats registered with the Canadian Goat Society under the herd name Green Goddess. *Goats are good on a small acreage.* Shannon milks her does and makes chevré [cream cheese], feta, and 'some kind of cheese.' She says, *Everybody starts with cream cheeses because they're supposed to be simple, but we had a terrible time making a good cream cheese!* 'Some kind of cheese' is an inside joke between my mother [Sandra] and me: "What kind of cheese are you making?" "Oh, some kind of cheese." *It's a really good, milky mozzarella.*

Shannon also sells registered does as dairy goats for breeding stock and milkers; and as a sideline, her wethers [castrated male goats] and cull does in the fall for meat mainly to South Asian buyers. Shannon is self-publishing a book on the goat business: *Lots of people are interested in raising goats.*

On the Hitt farm, mother and daughter also planted a vegetable garden that included herb beds, and they paid respectful attention to dandelions: *Dandelion root is a really good liver tonic and blood cleanser. I feed it to the goats, I feed it to ourselves, I make soup out of it. You can roast it the way you roast carrots and potatoes. We dry it, as we use it mostly in the winter. We collect the leaves as well.* A garden feeds them year round. *It hearkens back to how small farms used to work – not many people feed themselves off their own land – in our case, off __his__ land. And you don't often hear people today talk about root cellars, but we would definitely not be able to eat off our garden all year without Raymond's good root cellars.*

Raymond's two root cellars are an essential aspect of his own farm management. They juxtapose opposite ends of the barn and are dug into the edge of the hill. Thus each cellar is buried on two sides by earth over six feet deep. You enter through a full-sized door that leads directly to a second door about three feet ahead. *We needed two doors to protect against the cold weather – otherwise, if it gets to minus 20 Fahrenheit for any length of time, everything would freeze.* A bin of McIntosh apples lies near the entry. The cellar space is divided into four rooms. Electricity supplies the light. The floor is hard-packed dirt. The air is cold. Clean turnips lie on a rack beside water taps. *We wash them in tubs here and put them on the rack to dry. The water drains away down the hill through this hole.* Along the rear wall, hundreds of pounds of turnips lie under a chute that feeds from a storage area built above the root cellar: *You're paying for a roof anyway, so you might as well have some extra storage space, but it isn't insulated – the roof is just rafters with tin laid over them so the snow will slide off.*

Since the Hitts have lived in Armstrong Spallumcheen for close to 100 years, Raymond's house holds some unique mementoes. Photograph albums display pictures taken by the family and by a neighbour, photographer Donovan Clemson: snaps of early Prices and Hitts in England; Knob Hill Church on Ford Road; Charles Hoover's sawmill at Hullcar; Raymond at age sixteen with his friend Jan Clemson leaning out the Dutch door of the Clemson barn;

Marjorie roughly the same age in winter coat and mittens; Mabel Louttit Ramsey – *Donovan took photos of her at different ages. He used us for subjects. I didn't realize how good he was – he was way before his time.*

Raymond picks up a little hand-held dial with short connecting wires. *Ever seen this? It's a voltometer. It measured the voltage in six- and twelve-volt car batteries and in radio batteries. The old radios had an A battery, two B batteries and a C battery. And you could tell with this voltometer if any of them was getting low.* Having the radio die on a dark winter night was exasperating.

Of archival interest are several publications. The first is a copy of number 31, *Weekly Market Review,* Saturday, October 19, 1929. *10 days later the stock market crashed! Not much indication in there!* In fact, the news in this pre-crash publication is upbeat:

Canadian Finance: The brisk recovery on the stock exchanges this week appears to indicate that another period of readjustment in speculative accounts has been completed. The air has been cleared in both the New York and Montreal markets.
British Columbia Mines: The mining market has on the whole held fairly firm during the past week though there has not been very much trading. We still advise the accumulation of carefully selected mining stock, for at present levels many of them are most attractive speculative investments. *Dad had some Noble Five stocks in the Kootenays.* Regarding Noble Five the *Review* stated confidently, "Development work in progress indicates the possibilities of the property are still very great." *The stocks went to nothing. They were not worth the paper you wrote on.*

I was telling a fellow from Okanagan [University] College about this newsletter and he said, "I bet my instructor would like to see that." So he showed it to him. The instructor thought it was great. Postage on the newssheet is one cent.

Of particular interest to Raymond is a telephone directory for the cities of Armstrong, Enderby, Kelowna, Penticton, Peachland, Revelstoke, Salmon Arm, Summerland, and Vernon for the period

July to December, 1932. *It came out on my birthday.* The directory measures six by nine inches, contains thirty sheets, and is one-eighth of an inch [2 mm] thick. It is published by *Walker Press* in Enderby. *Imagine Enderby publishing the directory for the whole valley!*

This copy is addressed to Mr. S. [Stan] Price, Hullcar District. The front and back covers carry advertisements, and the initial pages give the Terms and Conditions governing telephone users. These include Party Line Courtesy, such as, hanging up immediately if the line is already in use, and not allowing "children or others" to listen in on conversations; the prohibition of "profane or obscene language" under penalty of losing both the line and the instrument; and the repeated dire warning in bold print:

Do Not Use the Telephone During a Thunder Storm.

245 homes in Armstrong Spallumcheen have telephones. The Business Directory which precedes the general listing carries eleven names. *It was Depression time and likely too expensive for a lot of people.*

Jean Gill still remembers her family's telephone number: *184L3. My dad was in partnership with Hawes so it was listed under Hawes and Harris, Hullcar Road. You cranked the telephone on the wall and told Central the person you wanted to speak to.* In 1932 Mrs. C.B. Wilson was the agent, and took only emergency calls between 10:30 p.m. and 7 a.m. *There was no telephone between our place and Hullcar, so my dad was always taking messages up the road to somebody: "Be at work at six o'clock tomorrow morning...."* Mr. R.M. Ecclestone's number is 55R2. *He was the manager of the Canadian Bank of Commerce when I started working there in 1941. A few years later it amalgamated with the Imperial Bank to form the Canadian Imperial Bank of Commerce. I worked in the bank for twenty-five years full time and eight years part time, thirty-three years in all.*

Raymond's third publication beats the drum in praise of

Armstrong Spallumcheen, "a million dollar community of 3200 people in 1943." It is a pale blue, two-page pamphlet dated September 1st, 1944, and issued annually by the Board of Trade [Chamber of Commerce]:

Salient Facts and

Information
concerning the
City of Armstrong
and the
Municipality of Spallumcheen
located in the non-irrigated part of the famed Okanagan Valley

The home of the largest dairy cow population in the Interior of British Columbia... The home of the Armstrong Cheese Co-operative Association – the only cheese factory of note in British Columbia... The home of the famous 'Armstrong celery...'The home of the Armstrong Co-operative Society – operating one of the largest Farmers' Co-operative stores in British Columbia... The home of Inland Flour Mills Ltd., manufacturing flour, breakfast foods, alfalfa meal, and handl[ing] all kinds of livestock feed... The home of the Interior Provincial Exhibition – the largest and best Exhibition in the Interior of British Columbia and the largest and best live stock show in the Province... The home of two thousand happy, contented and prosperous farmers in the Municipality of Spallumcheen and another twelve hundred in the city of Armstrong.

Overleaf the reader learns that Spallumcheen has "one hundred and fifty miles of good gravelled and surfaced roads all leading to the City of Armstrong... as well as reaching out to Salmon River and Deep Creek valleys; thirteen-hour rail service [to and from Vancouver]; dining- and sleeping-car service both East and West; [and] Armstrong ships more hogs than any shipping point in British Columbia.

"[The Municipality comprises] something over sixty-five thousand acres, with twenty thousand acres under cultivation on some six hundred farms; is dependent upon no one type of crop or agricultural return, [and] the combined assessed value of the City of Armstrong and the Municipality of Spallumcheen is over three million dollars." *That's peanuts today.*

The amenities boast: "a domestic water system which... furnishes near ice cold, pure water to the City... and supplies a goodly portion to Spallumcheen; comfortable... church edifices; a Consolidated School equipped with the latest and best of everything for its nearly six hundred students; a well-equipped High School with four efficient teachers and a full-time School Nurse; [and the Armstrong Spallumcheen Hospital] surrounded by spacious lawns... self-sustaining through sales of Hospital Insurance... and efficiently conducted with a matron and staff of seven."

Concluding the brochure, a full-page map of Armstrong Spallumcheen features Deep Creek, Davis [Fortune] Creek, Meighan Creek; the CN and CP rail lines connecting the district north, south, east, and west; and mileage to Vancouver, Calgary, Revelstoke, Kamloops, Sicamous, Vernon, and Enderby.

This same autumn the community received a further accolade in the Saturday, November 25, 1944, *Vancouver Daily Province* – an article titled "They Also Serve." It includes, among several women from British Columbia, the photographs and war effort of three senior residents of Armstrong Spallumcheen. *This is a picture of Granny Price.* The other two are Mrs. Pyott *(You remember Pyott Road)*, and Mrs. Ehmke, a relative of storyteller Genevieve Culling.

There is an army of women in British Columbia whose voluntary devotion to duty ranks with the heroes of the war. They are just ordinary women... mothers, wives, sisters... there is nothing to distinguish their service. But they live and work in the knowledge that there is a war to be won, and in the books of the provincial Red Cross there is a tabulated statement that tells of the heroic amounts of work accomplished. It is these women who have knitted and sewn the four million articles shipped out of B.C. Red Cross workrooms. With their men folk overseas, they have learned to cope cheerfully with their families, their housework, their gardens – and then to sit down for a few rounds of knitting or to stitch up a seam, between chores.

"Granny" Price is one of these hardworking older women. She is 77 and a member of the West Hullcar Circle. Her specialty is army socks, and she has knitted more than 400 pairs in three years. **Mrs. Pyott** is another Armstrong woman who has turned in an almost unbelievable amount of work – all knitted articles. She is 85 this month and badly crippled with arthritis, but that doesn't deter her from her job. She's a member of the Highland Park Circle No. 2, and she has turned in many knitted afghans, as well as sweaters, socks, and washcloths. One of the oldest active workers at Armstrong is **Mrs. Ehmke**, aged 91. Washcloths are her responsibility and every time a shipment of these goes out of Armstrong, Mrs. Ehmke can claim the greater proportion of it. These are all Armstrong women…. These are only a few of the women in silent service. Every town, every village has others.

When Raymond started school, of necessity he rode the school bus. *In my time there were seven buses. I rode on Bus 2. 'Gasoline' Billy Smith was our driver. Ewart Price built the frame for the bus and set it on the back of a two- or three-ton truck that Billy owned. Charlie Patten drove Bus 1; Buster Cave drove Bus 3; Gordon Grey, Bus 4; Joe Glaicar, Bus 5; Bus 6 had several drivers over the years – it was newer and had a silver-coloured top; and Len Wood drove Bus 7. Two buses were out of Fletcher's garage, two were out of A. Smith and Sons garage (where the Bank of Commerce is now), and one was out of 'Gasoline' Billy Smith's garage (Co-op gas station). The other two buses were each parked at the driver's home.* Seating arrangements varied with the vintage of the bus. *In our bus the boys sat on one side of the aisle and girls sat on the other. Other buses had benches along the side and seats back to back in the centre.*

A few of Raymond's schoolbooks survive. The prices are friendly: *Highroads Dictionary,* forty cents; *Abraham Lincoln* by John Drinkwater, a play with study helps, forty cents. *We weren't supplied with books – we used to buy them at Blumenauer's drugstore, or try to get them secondhand from the older kids. I was in school in 1949 when Newfoundland became the tenth province of Canada. [Before that] we'd always learned there were nine provinces. The schools in Armstrong were quite a high calibre. I am surprised the government dropped this school district because the Brick School was one of the first consolidated schools. They should have kept this district separate for that reason. It was historic and could literally have shown people how far we have come.*

Raymond's memories of the Brick School are ink-spattered. *Helen Sidney [Miss Sperling] was one of my teachers and Mrs. Floyd Parkinson was another – she was a Miss Lewis. Mrs. Marion Hope was around too – Miss Pickering – although I never had her – and she remembers the McLean's Method of Writing.* While attending Vancouver Normal School, Miss Pickering was McLean's top student in her class. *I can remember the old dip pen, and the teacher in front of the class showing us the McLean's Method: "Point your pen back over your right shoulder!" I'm left handed. So, of course, when I pointed my pen over my shoulder and wrote, my hand would smudge the words, and the more I pointed my pen over my shoulder, the worse it got! No teacher took any account of left-handed kids. I can remember going into the bank to write a cheque – they had those stick pens with a nib. For a left-handed person, of course, the nib was worn down on the wrong side. It would stick right into the paper. It was a pain in the ass.*

I remember the fountain pens. You'd crank a lever on the side to fill it up with ink. I had a fountain pen at school and somebody asked to borrow it. It was worn down on the wrong side, so after that I never had to worry about somebody wanting to use my pen. Then my mom got me a ballpoint pen. They were just coming out the year I quit school and they left a lot to be desired. You could tell what I had written but it left gaps. Nowadays you just type, and you don't use your head for math, just a calculator.

A well-thumbed yearbook is the 1951 *Ayaitchess* published by the Journalism Club of the Armstrong High School. *Marjorie was in the Journalism Club.* The annual is dedicated to Richard 'Dick'

Thomas who "symbolized the continuity which cannot be maintained by teachers who come and go." He had been caretaker at the school for forty years and had died that year at age seventy. *Beaky, we called him.* The editorial and the valedictory are by Donna Runnalls, Jean Lockhart's sister. A cartoon of a woodpecker introduces each section of photos. *The woodpecker was our mascot. You'd hear him digging holes in the school.* The school's Latin motto states "E labore est praemium," loosely translated "From work is reward." *Girls had to take Latin in those days if they wanted to be a nurse, so every second year [the school offered] Latin.*

We had grades 9, 10, 11, 12, and 13 in the school south of the Odd Fellows Hall [Bridge Street], and industrial arts in the one in the [Memorial] Park. There were only 150 kids in high school – thirty-odd in a class. Grade 13 had a dozen or so. Grade 13 was just like first-year university – you could [follow with] one year of Normal School and then, with summer schools, you could teach. In grade 7 and 8 lots of kids quit, and you lost more as the grades went higher – they could go out and get a job. In the '50s there was more money in loggin' than in teaching. I quit in 1949 at the end of grade 10. My English was no heck. Then we got into this darn algebra. I could figure it in my head but I can remember the teacher giving me hell for not working it out on paper. I knew darn well that if I kept going and it got tougher, I couldn't do it.

Flipping pages of the yearbook, Raymond muses over photographs of the high school staff: *Arthur Linfield, principal – he was in the RCAF in the Second War – smart beggar. R. Smale – he'd been in the army in the First War. Terry Moore was our industrial arts teacher except in grade 9 when we had Reid. Miss Reith – she was a good old girl. There was a stage in the old Rec. Hall. You could go up one stairs, cross behind the curtain and down the other stairs. We'd make a noise and watch which way she'd come, then go the other way.* It was a game of hide and seek she never won.

Miss Winskill: we had Bible reading in school – she was supposed to read a little part each morning to the class and then [lead] the Lord's Prayer. She was never in the room – she'd designate someone to do it. You'd start down one row and go on to the next – so the kid that was supposed to do it would know for the next day. Our bus would be late getting in – right on the bell – and I'd forget about this job. I didn't know where to find the darn [passages], but there was a good Baptist girl sitting right close to me in class. She'd save his bacon. *You'd read a little bit and then we'd all stand up and say the Lord's Prayer.* Beginning the school day with readings and prayers was not universally supported. *The parents of a friend of mine wrote and told the teacher that he was not to be in that room when Bible reading was taking place. They didn't believe in religion, period. You didn't have much of that [attitude] back then though you have lots of it today. I wasn't brought up religious either, so it didn't surprise me.*

Miss McConnell – Mrs. Jim Nelson: She was well liked – she was only a young gal – she would have done her rookie year in 1949. When we went from grade 8 into grade 9, we had to go into a club. Cadet Club was [held] in school in those days, but some of us boys didn't want to go into cadets – it was after the war – there wasn't a need for it. We got the brilliant idea we'd go into Costume and Makeup Club. Good gosh! When Miss McConnell saw us come in, I don't know what she thought. You can understand boys making up girls today, but not fifty years ago! They didn't last long with Miss McConnell and reluctantly entered cadets.

I stayed in cadets for the year, and when Inspection Day arrived, Mom and Dad let me stay home. Several of the boys must have had the same idea. *They changed the date to the following day and I come to school without a uniform on, and of course I was relegated to the back [of the parade]. The next year I said, "To hell with this!" so I just wrote in my schedule 'Study Period.' I might have told somebody else – and by February or March there were about a dozen of us boys in there. Linfield started talking to us one day: "Oh, you should be in a club." He was real nice until he found out we weren't going to budge. Then he got mad: "I don't care if you join a Horseshoe Club or what!" I quit school at the end of the year.*

182

I always say I got kicked out.

In this issue of *Ayaitchess, Walter Block* is president of the Students' Council; *Alan Gill,* of the Athletic Council. After a busy and successful year the *Red Cross Club* is $1.11 to the good. Class photos in grades 9 and 10 are gender based, and each student is given a line of print. In Grade 9, *Carolyn Hoover* "plays the piano and likes dancing." *Betty Brown* "is known as 'Liz,' and likes sports, especially swimming," and *Diane Hope* "is good at school and sports." *Dennis Lyster* "is always laughing," and *Harold Norris* "sees all, says nothing!" *Eric Hornby* "is one of those tall boys so useful on a basketball team," and *Dick Ramsey* "is a good guard on the Junior basketball team." In Grade 10, *Bob Bigsby* "likes tinkering with motors," *Tom Nordstrom* "is a promising track star," and *Jan Clemson* "is an actor." *Norman Huggins* "designs aeroplanes and climbs mountains," and *Ernie Heighton* "hunts big game!" *Dorothy McNair* "does a good job as Captain of C Team," while the attribute for *Nora Bell* states unequivocally, "Good things come in small packages!"

Marjorie Hitt has graced with a rhyming couplet the name of each student in her grade 11 class, including

Jack Noble:
Don't be fooled by his innocent smile,
For he's full of mischief all the while.
Jim Jamieson:
Our photographer Jim is tall and slim.
The witty answers come from him.
Dick File:
He's the greatest curling fan in our room,
But which curls the most, the smoke or the broom?
Marjorie Hitt:
If these personals you'd like to abridge,
Put the blame on me, just 'Midge'.

Scotty Dodds named her Midge. The nickname referred to her petite size.

Befitting their senior status, students in grades 12 and 13 have longer attributes. *Tom Sidney* is Captain of Cadets, "quite expert in the shot put and discus throw [and] quite a shot with a rifle." *Art Maw* is "our Track man, winner of the Mile and Half-mile." *George Bowie* "has been Team 'A's captain for two years and also played softball, soccer, and basketball." *Pat Thompson* "is a member of the Jersey Club and won a trip to Toronto in 1950." *Agnes Dodds* "has been in Drama and Glee Clubs [and] is clerk of Teen Town." *Bert Scott* "has belonged to Badminton, Cadets, and Drama." *Larry Slapak* has written a short story, and *Don Little* describes "My Trip to England." Clubs and sports teams receive praise.

The Armstrong Co-operative Society has purchased a full-page advertisement located prominently at the front of the annual, and someone, likely Marjorie, has written '$15.00' in the margin. *Marjorie contacted all the advertisers and kept a running list from year to year.* Other local advertisers include Golden Gate Café, Shepherd's Hardware, Harrison's Groceteria, Armstrong and Spallumcheen Credit Union, The City of Armstrong, the *Armstrong Advertiser*, Overwaitea Ltd., Mat. Hassen & Sons, H. Comber Greenhouses, and Star Theatre. One page carries Vernon advertisements including "CKOV... 630 on your Dial," and Bulman's Limited, processors of Okanagan fruits and vegetables. Marjorie has written follow-up reminders for next year on these pages.

In addition to a flair for writing, Marjorie still loves to paint. Raymond's house displays some canvases. A Donovan Clemson photograph of a teen-aged Marjorie painting clay models made the March 6, 1952, edition of the *Family Herald and Weekly Star*, a fat newspaper published in Montreal and distributed weekly in Canada for $1.50 per year; in Britain, $3; and in the United States, $4.50. *I think that's how Marj got her pen pal in England – Sybil Hackett, I think her name was – she saw Marj's photo. She came to Vancouver about ten years ago. It was the only time they met.*

Further items of interest to Armstrong Spallumcheen surface in

184

the same issue:

- Foot and Mouth Disease hits Canada, and drastic quarantines have been set up around Regina. Map provided.
- Canadians are the leading buyers of Aberdeen Angus cattle at Perth (Scotland) sales.
- *Case* tractors make good use of short growing season; just right for snow and mud.
- The importance of exercise for hens: a 12-pound Barred Rock was raised by Holley Skelton, RR2, Armstrong, B.C.

Also featured are short stories, A Quiet Hour for Sunday Reading, Just for Girls: figure trimmers, The Maple Leaf Club for children, a children's page, comics, recipes with accompanying photographs, and the advice of Dorothy Dix. Many pages of advertisements conclude the publication. It was widely popular.

After the Second War the Price-Hitt family became especially interested in the community's decision to build a swimming pool in Memorial Park. As the first pool in the Okanagan, it would present advantages for local youth, and Ewart Price was in charge of its construction. *Ewart Price was the construction and maintenance man at the Pea Growers. He did some of the building of the Pea Factory. He worked [also] at Portage La Prairie [Manitoba] where the Pea Growers had a farm. During his trips to the Coast and the [American] Northwest, City officials asked him to visit swimming pools to get a few specs on pool construction for them. I can remember the Kelowna Courier [complaining]: "Even the little town of Armstrong has got a pool." Boys and girls in the early '50s were getting Red Cross training for lifeguards. They could go to other places and get summer jobs. They were in great demand.*

In the early '50s Raymond was in his late teens and farming with his father. The weather occupied a significant amount of attention in his recollections.

In November of 1955, I remember I was pulling turnips on a

Friday afternoon and it was around 50 above [Fahrenheit]. No snow on the ground at all. By Saturday morning, which was Remembrance Day, it was down to 10 degrees – an absolute contrast. It went down to at least 10 or 15 below zero F. at night for about a week, and then it snowed like heck. It did a lot of damage – you can imagine. Suckers come up from the [plum] trees and some of them have fruit. They'd grow fast and then couldn't stand the cold – they'd freeze off at the snowline. Only hardy varieties survived. 1968-69 was the last real cold winter we had. There was three kicks at real cold snaps that winter – one in early December, one around New Year's and the third in late January. It was around 25-30 below zero F. We haven't seen that for years.

Cold weather also meant taking extra precautions with machinery. *[In early days] we used little gas engines. If we went to visit someplace on a cold night, Dad always covered the engine of our Model A [Ford] with a blanket to keep it warm. And every so often he'd go outside and start the car – let the engine run a few minutes. When he got home, he always drained the engine, and in the morning he poured warm water into it before he turned on the ignition.* A similar procedure might be used on any gasoline water-cooled engine.

Set on a hilltop like an eyrie with a 360-degree vista of the Okanagan Valley, Raymond's farm feels spacious. He says the night sky is brilliant. In the daytime one sees to the east, Enderby Cliffs and the Monashees; to the southeast, Fortune Creek and just the tip of Silver Star Mountain; to the south, Stepping Stones Estates and the road to Vernon; to the southwest, Rose Swanson Mountain – *see the red trees – the dead trees – on the mountain;* to the west, Salmon River Valley Road; to the northwest, Hullcar Mountain and Mount Ida.

Neighbouring farms, past and present, are visible too. *Spanning from south to north, you see Maw's first, then Docksteader, then Dennis Frederick's on Salmon River Road. That used to be the Brydon place – Lew's parents – Mildred Hartman was a Brydon.*

Next you can see the antenna on that roof – William Anderson (Bill) on Ford Road is an amateur radio [enthusiast]. In fact, when the fires were burning in the summer of 2003, he was relaying messages about them. Bill's property was part of the Brydon place. Then there's Knob Hill Farms asparagus patch on Ford Road – the old Ford place was 320 acres originally. I can remember as a kid Dad and I hunting pheasants there, and a lot of the land wasn't being worked – dry years in the '30s along with the Depression. The United Church had the lot on the northeast corner of Ford and Salmon River Road where they built Knob Hill Church, and when Ford left, they found out that the church didn't own the land. Ford had given it to the church but never registered it. Luckily Steve Heal had bought the Ford place and made arrangements to make it legal.

Knob Hill School, later Knob Hill Hall, was kitty-cornered from the church on the southwest corner. *When they took the church down, they put the organ and the pews over in the hall.* Knob Hill Hall was the activity centre for local residents. *We always played whist on Friday night – us, Donald Louttit, Docksteader, Casement, Lester Babb, and others, wives, and sometimes kids – as stores stayed open to nine o'clock on Saturday night then – Saturday was the big day for coming to town. But by the end of April we'd quit playing because fifty years ago people had asparagus to pick. Knob Hill Hall burnt in 1998 – it was rented on a cold night and they put too much wood in the stove.* Today the action is at the Seniors' Activity Centre on Patterson Avenue. *It's much easier for people to get to. We have booked the first and third Saturday nights of the month, the United Church has it on the second Saturday, and the Anglicans, on the fourth. We play regular whist and the other two groups play court whist.* Whist resembles bridge without the bidding. *Last Saturday [summer 2006] we had eight tables.*

Raymond Hitt has never married. *I was so darn shy. If somebody was to say twenty or thirty years ago that I'd get up and announce winners and dish out prizes at the [Seniors'] Activity Centre, nobody would believe it. One time they asked me to be president of the Knob Hill Society for a year, and I said, "No way I'd do that!"*

187

*Last year at the Armstrong Farmers' Market, the elementary school
kids did a Maypole Dance, and it reminded me of the time they tried
to teach us the French Minuet. I thought to myself, 'There's twenty
boys and twelve or so girls, so if I make some mistakes, I can get out
of doing this.' So I made some mistakes!*

Religious affiliation also limited choice of a marriage partner.
*You'd never look at a Catholic girl – you'd never look at a Baptist girl
– [because] I wasn't brought up real religious. And there wasn't a lot
of girls available. Then you got all kinds of displaced persons coming
in the fifties – more guys than gals – and it upset the balance to some
extent. You know the Melvins. I went out with their cousin. This is darn
near fifty years ago now. When I'd take her out, her youngest brother
used to come along to chaperone. There was nothing wrong with this
cousin – she was the same religion as some of the Prices: Seventh
Day Adventist. I went off to some of the meetin's that they had, but I
couldn't get into it. And to top it off, the goldarned preacher was my
cousin Jack Price! In fact, I think that was the only reason I got to go
with her at all. In a small community like this, it was tough.*

Friendships and familial networks have been nurtured over
many years and are significant aspects of Raymond's life. An important figure is his small, multi-coloured dog, an energetic harbinger of
any interloper inside the house or on the farm – *Tippy is a Heinz 57
variety.* Several friends celebrate birthdays together and play cards:
*Bea Whittaker, Jean Howard, Jean Gill, and Rika Jackson when she
was alive.* Raymond can rely on other friends for farm work: *Craig
McKechnie cuts the alfalfa for me. No point tyin' a whole bunch of
money up in machinery – you only use it once a year.* His niece and
nephews and their children are familiar visitors. Rae is the youngest
of Marjorie's three sons. His older brothers are Darcy and Reginald.
Marjorie married Richard Gordon from out of town. Rae recounts
the story:

*She met my father at her high school graduation. My father's
sister Heather was married to Vern Smith [son of 'Gasoline' Billy]
and living at the time in Armstrong, and my dad came up from*

Vancouver to visit her. There was a dance and he took another lady to the dance and went home with my mother. He said he knew at once that he was going to marry her. She married from home at nineteen.

Because he worked so closely with his father on Valley Vista Farm, Raymond learned at first hand one of his secrets – the art and craft of water witching – and his dowsing talents are in demand. His tools are simple: one ordinary wire bent into a V, the sides of which are roughly sixteen inches long, and a single wire about a yard in length called a bobber. First he holds the ends of the V-wire firmly in his grip. *I know where our water line is. It's coming that way, you see?* The V bends downward. He turns 180 degrees. *I can't feel anything if I face downstream – see? – I have to face the direction the water's coming from. With the bobber, about a foot each bob will tell you the depth of the water.*

Since counting the number of bobs may be tedious if the water is located far below the surface, Raymond has developed a shorter method. *Dad didn't know some of the things that I've found out. He didn't realize the wand would turn over [point downwards] so many paces outward from the centre of the stream in one direction, and the same distance out to the side in the opposite direction. The paces give you a rough idea of the depth of the water – so many paces to the side mean roughly so much depth. 20 paces would be about 150-160 feet, roughly 8 feet of depth to a pace.*

I've found that, in some of the places I've water witched, they've tried to drill where it turned over, but it was just showing the depth and not the main stream. He demonstrates on his water line. *It turns over here and then it turns over again here, and I've walked eight paces to the side. You could drill here, but you wouldn't be right on the stream. As I come in [towards the centre], it turns over on the main.*

During this demonstration Raymond's manipulation of the wand involves 'connecting' and 'disconnecting' the energy flow. *If I disconnect, there's nothing showing there now even though [the wand] turned over a moment before in that spot.* Again he 'disconnects,' or 'breaks the circuit' after the wand has pointed downwards. *[Also] the wand will still point if there's no water there now, but it's been running and has gone dry.* Being able to distinguish dry streams from active watercourses is essential.

Another aspect of dowsing appears to relate to types of rock. In this case the bobber is the tool, and the rocks are lying in Raymond's driveway. *I've found out that certain rocks will 'show.' See that rock there? It's bobbing on that rock. And [unlike water] it will do it from any angle – you see? It bobs to beat heck. There's got to be some mineral in that baby. And the same with this one. See? But this other rock doesn't.* The bobber remains motionless. *So that's why I think some of these old prospectors knew something about dowsing – that's how some of them found their ore. But you can be damn sure they never told anyone – it was their secret.*

The wand will 'turn' for silver and gold. Remember, your old coins were silver. If you buried them in one of three holes, Dad could tell you which hole they were in. I've just discovered this rock here because I watched him locate silver coins. Whether there's a certain amount of silver in it.... He hefts the rock. *Heavy beggar! Something's in it! Bobbers don't work on loonies or toonies – dead metal. So you couldn't go around with a bobber on the beach looking for them. You could crush the good rocks, though, and leave the other ones.*

I've tried witching out in our field and discovered there must be a rock six or eight feet down because I know there is no water there. It must be to do with the mineral that's in it, you see. There used to be a watercourse there, so the water may have been dragging some of these rocks along, and that's what makes the bobber respond.

Dowsing is a skill that takes practice to perfect. Raymond thinks dowsing and living have something in common. *Dad did it. I learned more. People show you things at different times. You never want to think you know everything.*

190

Teenaged friends Jan Clemson, left, and Raymond Hitt leaning out the Clemson barn
Photo by Donovan Clemson

191

Chapter Five

Nanny's Story

Doris Adelaide (Harrison) Hassard

I remember my first party dress. Gosh, it was a beautiful dress – lace with satin underneath. The rust colour suited me because my hair was brown and I had hazel eyes. It cost $15 and I had to buy it 'on time' – so much a month. In those days you got nice clothes for $15 at Piggott's ladies' wear. They let me have it before I finished paying for it because they knew I was 'good' for it. (I worked at their house, and every once in a while I'd come and help out at the store.) The dress had a turn-back collar – very fancy – and big, lace, puffy sleeves. It fit me around the hips and flared out at the bottom. I just loved that dress! I was slim in those days too.

Nearly 92, Doris was still slim and upright, a vivacious, pretty woman. At home in Abbeyfield House on Wood Avenue in Armstrong, she enjoyed entertaining family and old friends – *'Mac' Thornton [Pull up a Chair] was in town just a short while ago and came up to see me* – and she took pleasure in looking her best.

My hair needs a perm right now, but I have a special hair-dresser in Vernon that I go to. I remember the time perms came in – the first perm I had. Oh, it was so heavy on my head! The whole set was attached to your head for heating the rods – you were so glad when the time was up – but it sure made a nice curl. My hair was quite thick at that time – certainly thicker than it is now – you can spit through it!

I have a picture of myself taken by Don Clemson when I was applying for a passport. I didn't go anywhere – I just wanted a pass-port. I would like to have gone places, you know. On the back of the small photograph Doris has written: "Taken by Donovan Clemson for my passport picture before my hair turned grey."

Doris did cross the Canadian border on occasion. Her niece Karen Hassard recalls, *When I was in high school, she and Uncle Al went with my mom and dad to Mexico a few times, but they were never very venturesome on their own. Living in small towns, I guess you're not so worldly in that respect. She did get to Reno many times on a bus tour – she loved to gamble. She'd save up her quarters and probably gambled more in the nickels and pennies than the quarters – she wasn't a big spender. It was an outing.*

Like many first-generation Canadians born in the early twentieth century, Doris had grown up in a country that tested one's mettle. Her parents were emigrants from northern England. Their story depicts the false starts newcomers to Canada might make before finding a satisfactory home in their adopted country. Her father, John Henry Whitfield (Henry) Harrison came from a hamlet called West Black-dean, near Stanhope in Durham. Although Doris Hassard never saw her father's birthplace, her niece Dolores Culling, the Harrison family's historian, visited West Black-dean in the mid-eighties: She says, *It consisted of a sheep enclosure surrounded by a fence and four or five houses.*

Henry followed three brothers to Canada and homesteaded first in a region of the Northwest Territories called Regina. That region would later become the northern half of the new province of Saskatchewan. He went back to England and early in 1904 he claimed a bride from Tanshelf, Pontefract, Yorkshire. Doris carried a permanent memento of that event: *I have a middle name and I don't like it – Adelaide. I was named after Mother: Mary Adelaide Swift.* The couple returned to the homestead where their first child, Eliza Lilian, 'Lily,' was born late in the same year.

Life was pretty hard out there in the early 1900s. It was bare prairie in those days, you know. Mary Adelaide's parents came out to visit their daughter and new grandchild, their idea being to remain with them in Canada, but they had second thoughts and all five returned to England. Finally, Henry and Mary Adelaide made the decision to emigrate permanently. Because Henry's brothers had left Saskatchewan for British Columbia, the Harrisons followed them to Armstrong. *One brother, 'Hank,' (John Henry) was born here [1907], and then in 1909 they went back to Saskatchewan.* The nearest business district to them was Neilburg, close to the Alberta border. They pre-empted a quarter-section (160 acres) for three dollars an acre fourteen miles from Yonker, a town that no longer exists, and eight miles from Winter. *And that's where I was born. There were six of us in the family. I was the fourth.*

Dolores Culling's account of the Harrisons' dozen years on their pre-emption is bleak. Three children were born in the lean-to farmhouse that consisted of two bedrooms, a kitchen, and a pantry: Frank on March 15, 1910; Doris on September 1, 1912; and Howard on February 11, 1915. By the time the baby of the family, Irene, arrived in hospital on September 23, 1918, Henry had of necessity built a larger house and a barn. With six children Mary Adelaide had her hands full: *Every time she received a letter from England, she wept buckets of tears.*

Henry was having a hard time too. In England he had followed a trade as a moulder in a steel mill. Consequently, he had little notion of farming. He broke his land with three or four horses and a plough, and his two older children picked rocks. He grew oats, wheat and some barley and ploughed fireguards around his buildings to hamper the ubiquitous prairie fires.

The family carried water to the house from a slough. Once a week Mary Adelaide administered a ritual bath in a tin tub sequentially from the cleanest to the dirtiest family member. Once a year she sent $500 to Timothy Eaton's Ltd. for twelve months' supply of groceries. She wrapped bread dough to rise in an old fur coat with heated flat irons around it. In the cold winter she and Lily sat up late stoking the stove to warm the house, and kept themselves awake by crocheting and embroidering. The children slid on shovels down a snow hill that extended from the barn roof to the ground. Sometimes

Hank threw a bucket of water over it to ice the slope. They walked two and a half miles to school. Their parents carted Mary Adelaide's piano by sleigh to the schoolhouse for parties and Christmas concerts, where Henry accompanied his wife on the violin.

Doris's childhood was tinted with these events. *Then in 1921 we came back to Armstrong for good. We first lived in a house just above the dump ground on Powerhouse Road. That house is gone now. The land was down below on the creek bottom and, of course, in those days they didn't clean out the creeks like they do today. The débris coming down the creek was just left there and in the spring the water flooded the land. The first crop that Dad put in was washed out completely. So that [property] wasn't any good.*

So we looked for another farm at the other end of Powerhouse Road towards Vernon. We lived in a house right at the corner of Highway 97A – the first house on Powerhouse Road. In the spring the basement filled with water and one brother got rheumatic fever. So they moved the house on rollers [farther] up from the corner. They'd move one roller ahead of the other, you know, and it took quite a while. We lived there [2092] until my brother [Howard] took over the farm.

I was at the [Armstrong] Consolidated School the first year it opened. We came in February of 1921 and the school opened in September. And in the meantime schools weren't very plentiful, and they were all full. So from February until June, I went to the old Baptist Church, where the present Baptist Church is located [3185 Becker Street], as I think they had classes there for grades one and two. I had started grade two on the Prairies, but they put me back into grade one.

Doris recalled walking to school by herself. *I was only eight and a half, so the younger two wouldn't be going to school yet, and I don't remember if my older brother Frank was going to school.* At eleven years he may have been helping the family settle in. *I walked from Powerhouse Road on the main highway up to Rosedale Avenue [and along] to the church. It wasn't too far. There wasn't much traffic then – very few cars in those days – everything done by horses – so walking wasn't dangerous. But one morning it was* cold. *When I got to school, I stood up too close to the big-bellied heater and burnt the front out of my dress.*

I went from grade one to grade eight and then to the old high school [Bridge Street] for the full three years. I finished around age seventeen. It was 1929 and the Great Depression was about to begin.

Like many young women of that time, Doris had three principal options for a professional career: teaching, nursing, or secretarial work. Her preference, nursing, required years of training and was physically arduous – lifting and carrying, and being continually on one's feet.

I worked in the [Armstrong Spallumcheen] hospital for a while, training in practical nursing like they do now, but you didn't get a certificate or anything. I worked in the summer mostly when they hired extra people as [holiday] replacements. It was within walking distance of our place on Powerhouse Road. I liked it. I'd have liked to go in for a nurse, but I was having trouble with my knees even in the early days. They tested me and [turned me down] because my legs weren't strong enough. You've got to have good legs for that job.

I didn't want teaching. The only other [career] in those days was stenography. And my folks had no money to send me to college. Everybody was struggling to get along. Times were hard and jobs were scarce. So I used to do housework because there was nothing much else. I worked for quite a few people for short periods of time – just on and off – somebody was sick and needed help for a little while. That was the only way [a woman] could make a living in those days.

Living at home as a young adult further curtailed Doris's independence. *My parents were strict – very, very strict Methodists – so I was held down at home. They were definitely against drink, so any drinking you did was away from home – I don't blame them for that though. The Methodist Church was on the corner of Patterson Avenue and the alley [Shepherd Lane] beside Fletcher's garage. It had tie rails all along the back and a shed for the horses. It was the same at [Zion] United Church. Another hitching rail [ran] in front of the old Co-op store [Rose Valley Square].*

Whenever I could sneak away from my dad, I went to dances and parties. After we came from the Prairies, my oldest sister, Lily, never stayed home any more. She was sixteen then and got a job. My brother Frank found work in the [Armstrong] Co-op store right after he graduated from high school. He went as manager to a co-op store in Revelstoke and then came back and bought out the IGA store [Independent Grocers' Association] in Armstrong and started out on his own. The IGA was located on Okanagan Street just south of the Armstrong Hotel. Of course, his nieces could bank on a summer job with Uncle Frank.

Doris, too, had a special relationship with her brothers' and sisters' children. As a baby her oldest niece, Dolores, Hank's daughter, couldn't manage the word 'Aunty.' She lisped "Nanny," and thereafter Doris was 'Nanny' to them all.

Since she was yet unmarried, her family had priority on Doris's leisure and labour. *Most of the time I lived with my sister Lily and helped her with her babies and kept the house. I also worked for my brother and a friend who had rented a house, and I cooked for them for a while. I never cooked at home. My mother did all the cooking. I learnt it when I had to.*

Whenever she saw an opportunity, however, Doris took other jobs. They gave her both her own money and greater freedom. *When I got a job in town, I [usually] stayed right with the people I worked for. I got $15 a month doing everything – cooking, cleaning, and looking after children too if they had them.* The purchase of her brown silk and lace party dress, therefore, represented a full month of hard work. The advantage was that Doris had fewer questions to answer about her off-duty hours. *They [employers] would let you go out "as long as you got home at a decent time."*

Dressing for a soireé was an exhilarating change from house-keeping. *I had short hair but I always had it permed when I was working – it wasn't much or I couldn't have afforded it. We wore lisle stockings – silk stockings for those that could afford it – so you would save until you could buy a pair of silk ones. Stockings last me a lot longer now than they did then! I used to like nice shoes. When I got away from home, I used to wear quite high heels. When you get dressed up, you need high heels.*

There were a lot of house parties, you know. You played a lot of silly games. For instance, they'd put up a curtain, and the ladies would stand in a row behind it with just their legs showing beneath it. They'd give the men a mirror and they'd have to turn their backs to the curtain and look through the mirror at a girl's legs and guess who it was. And, of course, some of the girls used to put on crazy shoes to fool them. Then, if the house had a piano, we'd dance. Was it crowded? *You crowded into a room anyway if you were going to have fun!*

Doris loved to dance and had inherited a natural musical talent. Karen Hassard recalls, *Her father played the violin and her mother, the piano, but Nanny played violin, piano, organ, mouth organ, button accordion – any instrument she got her hands on. She kept really good time. Yet she never had music lessons and learned to play by ear. She had this red button accordion that I used to like to play – I don't know where it ever got to.* Doris's skill was in demand at parties because she could play whichever musical instrument was handy. This joyful and imaginative side of her nature gave respite from her usual jobs.

The most I ever got for working out was $25 a month at the Big House – I worked for Mrs. T.K. Smith for a year and a half. And I *didn't stay there. I lived nearly a quarter mile away in a little house that was on my brother [Hank]'s property and walked to work. I paid him $5 a month rent off my $25. Well, everybody else was living under constraints too so I didn't feel bad.*

Some people used to think you could go on forever without a day off. At this one place I never got time off. Once I asked to go for the day to Revelstoke Mountain with my brother Frank and his wife to see the spring flowers. The woman finally agreed, but when I came back the next morning, all the dirty dishes from the day before were sitting there waiting to be washed. And then I got sick. I had what they called 'quinsy.' Your tonsils swelled up and got pus-y. Then that gathering broke one night and I swallowed it, and the poison went through my system. Arthritis started behind my ankles. It hurt me so much to walk.

At this juncture Doris accepted a job offer that sent her life in a new direction. She was thirty. It was the summer of 1941 and World War Two was nearly two years old.

Al Hassard and I had been going together for some time. His sister had been cooking and keeping house for their parents, but [the Hassards] moved to Vernon, and she and her husband decided to go to Vancouver to work in the Boeing munitions factory and make some money. They were leaving the farm, leaving the cooking, so they needed a cook. I'd been working in Kelowna at a 15-cent store while the clerks were on holiday and I was back in Armstrong between jobs, so Al asked me if I'd go down to the farm. The Hassard farm was located on Back Enderby Road in Spallumcheen, and Alers Hassard and his brother Gordon were running it with hired help. *It was haying season, and the first crop was off, but the second crop was coming on. They had fourteen hired men.* Add Alers, Gordon, and herself. *I thought, 'Gosh, I've never cooked for that many people before!'*

It was one of the biggest farms in the area – 640 acres [a section] plus rentals. The house was large – after all, it had housed *eighteen children somehow. (Now, mind you, when the youngest was born, the oldest one was married, so maybe they weren't all there at the same time.) They had a big barn with workhorses in it, and a herd of registered Shorthorn beef cattle. They were growing grain and alfalfa and some timothy because they used to ship hay to the Coast for the racehorses. At that time they coiled the hay out in the field and used horse teams and drivers to haul the hay to the stack. So there were all these men coiling the hay and working on the wagons and the stack. They'd stack it raw and it would have to sit for a while – and then in the fall when the farm work was done, the stationary baler would come and sit beside the stack and bale the whole thing – square bales like they have today. (They didn't have the movable balers as they do now.) There was a spur on the railway back at Stepney – Stepney siding – and they used to ship the hay from there. They'd order in boxcars and load them – hay all baled and hauled to the buyers in Vancouver and Victoria for $35 a ton – a far cry from today's prices.*

So that first summer I arrived, the second crop of hay was coming off and what was I to do? All those men! It was a nightmare, I'll tell you that!! I didn't know how in the world to tackle it! And, of course, they were getting three meals a day! They were practically all Indians [natives] from the Enderby Reserve and it was during the war and we were rationed. Sugar, tea, coffee – all that stuff was rationed. Well, you couldn't get the men to bring their ration books: the wife had it in her purse... or somebody had taken it somewhere else... every excuse under the sun.

I'd be up before five o'clock in the morning getting stuff ready for breakfast: porridge, pancakes, bacon and eggs, toast and jam – you name it. The full course! There wasn't so much dried cereal then and men working in the field don't want dried cereal.

I fed the hired men in the outside kitchen. It held a big stove with a wide, flat top, a warming closet up above, and a reservoir for warming water on the side. I had a sink with a drainboard, a flat counter and cupboards. I managed everything out there, but, you

203

know, in summer it was hot, and you were poking wood into this darn stove. Anyway, I got through breakfast. And everything was eaten too. You know, those Indians, they really ate a lot, but they were good men... they were good men [workers].

We had an outside platform where I went up two steps to hang out the washing, and where I used to put the basins for the men to clean up... the soap, and the towels. We were very short of towels, so we made them out of feed sacks – the coarse, canvas feed sacks. I would split one of these and make two towels. And they were quite good – you could bleach them out to pretty near white. I didn't get my first towels from a store until 1945. World War Two had ended.

We had an old washing machine that did a good job, but you had to do it by hand. You worked a lever to do the washing, and you had to pull that lever for quite a while to get the clothes clean. It's surprising what you can do when you have to do it. Later, some time during the war, we got the first electric washing machine. That was a blessing.

By eight o'clock in the morning the men had gone to the fields. *I did the washing up by hand. We had running water in the kitchen – a tap, but we also had a [hot water] tank. It's so much easier now – dishwashers, and so on.*

At that time I didn't have a fridge, just an icebox. We didn't get a fridge until 1945. The boys used to go out and cut ice in the river, stack it in the ice house under sawdust, and every day or two I'd holler, "I need some ice! I need some ice!" And Al would go and get a block of ice and bring it in, and – sure – it would be too big to go in the icebox – and he'd have to take it back out in the yard and chisel it off – and, of course, the air was blue around there! And you'd have to remember to empty the darn pan underneath the icebox or you'd have a flood all over the kitchen floor. So I couldn't keep a lot of meat and had to shop quite often. I never baked bread. I just said, "No, I'm not going to bake bread." So we had to buy bread, and we used a lot in those days. A working man could eat half a loaf at a sitting.

The big meal was at lunchtime. Doris laughed at her convolutions to get the food on the table. *You're kind of thinking when you go to bed: 'Now, what are we going to have tomorrow?' You're planning all the time. I drove myself to town for groceries or I couldn't have existed – the men were always busy out in the fields. I just got what we needed – things were a heck of a lot cheaper than they are now. You'd serve your meat, and vegetables that were in season, you know. I didn't make a lot of salads – heavy eaters like that don't like salads – [instead] I sliced up tomatoes and cucumbers and celery. It was a lot of work peeling and slicing up vegetables. And they didn't have peelers like they have today – just a knife, you know.*

The men seemed to go for solid foods. Chicken… roast of beef or pork. I don't know how many pounds the roasts were, but they were big! Because you had to have some cold meat left for supper. Supper was just about as big a deal as lunchtime. You'd fry potatoes left from the boiled ones at lunch – always make enough to carry over!

I baked a lot of pies. I'd make the pastry at night and then do the pies in the morning. There was never a dull moment – you were always doing something. We had a prune tree and an apple tree, but it wasn't very good – a Flemish Beauty. Some people like it for cooking but I didn't – for cooking pies I liked the 'Macs' [McIntosh]. I made a cake pretty near every day – plain white cake – they liked that just as much as chocolate. If I had time, I'd ice it. Oh, I was tired when I went to bed at night! The boys had their end of the house and I had mine – I was up in the morning before they were.

That first summer at the Hassard farm was Doris's trial by woodstove fire, but in September, 1941, Gordon married Mary Dixon and brought her to live in the farmhouse. A second pair of female hands made life easier.

We divided the hired men. But I felt kind of sorry for Mary because she had never done any cooking before – she was a book-

keeper and stenographer in George Smith's hardware store [3530 Okanagan Street] where Margarieta's Place is now. Mary had quite a time breaking into that kind of life, but we got on well together.

The women also organized the household chores. *We each took a washing day – one would do it on one day and one on the other because we only had one clothesline. We had one cow – usually a Jersey. Gordon milked in the morning and Al milked at night. Gordon kept the morning milk and Al kept the evening milk. They used to keep it out in the milk house where they had water running all the time and the milk hanging in a vat in the water. The cream would come to the top and we'd skim it off ourselves. (There was a cream separator in there too but they didn't use it any more because they only had the one cow left.)*

Naturally, along with an ice house and a milk house, the Hassards had a hen house. *Mary had some chickens, and I raised about fifty laying hens. That was my pocket money. On a Friday afternoon when we weren't too busy, I used to take my eggs down to the Egg Pool in Armstrong and then go visit my mother, who lived in town. I'd be there for a little while and then back to work. There was no socializing or anything like that in those days – we were just too busy! So that was my little outing on Friday afternoon except when I had to run to town to get groceries.*

Karen Hassard remembers Doris's fondness for chickens: *Nanny liked farm animals and her favourite were chickens. She always had chickens, and when we visited, we'd get the opportunity to gather the eggs. It's nice and warm underneath the chickens. It's exciting too because when you're sticking your hand out, you don't know if the hen's going to peck you.*

Doris expanded her chicken business. *[Sometimes] I raised fifty male meat birds and fed them with our own grain. I'd get them in the spring and keep them over the summer. In the fall I'd have somebody kill them – one of the hired men. I'd sell them fresh killed or on the hoof – people could take them home alive and kill them when they* *wanted to. At $1.50 apiece a lot of people wanted them. You wouldn't get anything* now *for a dollar and a half.* For a summer's work Doris pocketed seventy-five dollars. *And you'd figure that was good!*

I didn't have much of a garden at the farm – as best I could I worked the heavy clay – but it was nice to have a little bit of fresh stuff. I'd grow a few peas or something. Of course, there were always the Chinese gardens in those days – they were flourishing in town. So we'd go there once a week to fill up with vegetables. You wouldn't know it now, but there were Chinese field gardens all around Armstrong – now it's all built up. Jong's vegetable field is the only one left. Karen Hassard recalls the same scenes: *I remember down on the Flats the Chinese people used to live and grow celery and lettuce. I remember seeing them carrying their vegetables to the stores with a pole balanced across their shoulders and a basket hanging down from each end of it.*

With Gordon's marriage came an alteration in the living arrangements. To accommodate the newlyweds, the brothers divided the farmhouse into two residences. *It was a plenty big house for all of us. We took one of the bedrooms on the ground floor next to the living room and made it into a new kitchen for Mary. I kept the old [inside] kitchen – it was a big kitchen – the full length was probably twenty-four feet – the table right down the centre. You should have seen that table – it was in the house when we sold it – you could seat sixteen or eighteen people around it. Lots of chairs too. [Off the kitchen] was a little pantry with glass cupboards and a counter where Grandma Hassard had done a lot of her baking, but I never used it. A couch was by the window, and I used to lie down there once in a while to get off my feet. There wasn't much room for anything else! It was a poor kitchen to start with, but I had it remodelled. We replaced the old sink and drain board and built new cupboards in a U. We put a stove in there with two ovens. It turned out I never used that second oven much. I didn't have to.*

In fact, over time new technology reduced the number of hired men stumping into the outside kitchen for their three square meals a day. *The automatic balers came in and we got one. I could manage feeding four or five men. And the second year I was down there, Hassards were the first ones to have a combine. That combine was $12,000. It was only a small one – twelve foot – but it sure did a lot of work.*

Just a few months after Gordon brought home his bride, Alers Leonard and Doris Adelaide were wed. *Gordon and Mary were married in September, 1941, and we were married in December.* Life was good. *One time you knew everybody – everybody had parties. The Hassards raised seventeen children and we'd lots of nieces and nephews on my side too, so we really had good times [in spite of] the war. Liquor was rationed, so if you wanted a drink, you'd bring your own bottle. It was mostly the men who drank. The girls weren't much for that. You shared your eats too and just had a good time. The town's grown – I wouldn't know anybody now. I drove through town when the contents of the Armstrong Hotel were being auctioned off [March 22, 2003]. My, it was crowded!*

I was on the farm eight years – from 1941 to 1949. During this period Gordon and Mary had two offspring, Earl and Wendy, but Alers and Doris remained childless. Instead, the farm became the cherished holiday destination for a stream of Doris's young relations.

Karen Hassard remembers these visits: *Of course, she took every niece and nephew in the summertime. She liked kids. It's too bad she never had her own – but she treated us all as her own children, you know. My two brothers, Lorne and David, and I used to come. We lived in Falkland when I was little, so we went by train to Armstrong. Now that was a big trip! I can remember Armstrong station looked huge! And Nanny and Al would meet us at the station and drive us toward Enderby to the farm for our two- or three-week holiday. It was exciting for a city kid. I can remember making butter. They used to have a creamery where they put the milk to cool, and they had a barrel churn. Of course, it was the highlight of every child's visit to make butter and ice cream.* (Not to mention the suspense in the chicken house.)

One time at the farm we were playing store – buying and selling stuff. We had set out all Nanny's cans from her pantry, and I can remember my brothers getting nails and hammering them through the lids to open them up. She came out of the house – and oh! she could have killed them! Poor Nanny – she always got over it! She was strict with us but there still was lots of love. Another time my younger brother David fell on a discarded can at the farm and cut his arm really badly. Of course, there was an uproar because it wasn't that easy to get to town to the doctor's in those days, but they did and got him stitched up. He was fine, but it was a nasty cut, and you don't want that to happen when you're looking after somebody else's kids.

On one occasion at the end of their visit, Karen's mother, Irene, took the sting out of leave-taking: *My mother drove us home. She had this old car, and Nanny and my mom were in the front and the three of us kids were in the rumble seat. And we drove all the way from Enderby, down through Armstrong to Falkland on those old roads, and the wind was blowing in our faces. It was fun.*

In 1949 the Hassard brothers decided to sell the farm. Alers was now in his late forties and Doris, thirty-seven. The farm's acreage, the brothers' shared management, and Gordon and Mary's growing family made the choice a reasonable one. *There aren't many chances to sell a place that size, so when one came along, they sold to Bud [Albert] and Arlie Pieper, Chris Pieper's parents. Chris was just a little boy when they bought the farm. Then the Piepers sold to the Pea Growers, which was run by Mr. [Steve] Heal. David Heal was the right-hand man and he lived in town. David is running the farm today [2004]. They've got huge machinery there now compared to the machinery we used – big wheels five feet tall! We didn't have much machinery at that time – not that big stuff.*

Al and I came to town and bought a little house up on Fred Street for $4,000. We sold it for $5,000 and bought a house on two lots kitty-cornered on Becker and Rosedale. It's there today.

There's a big house built right beside it now – a little too close. Then for $5,000 we bought the Dr. Van Kleeck house on the corner of Okanagan Street across from Judge Behncke's house, and we fixed it all up. It was a three-storey building, but we didn't want one that big so we cut it down to one storey: At the first level, we took some boards off and put in a second roof inside the house; then we took the top off. After he left the farm, Al was always happy at carpentry and he followed that trade for quite a while. Renovating that house was his first big experience. Karen recalls that the original Van Kleeck house was beautiful and had hardwood floors throughout.

For the first time in nearly a decade, Doris was located in town and had the leisure to follow her own interests. She shared them with her younger sister, Irene Hoover, with whom she was especially close.

When I worked in town before I was married, I used to belong to the United Church choir. When we were on the farm, we never had time to belong to clubs or groups, and I never saw the inside of a church for a long while – I was too busy. But when I came back to Armstrong, I went back into the choir and stayed in it until about 1970. I went practically every week to church and choir practice. I haven't been able to attend lately. I began to be short of breath. Karen adds, *Nanny could sing really well. She sang alto and my mother sang soprano. That was their thing for a long, long time.*

Doris and Irene also shared a love of the outdoors, which they put to use for the church. *We enjoyed the Drone Circle of the United Church women. I think it is extinct now.* Karen suggests the group was called 'Stitch and Chatter.' *The church always had a Christmas bazaar in the fall, and the Drone Circle used to serve the tea and refreshments. We didn't seem to take in very much – about $30 to $40 on the bake tables. My sister and I were hobbyists, you know, so we got the idea of adding a craft table. We cleared $100. So we decided to do that instead of helping with the tea.*

Irene used to drive a car more than I did, and we went hiking around the lakes. We'd go out after the high water in the spring and find driftwood. And we'd pull all the weeds on the roadside and dry them and sell the driftwood with wild flowers wired on them. We'd pick the bulrushes before they got to the stage of breaking, early in September, and take them home and put them through a little process – rolling the bulrushes in a mixture of furniture glue and then in coloured flocking – the powdered stuff – and sell them in bouquets. They were pretty – nice to have over the winter. And we'd make tissue flowers too – great big ones, seven or eight inches wide – three or four would make a bouquet. The others in the Drone Circle didn't make crafts – my sister and I were the only ones that did those crazy things. She died at age sixty of Parkinson's disease.

Her sister's early death left a painful vacancy. *I had another sister in town – Lily Hallam – but we lived different lives. I love nature. I really like gardening – flowers mostly, but I like vegetables too.* In town Doris kept a large garden and always preserved for the winter. *I can't do it anymore but I still like it.* She searched the seed catalogues for unusual plants and started them in the house. She grew beautiful zinnias. Lily also had a green thumb. Karen declares, *She could grow anything!*

Another skill Doris shared with Lily was needlework. Karen says, *Besides towels, women used feed sacks for pillowcases, teacloths, and tablecloths and embroidered on them. I still have some my Aunty Lily made – she was wonderful at embroidery. Nanny was good too but Lily was exceptional. Wherever they got time to do that work, I don't know.*

When Gordon and Mary left the farm, they bought a hardware store in Enderby. Tragically, Gordon drowned in Mabel Lake. Alers died in 2003. *My husband made the century. He was 101. It's fine when you've got your faculties, but it's not so fine when you don't know what is going on. They're sleeping and you go to visit them and they're not with it. I don't want to be like that.*

It was not a likely possibility. In her early nineties Doris was alert and enjoyed conversation. She looked back and laughed at her first months on the Hassard farm.

That was a real initiation. I was really nervous when I first started. I never dreamt I could do it. I'd never want to do it again either! I got $20 a month, room and board. For the way you worked!!

[A few months after recounting these memories, on August 20, 2004, Doris Adelaide (Harrison) Hassard passed away peacefully at Vernon Jubilee Hospital.]

Doris Hassard's passport picture taken by Donovan Clemson

Chapter Six

A Life in the Outdoors

Glen Howard Maw

The large framed photograph is titled 'Maw's Orchard 1947.' A section of rail fence in the foreground; a young woman and child wandering downhill toward blossoming apple trees and a house; in the far background the suggestion of a town and a mountain.

Donovan Clemson took that picture from above looking east. Those apple trees are not there anymore. And the house isn't there anymore – or this woodshed. That row of houses in the distance is the main street in Armstrong. Beyond it is the bottom part of what they call Memorial Mountain. See, it's basically bare – it had burnt in 1925.

My grandparents and their four sons [Gordon Lister, Arthur Edwin, Harold Stovin, Joseph Goodson] came to this place early in 1911. My grandfather had bought the house and farm – 200 acres – from John Docksteader in 1910. There was some Frenchmen from Quebec on it, I think, before we came, but they only stayed a year or two. The house was probably built in 1898 – newspaper from that date was glued to the rough lumber between the rooms before they added the wallboard. Five or six years ago it took me an hour with my bulldozer, and the house and woodshed were in a pile. Neighbour kids used to go in there and I was afraid they'd fall through the floor. Some heritage people were looking at it too and I didn't want any part of that: those old-time houses, they're not insulated – there wasn't a basement under it – it was setting on stone.

When Dad [Arthur Edwin] and Mother were going to get married, he built up on the old place too. A small white house sits at 4300 Maw Road. *That was the house I was raised in. Vi [wife] and I have never lived on the home farm. It's over a mile as the crow flies from where we live now [4094 Salmon River Road]. You wouldn't believe the amount of people that would like to build a house up there for the view.* Located high on the flank of Rose Swanson Mountain, and stretching half a mile west and three-quarters of a mile north and south, the farm overlooks the wide Spallumcheen Valley, and from its eastern end, the city of Armstrong.

From his dining-room window, Glen can see the farm. *My son Will and his wife, Leanne, live just to the right [4305] in the house my brother Art built. Swing to the left and you can see the roof of the original barn. As far as I can figure, it was built at the turn of the [last] century. (There was a water-powered sawmill down in Deep Creek in the early days – they sawed lumber in the daytime and ground grain at night.)* The barn's interior from floor to high-peaked roof is stacked with Glen Howard's round hay bales. *The frame on that barn has long 10- x 10-inch beams dowelled to wooden braces, not a nail in it – I don't know how they ever got them raised up and in place. To the left those openings through trees are also part of the property.*

Grandfather and Grandmother Maw came here from Manitoba. My grandfather – Howard Stovin Maw – was born in England [1849], and he came pretty young to the United States [St. Paul, Minnesota, 1868] and then up the Red River to Winnipeg where he married my grandmother, Maria Goodson [1876]. They built up the largest poultry farm in Western Canada. An artistic chicken icon on the front cover of a commercially printed, illustrated catalogue dated 1910-1911 advertises the family business:

Maw's Poultry Farm

Acclimatized Utility Breeds
Turkeys, Geese, Ducks, Chickens
Poultry Supplies

Parkdale P.O., Manitoba

We ship C.P.R., C.N. R., and G.T.P. [Grand Trunk Pacific]

The inside cover pledges,

We have been breeding poultry in Manitoba over 20 years and have learnt by experience the best paying varieties adapted to our climate. We have aimed to get the best of each variety both as winter layers and for table purposes. During these 20 years we have exhibited our stock at the leading shows in competition with many of the leading Ontario and American breeders, and have secured hundreds of prizes, also numerous Silver and Bronze medals, Diplomas, Ribbons, and one Gold medal at the Winnipeg Poultry Show, 1906. At the Winnipeg Industrial [Show], 1909, we won the Silver Medal, Diploma for Best Display of turkeys, and Six Specials given by the Canadian Turkey and Water Fowl Club of Canada, this in addition to a great number of the regular cash prizes.

Since the purchase of live birds is order-specific, the catalogue instead quotes prices for hatching eggs and gives detailed instructions for the correct care of each poultry breed. These include cotton instead of glass on the front of housing for air circulation, the advocacy of free-range conditions during the day, and an admonition not to feed poultry at the back door or allow them to stay around the house, but rather to feed at night at the coop so they return home. Poultry supplies include:

Double Lock Leg Bands, one dozen, 30c;
Incubator thermometers, Doubly tested, by mail, postage paid, $1.00;
Perfect Balanced Chick Feed, 50 lbs. $2.00; 100 lbs. $3.75;
Edwards' Roup Cure, a Poultry Keeper's Necessity, ½ lb Tin, mailed, postage paid, 50c; and
No.1 Poulterers' Mill, The Most Useful Necessity in the Outfit: A Combination Grit Crusher, Bone Cracker, Grain Cracker, Makes Bone Meal, Meat Meal, Cracks Shells and Charcoal, $6.00 f.o.b. [freight on board] Winnipeg. An Unsolicited Testamonial from W.B. Asquith, Moose Jaw, Saskatchewan declares: "I tried it on some boulder rock and it crushed up splendidly."

Maw's catalogue also advertises a guard dog:

We have a great strain of Wolf Hounds, sure killers. When we came to Parkdale, wolves were everywhere. Now we can let our turkeys roam. Write us, we have pups and young dogs for sale during each year and will give full particulars and prices.

They shipped all over the Western provinces. I've got two of his record books that show orders from a lot of those old mining towns in the West Kootenay: Sandon – Beaton – Halcyon – they're not there any more. And customers gave shipping instructions: In the Cariboo, for instance, they had to catch a stage at Ashcroft for Lac La Hache and 70 Mile. In early days some stagecoaches from Ashcroft had three wagons in tandem and about a dozen horses pullin' them [CHBC Mike Roberts: "Gold Trails and Ghost Towns"]. I've spent hours lookin' at my grandfather's record books.

The earliest record Glen Howard possesses is a hardbound, lined Student's Book on the cover of which Howard Stovin has penned the words **Egg Orders 1908**. Abbreviations for egg sales refer to *Mammoth Bronze turkey, Toulouse goose, Imperial Pekin duck, Barred Plymouth Rock* and *Buff Orpington chicken*. Turkey eggs at 37½ cents apiece are the most expensive. The two sides of the first page list a dozen orders for the period January to July, 1907. Orders for the ensuing years are extensive. A page contains approximately seven entries in small, neat penmanship, a line separating each. In general, orders are sparse in January or February, and increase until the end of the season in June. In addition to the western provinces, customers are from Ontario, and one, from Nova Scotia. The recording of each order is consistent: egg type, receipt date of order, shipment date, client's name and address, price, comments or shipping instructions, as necessary. A cumulative income total appears at the top of each page. All communications appear to be by post; therefore, each transaction requires at least two letters. A tick-mark indicates the successful completion of the order, and a large X drawn through the page consigns the business to the past. The egg orders in this book continue through to June, 1914.

8B.T.	21.2.7	[27.4.7]	Mrs. W. Duck	3.00

Rocky View, [Man.]
Will send cash as soon as possible.
Cash received 27.4.7

12T.G.	13.3.7	23.4.7.	Robert Shiel	4.00

Needles, Arrow Lake
B.C.

100P.R.	12.3.7	[3.4.7]	Tom E. Richards	7.50

St.Swithin's, Canford
Nicola Valley, B.C.
16.3.7   Wrote for further instructions as Ex.Co
only go to Spence's Bridge.
Received letter stating to ship eggs about middle April.
Notified OK 3.4.7.

6T.G.	4.3.8	14.4.8	John H. Paul	2.00
15P.R.			Chilliwack, B.C.	2.00

Notified would ship as soon as geese laid.
Notified shipped 13.4.8

8B.T.	11.3.8	30.4.8	Mrs. John B. Bueller	3.00

High River, Alta.
Mrs. B. lives 15 miles from town and wants notifying a
few days before we ship. Notified OK.

8B.T.	13.3.8	25.4.8	Frederick William Kay	3.00
30P.R.			Saskatoon, Sask.	3.00
10P.D.				1.50

Lives 40 miles from Saskatoon.
Eggs must be at Saskatoon April 30.
Wrote OK they should be there.

15B.O.	21.3.8	8.4.8	H.J. Parr	2.00

Bradwardine, Man.
Ship as soon as safe.

12T.G.	10.4.8	23.4.8	Harry McIntosh Halcyon, B.C.	4.00

Notified OK. Ship as soon as turn comes.
23.4.8 Notified shipped.

15B.O.	13.4.8	15.4.8	Thos. Thompson	2.00
10P.D.			Foxwarren, Man.	1.00

Send catalogue. OK

30P.R.	1.5.8	8.5.8	[Miss Nellie Edwirthy Gladstone, Man.]	3.00

No name given. Wrote postmaster for name,
enclosing postal card for reply, P.O.O. number 4979.
Notified shipped.

15P.R.	2.5.8	15.5.8	Mrs. J.V. Dickens Patience, [Man.]	Free

Had poor results last season.
CPR Ex. to Millet.

20P.D.	11.5.8	13.5.8	D. Denny Beaton, B.C.	3.00

Ex. to Arrowhead. Notified shipped.

30P.R.	19.5.8	22.5.8	Wm. Adams Trout Lake, B.C.	3.00

Notified shipped.

26B.O.	22.6.8		Mrs. Bessie Howe	3.00
10B.T.			Watson, Sask.	
10P.D.				

Sent her these extra eggs as she had bad

luck previous year.

A bank deposit entry following 1909 compares income with the previous year:

	1909	1908
March	$188	$143
April	262	471
May	286	284
June	80	143
	$816	$1041

Egg sales in 1910 have returned to 1908 levels and the record book includes a detailed breakdown:

> Toulouse geese 56 settings
> 564 turkey
> 495 Pekin duck
> 1526 Buff Orpington
> 1800 Plymouth Rock in 100 lots
> 1500 Plymouth Rock in 30 lots
> 427 Plymouth Rock in odd lots
> Total $1004

However, in 1910 Maw & Sons has increased the price of turkey eggs to fifty cents and some repeat customers are taken by surprise:

8B.T.   5.4.10   5.5.10   Mrs. John Grasley   4.00
Crossfield, Alta.
Only sent 3.00. Notified her. Eggs 4.00. Asked for
instructions. She sent 1.00 19.4.10.

Some customers think that ordering a setting of eggs may be cheaper than single units:

3 set.T.G. 4.4.10   21.4.10   Mrs. John B. Graves   6.00
Barnhartvale P.O.
Via Kamloops, B.C.
4.4.10 notified Mrs. G. goose eggs 2.50 per setting.
Notified shipped.

In 1910 Maw & Sons is losing patience with carelessness and complaints:

30P.R.	5.4.10	14.4.10	[E.W. Cripps	3.00
5B.O.			Gainsboro, Man.]	2.00
10P.D.				1.50

Eggs to be at Gainsboro 15.4.10. No name to order. Notified if he sent his name, eggs would be there.

15B.O.	4.6.10	9.6.10	Mrs. Fred Bard	2.00
6T.G.			Monarch, Alta.	2.50
10P.D.				1.50

CPR. Goose eggs smashed and wrote Mrs. F.B. to make claim on agent. [Either before or after this notification, Mrs. Bard cancelled her order for 50 leg bands and catalogue.]

In 1911 the orders were nothing much. They're in Armstrong and too busy – they started farming that spring. There was already seven acres of orchard on the place, and I think over fifty varieties of apples. But my grandfather didn't want to give up his poultry business. Things were pretty tough in those days, you know – in the old house I found packing house receipts for crates of strawberries at fifty cents, cucumbers for a cent a pound. No, my grandfather carried on for about sixteen years after they moved here. An undated poultry catalogue printed in Armstrong still advertises Wolf Hounds.

The second record book in Glen Howard's possession lists prices of live birds, Oct 1st to Dec 20th 1920:

Yearling Gob a grand bird	$20.00
" " not so large	15.00
Gob Hatched a grand bird	12.00
Gob " not so large	10.00
Old hen	10.00
Young hen	10.00
Goslings	5.00

A faded letter tucked inside this book reveals a memorable transaction from twenty-five years earlier.

> *Canington Manor*
> *Assa*
> *N.W.T.* [North West Territories]
> *Oct.21/95* [1895]

M. [Mr.] *Maw Esq.*
Winnipeg

Dear Sir
   In reply to yours of 18th re Turks
I have to say our people would like very much to get the
*Two hens and Gob at $25 deliv'd in Moosomin but I cannot & *
will not pay that amt in Cash, but as they are so anxious
to get them I will do the best that I can. I have a pure
bred Holstein Frisian Heifer home bred will be 2 yrs
in Dec. & is in calf for April. She is a good heifer in every
respect & is the only home bred one we have in calf. The rest
are all imp except two calves our herd number 16 head. This
heifer is in calf to a G.son of Colantha butter rec'd 31 lb in 7
days. She is dam of bull that took 1st at Worlds fair. To satisfy
them I will offer you this Heifer on Cars at Moosomin
for your 3 birds if you can give proof of their being not over 2
yrs old. I do not care for you to accept. I simply make the offer
as they cannot have the money.
>   *Yours*

J.F. Hindmarch

Our mail leaves Moosomin Friday morning at which time it is
possible to get an answer in from Winnipeg.

They made the deal too. My dad said they had to go pick that
heifer out of a [rail]car of Prairie steers that was unloaded at
Winnipeg, and I guess those cattle were pretty wild!

The letter writer, J.F.Hindmarch, had a tenuous connection to Armstrong Spallumcheen. *As a boy Dr. [J.J.] Murison worked for*

Hindmarch – apparently, he was an educated Englishman – and one day he asked Murison what he'd like to do for a trade when he got older, and he said he'd like to be a veterinary surgeon, and Hindmarch put him through vet school. Murison practised veterinary medicine here for a long time. He was the official veterinarian of the Armstrong Fair for over thirty years, and the longest-practising veterinarian in Canada – nearly sixty-six years.

When Grandfather Howard Stovin died in December, 1926, with one notable exception the poultry business on Maw Road came to an end. Maw's Instant Louse Killer continued to sell widely, one half-pound box in powdered form for fifty cents, post paid: "Enough to kill the lice on 1,000 birds." *Even when I was a kid, people used to send money orders for this louse killer. My dad used to mix it and ship it by mail. Customers added water and put it on the chicken roost, and the heat from the roosting chickens [activated the mixture] and the vapours killed the lice.* Maw's Instant Louse Killer was equally potent against lice on "horses, cattle, pigs, and bedsteads."

Glen Howard's father, Arthur Edwin, born in Winnipeg in 1886, was physically unlike Howard Stovin. *Grandfather Maw was tall – six feet, apparently. Dad was a little guy but he was tough.* The family had been on Maw Road only three years before the outbreak of World War One.

My dad enlisted in February, 1916 – he was with the Rocky Mountain Rangers to start with, and then in a Kootenay battalion [54th Battalion Canadian]. We've got a whole album of letters that he wrote from overseas – they came from the old house too. Some of them were in poor shape, but my sister Margaret went through them, photocopied and deciphered them, and typed them out. He talked mainly about things back home and didn't say much about the war – didn't want to worry them, I guess – he always said he was fine. Long after the war in a conversation taped by his nephew Earl Dixon, Arthur Edwin recounted that the winter of 1916-17 in Europe was very cold. The troops froze and nearly starved. However, a letter to his mother in January of 1917 refers only in passing to their dire straits. It is written on army issue notepaper imprinted with the YMCA crest and inscribed **On Active Service With The British Expeditionary Force.** Arthur Edwin gives no location and across the top of the paper has pencilled the words,

"Can't use pen no ink, but it sure works fine."

Jan 24th, 1917

Dear Mother,
                    Just a few lines this time as its late & I have some clean-
ing to do. We are out on six days rest & it sure is good. I had a letter from
Auntie she writes pretty regular. I sent her that Postal note for $16 you
sent me as I could not cash it over here so I sent it to her & told her if I
wanted any thing I would write her. Things are very quite here just now the
weather is very cold and there is quite a lot of Snow. Our draft has had no
loses yet. I had a visitor last night in the person of Joe Tapner he looks
fine he has been out here two years he was very pleased to hear all about
Armstrong. Oh say, Mother that cake was the finest ever. The tin was pretty
badly battered the cake was in good shape. It was the best thing I have
tasted this side of home in fact I ate so much it made me sick not very
bad & I soon recovered. Harold must be doing fine with the cows, how much
did the steer dress. I got Lills letter tonight & must answer tomorrow. I will
write to Harold then too. I got all the parcels but the chewing but am not in
need of it as I got sixteen plugs this week. I had a card from uncle Tom Mr
Lee. Very nice of him to write but have not heard from Mrs Hopkins or the
Docksteaders yet, nor Mrs Hichen. Well I guess you will think this letter
not very interesting but we have nothing much we can write. Dad is right the
War will soon be over & we will be home for Xmas & to stay in Canada for
Evermore amen. Well bye bye Mother dear don't worry over me. I'm quite
happy.
Believe me as ever
Your loving son   Artie xxxxxxxxxxxx

The Rangers were pretty badly shot up – lots of casualties – they disbanded them over there, and I think [survivors] had the choice of the regiment they went to. Dad suffered poison gas [Passchendaele Ridge, March 1, 1917] and went back to the Front after he recovered. He didn't get home until the spring of 1919.

Arthur Edwin Maw married Ruby Crawford in 1926 when he was forty and she, thirty-two. *Crawford Road in Spallumcheen is named after Mother's family. They were of Scottish descent, but I heard stories that they'd been in Ireland too, and they left because of the potato famine there [1846]. They crossed the border from the United States at Hamilton, Ontario, and that's where my grandfather Alexander Crawford was born in 1848. He was always known as Sandy.*

Grandfather Crawford was involved in the [first] Riel Rebellion. In 1870 Louis Riel focused the opposition of the Métis to the survey of Hudson Bay lands prior to the formation of the province of Manitoba in 1871. *For his part in the action, my grandfather received a land grant on the Red River near Winnipeg. He was a carpenter by trade, so he built a house on his land and in 1876 married my grandmother, Elizabeth Rollinson, who had been born in Kentucky. But in the spring of 1882 the Red River flooded, and their house floated away.*

Nature having taken the initiative, the Crawfords headed west along with Elizabeth's sister Ruth, who helped look after the children and planned to return to Ontario as soon as the Canadian transcontinental railway was completed. They went down through South Dakota and across to San Francisco by train, and then by boat through rough seas up the west coast to Victoria. That winter they spent in Yale. *Grandfather Crawford worked as a carpenter there. Then in the spring of 1883 they came up the Fraser Canyon by wagon because the railway wasn't finished, and he took up land in Knob Hill – 320 acres originally – now the greater part is the Ternier place [4683 Crawford Road]. That property has only had two owners – Grandfather Crawford and his son Alex – and then Mr. Ternier and his son and daughter-in-law, Robert and Lillian Ternier. The houses at the top of Hallam Road and others further east were all part of the old Crawford place.* Ruth Rollinson never returned to Ontario. Instead she married Donald Matheson and remained in the community.

When Grandfather and Grandmother Crawford settled in Spallumcheen, they had two school-aged kids – my mother's older brother and sister, Jack [John Henry] and Pudge (Susan – she later married Bob Tilton) – and they walked from the far end of Crawford Road to Round Prairie School on the Augustus Schubert place. My grandfather was the contractor that built Knob Hill School, and then my mother went there with another sister, Myrtle, and a brother, Alex. When the Consolidated School opened in 1921, Knob Hill School was given to the community and became Knob Hill Hall.

Alexander Crawford was also a musician. *There was quite a big band in Armstrong around the turn of the century, and my grandfather played a saxophone.* The band supplied music at civic events; such as, the opening of the Armstrong Fair. *Grandfather Crawford died in 1924, and Grandmother Crawford died on August 26, 1927, the day after I was born, so I never knew either of them.*

Arthur Maw and Ruby Crawford had four children. Glen Howard was followed by Meryl Ruby in 1930, Arthur Crawford in 1931, and Margaret Lynne in 1942 – *my mother was just about fifty years old then. I was actually a full seven [years] when I started school. You had to be at least six and a half 'cause they were havin' a hard time in the thirties to pay to keep the schools open. 'Course, in 1933 I'd just come six, so I had to wait another year – I was quite happy – I never regretted the late start.*

As the oldest child, Glen always worked. *That was when the Okanagan Valley was really goin' into fruit, and they cleared the land. Apples, pears, plums, cherries – there was twenty acres of orchard on the farm when I was growing up. East of the farm road was what we called the 1916 Orchard – west of it was the 1920 Orchard. In one three-quarter acre we had about 100 peach plum trees. They had to be gone over every second day once they started to ripen – they were all shipped to the Prairie through McDonald's packing house at the east end of town. As kids we used to pick cherries too – that kept us busy! You've got to learn the knack of it, you know – you can't pull 'em – you've got to twist 'em off – leave the stems on, or they rot.* An ad in the July 19, 1923, *Armstrong Advertiser* entices:

Cherries – 50 cents per large crate.
You can come and pick your own.
Bring containers and scissors.
Good picking – fine fruit.
Maw and Sons, Knob Hill

You'd probably get close to twenty pounds of cherries in a crate. That was a tin-top, four-basket crate. Simpson had a sawmill in Kelowna and made these tin-tops. They were thin veneer about ten inches square, tapered slightly, with a tin top running around the upper edge to hold the sides together. Apparently, it was real hard on the workers' hands making them. The baskets fit one inside the other and came in a big crate that held a few hundred. When we shipped the cherries, we put four baskets in a wooden crate with a lid. Today these baskets are made of green papier mâché.

I made apple boxes when I had to stand on another apple box at the bench to do it. The sawmill in town sawed lumber until June or so and then they started makin' boxes – that was a big part of their business – apple boxes, celery crates – no bulk bins like there is now. They cut and bundled the pieces. Apple boxes were two feet long and a foot square. 1,000 apples boxes came on a flatdeck truck, and you had to nail them together – two ends, two sides, and the bottom. Plums were in crates a third the width of an apple box but the same length and height. You tipped the crate up, and you poured the prunes into it on a slant so they were packed solid.

In contrast, packing apples was piecework. *Ordinary apples were loose – Fancy and Extra Fancy were wrapped in nine-inch-square paper. [But] they were all sized, so you were packing three or four boxes at a time and sizing as you went. You had to have so many rows and so many layers in a box that held so many apples of a certain size – I still remember how many were in a box: 66 (that was a big apple!), 88, 100, 113, 125, 138, 150.... You [first] laid corrugated cardboard in the bottom of the apple box, and you filled it about an inch and a half above the sides and then nailed on a padded, flexible lid. We had little inkpads to stamp the outside of the box with the number of apples it held, and another stamp for the kind and grade.*

I left school after grade 10 – 1944 – and that fall we had 9,000 boxes of apples, so I wondered whether I should have stayed in school! I was pickin' apples until the 20th of November – snow on them and all!

And we always kept some beef and milked a herd of dairy cattle. I milked as well. At first we had Jerseys, Holsteins, and Red Polls (dual purpose), but Dad bought his first purebred Ayrshire cow in 1939. You probably heard about Captain [J.C.] Dunwaters' ranch at Fintry? Dunwaters brought Ayrshires into the country, and there was quite a few of them around the neighbourhood – Docksteader had Ayrshires, Nigel Rees had Ayrshires, and Husband too. Some guy in Enderby had Ayrshires. He'd been in the British Army, so as soon as the Second War started, he joined up and sold off his cows, and my dad bought a female and built a whole herd of Ayrshires from her. That herd was my dad's hobby – he liked to have good production so he fed them good. Eventually some cows were on ROP (Record of Production), and we got a shield for the highest-producing three-year-old in Canada. She was Orchard Brook Rose. The wooden shield carries the raised profile in brass of an Ayrshire cow and the following citation, which Glen interprets:

Ayrshire Production Star 1954 Senior 4 *(age)* 365 days Orchard Brook Rose 336045 *(her number)* 16,133 *(lbs)* milk, 602 F *(lbs butterfat)*, 3.73% butterfat. Owners Maw Brothers. *(Dad and Uncle Joe stayed with the farm.)*

All the farming was done with horses too until the 1940s when we were able to buy a Caterpillar tractor. That experience would later come in handy.

Glen Howard's heart, however, lay in hunting. *My dad was a bird hunter. I guess where he grew up in Winnipeg there was lots of ducks and geese. When he wasn't very old, he worked weekends at the Winnipeg Free Press, and he made enough money to buy this double-barrelled shotgun. I still have it. He was expert with it. So Dad got me hunting. We did lots of shooting because there was predator birds on the farm – hawks used to get our chickens – magpies and crows ate the cherries. I shot two deer when I was twelve years old. I had a hunting licence – a deer tag cost twenty-five cents then.*

*It started out with the neighbour's cow getting into our hay-stack at the far end of a field past the orchard, and the guy came for his cow. We caught it, and while we were there, I saw this deer track through the orchard in the snow and I asked my dad if we could go after it. He was supposed to go with me – my licence stated, **Must be accompanied by an Adult**. Anyway, we started out, but the cow had broken the rail fence down and he stopped to fix it: "You go on ahead." So I followed the track and here's this buck deer layin' down, and I shot him. That was Sunday afternoon. Monday after school I saw all these other deer tracks, so I went out first thing Tuesday morning and found another three-point buck with a bunch of does and I got him too. He went down with one shot but I was just a kid, you know, and I wasn't goin' to have him get up again, so I gave him a couple, three more!*

That was the start of it and I'm still doin' it. But we grew up butchering – we butchered cattle and pigs for meat, and Dad shot deer for meat, but not as many after I started. But there's probably ten times more deer around now – in those days everybody hunted. They hunted to eat. Guys used to walk two miles from Armstrong – (they often didn't have vehicles, you know) – cut across the fields – and then up Rose Swanson Mountain either past or through our place. In those days we didn't have refrigeration either. We'd kill a beef every winter, and Mother kept it frozen as long as she could and canned the rest in sealers, and that's where the deer meat ended up sometimes too.

*Pheasant season opened on October 15th – **Pheasant Day** – and I always stayed home from school. There was pheasants everywhere – thousands of them. The farms were more spread out than they are now, and in those days everybody had a straw stack where they threshed the grain, and that's where pheasants hung around in the wintertime scratching into the screenings. And all the roads were lined with bush – cover for them. Now that's gone, so there's nowhere for them to hide. But years ago everybody hunted pheasants...*

ruffled grouse! In the springtime they stand on a log and clap their wings – you can hear them drumming for miles! We ate 'em all! The Armstrong Hotel was full of Coast hunters. They'd send their birds out on the train at night and they'd be in Vancouver by morning.

Shooting or trapping and skinning animals was a good way for a boy to make some money. A letter to Glen Howard from the Fur Purchasing Department of the Hudson's Bay Company in Vancouver indicates he was a supplier:

February 8th, 1943

Mr. Glen Maw,
Armstrong, B.C.

Dear Mr. Maw:

We are pleased to advise you that your name was the one drawn from amongst our B.C. Shippers on our radio broadcast on February 6th. This entitles you to a H.B. "4 point" blanket free provided you answer the following question correctly:-

"Name two fur animals that are classed as having long haired fur."

We are sure the above will present no difficulty, and when answering, please advise us of your first and second choice in these three colours:- Silver, Green, Scarlet. *(I picked scarlet – I still have it.)* Also state whether you wish the blanket shipped by parcel post or express.

Thanking you for your interest in this matter and trusting you will continue to favor us with your business, we are,

Yours faithfully,
For the Hudson's Bay Company,

(Signed) *R. Carey*
P. Manager, Raw Fur Department

There was a demand during the Second War for fur-lined mitts and caps for the pilots and crews in the bombers – so squirrel, weasel, muskrat, lynx were popular. The first lynx I shot was on towards spring. The price list quoted $110 for the top hide. I skinned it and got $10. Back in the '40s that was something! I bought my first rifle at seventeen – paid $100 for it – a lot of money in those days! Photographs of a teenaged Glen Howard posing with his new 6.5mm Steyr Jeffrey Mannlicher rifle beside his quarry attest to his proficiency.

Glen found another use for his hunting skills. *When I was in high school, I joined the Pacific Coast Militia Rangers [PCMR]. After the Japanese attacked Pearl Harbour, December 7, 1941, people believed that a Japanese invasion was imminent – so the PCMR was really active at the Coast and on Vancouver Island. Most of the guys in it up here were First World War veterans and farmers exempt from enlisting – fairly old – so they wanted young fellows too that were outdoorsmen and knew how to hunt and shoot. So in 1943 seven or eight of us teenagers volunteered – I remember Gerald Hallam, Louis Canuel, George Austin. George had been a Boy Scout and knew the semaphore – signalling with flags. We didn't have a uniform but we wore an armband with PCMR in big letters.*

It was a guerilla outfit. We were going to take to the hills and do what we could to hunt out or escape from the Japanese in case of invasion – we were a defence force. Our instructors were from the Vernon army camp, and they were serious about it. They taught us how to make black powder for pipe bombs... how to kill from behind... things I shouldn't even mention... things I never forgot. It was pretty realistic for a bunch of kids. Our firearms instructor was H. Page-Brown. He was a farmer, British Imperial Army, and a crack shot. He owned the place on Otter Lake Road [2475] that was later owned by Jim Gill and then became Matheson's dairy [presently Johnstone], and we shot towards the [current] health centre across Deep Creek and into the bank on the other side. They had dug a pit there, and guys in the pit put up the targets. By 1944 things had quietened down because the Japanese were busy in the eastern Pacific.

In addition to working with the orchard and the purebred dairy herd, Arthur Maw introduced Glen Howard to the business of raising bees. *He was into bees when I was small, and people would come with a can or a pail to get honey. He had about thirty hives. Every Sunday morning in the summer he had to go through them to cut out the queen cells or they'd swarm. And after lunch during the week, we'd take some honey off the hives. The bees were really doin' good in those days. There wasn't DDT and all those spray chemicals, and the top of Rose Swanson Mountain had burnt off in 1934 and grown up to fireweed. Some of the hives produced up to 400 pounds of honey – and you had to keep takin' it or they plugged up.*

Dad used the old creamery on the place for a honey house. It was fly-proof and cool because it had a concrete floor and insulated walls. The foundation was mortared stone, and it was sunk like a root cellar at the back – just the entrance was above ground. I operated the extractor. It was a big drum. You had to cut the wax off the outside of the honeycomb and put 'em in the extractor, then turn the handle, and the centrifugal force blew the honey out. When the weather is warm, honey is quite liquid, so if you extracted it then, it didn't take long. The honey ran down into the bottom part of the drum, and we'd [detach] it and set it up on some heavy boxes about twenty inches off the floor, slide a pail underneath a little gate in the bottom of the drum, open the gate, and fill the pail. A pail held about thirty-three pounds of honey, and he sold it for $3. He used to call it a thirty-pound pail – ten cents a pound. He could buy a not-too-bad pair of shoes for the three dollars he got for the pail of honey.

Dad also used to sell honey at the Armstrong Co-op in four-pound cans that he bought by the case. You had to be clean – spick and span. His labels were white as snow. I've still got some out in the shop. My mother used to put a little egg white in a saucer, dab a bit on one end of the label and bring the other end right 'round the can to cover it.

British Columbia

NO. 1 WHITE

Pure Honey
From Knob Hill Apiary

Arthur E. Maw
Armstrong,   B.C.

Net Weight   lbs   *(He'd fill that in.)*

I did that job until I left home and Dad went out of bees. He was gettin' old by then. I was the one who ended up bulldozing the honey house too....

Those old hives sat out there for a long time, and a swarm came from somewhere and went into one. Dad was in his nineties – gettin' 'round with a walker at that time – and he got quite interested in this hive. Anyway, I went up there a Sunday afternoon in September – it was hot – and I asked Mother where Dad was: "Oh, somewhere up around the buildings." I walked up and met him, and his face was red as a beet! "What's the matter, Dad?" and he says, "I've got about fifty bee stings in my face." What happened was – a bear had got into the beehive and wrecked it. My brother Art shot the bear and then told Dad what had happened to the hive. Well, I guess Dad went up to have a look and saw all the frames scattered around. He was pickin' them up, and the remainder of the bees were underneath one of them. They came after him, and he had no veil or gloves on. He probably used one hand to try to keep them off his face, and he crawled away from the frame and dragged the walker with him. And when I caught up to him, he was standing up in it. "Fifty bee stings in my face." That was an underestimation – he had a dozen stings in each eyelid. I figured it was goin' to kill him. I phoned the doctor. The doctor says, "Is it bothering his breathing?" "No." "Oh," he says, "he'll probably be all right." Vi and I went up there after supper that night and he was sittin' there readin' the paper – no ill effects. If it had been me, I would have been dead!

When he was in his nineties, they used to have to hide his boots to keep him indoors in icy weather, or remove a piece from the tractor so it wouldn't start. Otherwise, he'd be wanting to disk around the fruit trees and in danger of being swept off the machine by the branches. He believed it was his job to keep the old woodstove going, and he used to split firewood at the woodshed and fill up some empty five-gallon oil tins with the wood. Then he'd roll the tins over to the house. Dad lived to be ninety-eight and a half years old. He died in the spring of 1985. My mother died at ninety the fall before. He didn't live too long after she was gone.

As the eldest son, Glen Howard might have expected to remain on the farm with his father. Instead, the bitter winter of 1949-50 changed his plans. *It really desecrated the orchards all through the Okanagan Valley. So there wasn't work for everybody on the farm and I left. The first year I drove a Caterpillar tractor building a road for a mining outfit in the West Kootenay. The mine had been abandoned some fifty years before, but after the [Second] War, things were picking up, and I worked for the guy who had bought the claim. The mine was at 6,200 feet elevation.*

In early days packhorses was the only way they could get up there. An aerial tramway used to bring the ore down to the stamp mill that was still there on Mohawk Creek at about 4,500 feet elevation and about a mile or two from the mine. Waterpower from the creek used to crush the ore and send air back up to the mine through four-inch pipes. The pipes were still there too. The sawmill was just a pile of lumber on the ground. The old mining town of Camborne was gone too – all grown up in trees – and Beaton was only a store and a hotel, as I recall. It disappeared too when they dammed and flooded the Arrow Lakes [1969].

Three of us lived for the summer there – an old prospector, a *guy from Vernon, and me – and a woman cooked for us. We worked a ten-hour day seven days a week. It paid good money – $1.60 an hour. It doesn't sound like much but I liked it there. I liked the outdoors, and I was supposed to go back – they were going to bring in a new bulldozer for me. But the neighbour 'Young' Fred Hitt – Raymond Hitt's cousin – was in the same boat we were. His orchard had frozen, so he had a logging contract with the Armstrong Sawmill at Proctor Lake above the gravel pits, and he was havin' manpower trouble. He asked me if I'd come and work for him: No, I had a good job and I was waiting 'til the snow was gone in the Kootenay to go back. I said I'd go for a week until he could find somebody else. After the week was over, he said, "If you stay, I'll give you the same wages that you were makin' at the mine. And if you do good this summer, I'll give you a bonus."* The bonus arrived in early December. *He gave me the team of horses and the job.*

I logged with the horses until 1954 and by that time I'd made enough money to buy a crawler. My brother Art worked with me from 1956 to '63 when he took over the farm for my dad and my uncle. By the end of my logging days, I'd gone through probably twenty pieces of equipment, mostly John Deere and Caterpillar, and I'd logged Rose Swanson Mountain in different places from one end to the other, along with areas in Mara Mountain, Enderby, Falkland, Westwold, Kalamalka Lake, and White Man's Creek down Westside Road. I worked for the same outfit – the sawmill in Armstrong – for about thirty-five years. Just the name changed.

The Armstrong Sawmill bid on timber sales. Look in the Morning Star now and you see advertisements for government timber sales: Timber Sale Number so-and-so. The sawmill would get an area – normally for about three years – and then told you where to log. You had to abide by Forest Service rules. They marked out the boundaries – a half-mile square, for example – and if you cut trees outside those boundaries, you paid triple the stumpage fee. We never clear-cut. Sometimes they marked with paint the trees you could take. Sometimes they stipulated what size trees you could take – depending on the timber sale, you couldn't log anything less than fourteen inches... or sixteen inches. So all the timber that was undersized got left. And you didn't dare damage it either! If you broke the rules, you didn't last!

We'd log an area and pile the logs in decks, and then the company would send in crews and logging trucks to haul them out. In those days they were all short logs – about sixteen feet. (Most of the logging trucks you see on the roads today are carrying logs up to fifty-two feet long.) When I first started, I got about $10 to $12 per 1,000 board feet – about $50 for a truckload. After a time the sawmill got out of the loading and trucking business, so contractors had to load and deliver the logs too. That meant I had to hire truckers. Originally, each log was measured and hand-scaled in the mill yard. Now they hand-scale a sample every so often to get an average. Scalers have to be licensed, and the Forest Service does its own check too. I sold the contracting part of the business in 1977 and worked for the company another ten years bulldozing and specialty logging. I hired a contractor to do the logging and I built logging roads, log landings, and so on.

Logging was my main occupation in life, and it was good money too for anybody that could produce logs. Lots of 'em went broke at it. You had to know how to get the logs out of the bush – and some of 'em didn't! Well, as a kid I learned to work! One needed to be practical as well and make the best deals at the time. *And you had to stick your neck out too when you bought a big machine. My bulldozer out there was $93,000 bucks – a new one now is $300,000 to $400,000. I signed the papers for it in December of '75 because that year there was a government incentive for anything bought in 1975 – you wrote 5% off your tax payable, which was a reduction of about $5,000. And since it was a new machine, I could write 30% off in depreciation for that year and I had never even used it – didn't use it until January, '76.*

Not all Glen's logging experiences were positive. *Any truck that's on the road is licensed, so a trucker has a licence to haul so many tons on his truck. A logging truck could also be granted a permit to carry extra weight. Sometimes a fellow working for me didn't have scales on his logging truck and got into trouble for being overweight. He'd lose his permit for a period of time and not be able to bring out as many logs as he should. Another time a trucker was going too fast around an inside corner and laid it right over on the road – the truck... the load... the whole bit.... If there'd been a car coming, it would have been six inches thick!*

I still log – a certain amount of trees die every year on the old place and I take them out. I bulldozed all the access roads – they weren't there when I was a kid. The farm stretches halfway up the mountain, so since the '50s I've always used four-wheel-drive trucks to get around. The terrain is rough and steep. Loops of single-track road visit cleared pastures, the occasional split-rail fence, and dense bush. A stand of cedar hugs the creek that runs for half a mile through the farm. *I've operated a chainsaw now for fifty-five years, but I have to be careful at my age falling trees. I skid them down behind the bulldozer to my landing place. It's big timber. It goes to the [Tolko] mill for saw logs. I took two loads of dead fir logs out this last winter – they get root rot and blow down or break off in windstorms – most of it goes for plywood and peelers. And I took two loads of cedar that had died from that real hot weather two years ago [2004]. I waited because earlier the market wasn't that good – it's picked up now. Actually, every evening a train goes out – five or six engines and up to 100 cars on it. There's a few grain cars in there, but pretty well all chip cars or lumber cars – you've got to sit a long time at a crossing! So that's what keeps the valley goin' – lumber!*

Viva McGhee Maw has shared Glen's logging life. *We married in 1958 when I was thirty-one. She was from Vernon and we met through friends.*

Vi elaborates: *My best friend since we were girls was Amy Anderson. She married an Armstrong man, Jules Picou. We all ended up at Pierre Vandenborre's house one night – something needed fix-ing and the guys were there to help – and that's where I first laid eyes on Glen. We went out for a year or two – I wasn't sure what I wanted – to get married or join the air force!*

At the time I'd been working for Rocky Mountain Transport in Vernon for six and a half years. I started there at sixteen when I'd finished grade 10 – it was called Muir's Cartage back then – Tommy and June Muir, owners. Both companies hauled many different kinds of goods: fruit and vegetables, groceries from W.H. Malkin and from Kelly Douglas – they were old-time businesses – and other items went from their warehouses to the stores. I kept the books, and all I had for education was Business Fundamentals and Record Keeping.

I did the payroll, unemployment insurance stamps and banking, weigh bills and trip reports. June Muir taught me how to do it. It took me over two weeks to learn! This big ledger with all these accounts and customers! Charge accounts... prepaid charge accounts... cash accounts... prepaid cash accounts. And who's going to pay cash or charge when they get their goods. We had charge accounts go right through to Revelstoke, and to Beaton, Ferguson, Trout Lake in the Kootenays. And all the arithmetic was done by hand – lots of multiplying! Goods went at different rates, so on the weigh bills I had to list the weights, indicate the shipping class, and calculate the cost. For example, milk and eggs because of breakage or spoilage went First Class, fruit and vegetables went Second Class, canned goods went Third Class, and plywood and lumber, Fourth Class. I remember one time my boss showed me a weigh bill: "You see anything the matter with this?" I look at it - $4.16. It was supposed to be $41.60!

I knew so many phone numbers by heart because the phone was always ringing – orders and pick-ups – and all these truckers from different truck lines coming in and out because we transferred goods onwards as well. And that meant I had to calculate the percentage our company would receive when the bill was settled. And I felt so proud when I had the right balance and they hadn't done their arithmetic right!

241

Vi gave up her career reluctantly. *I knew more or less that I wouldn't work after I was married. Glen didn't want me running back and forth to Vernon. But I was a stranger out here and at first I was so lonesome looking at four walls all day. Then I became chums with my neighbours Emma Smith and Marg Bigler, and when I had my first child I fit in even more because we all had babies. But Glen wouldn't let me do his books!*

Glen says firmly, *I did my own. Payroll... income tax... Canada pension... unemployment insurance... I did it all.* He credits his expertise to a lucky accident the first week of high school. *When I started grade nine in the downtown school [Bridge Street], during wartime they opened a couple of weeks late so farm kids could bring in the harvest while the men were away. I was pickin' apples and didn't go back for another two weeks after it did open. I get down there, and the other kids had already settled on what they were going to take. At the time the language [elective] was either Latin or French, and that year they were teaching Latin. I took it for one period and didn't like it a bit! Some of the others that weren't taking Latin were taking a course called Junior Business so next time I went there, and an old girl was teaching it, and I wasn't too keen on her either! But then I realized I had to take one of the two, so I went back to her and it was the best thing I ever did in school. We learned to balance books, write cheques, and I was fairly good in math. I learnt more there than in all the English prose or other subjects I ever took!*

As a married couple Glen and Vi have always lived at their current address on Salmon River Road. *I don't remember very much before 1933, but there's quite a bit of land that's been cleared in Spallumcheen since that time. This place, for instance, was mostly bush. The ground was really hard and had some big trees. After Vi and I were married, we rented the original house for six months at $35 a month from Ed Schultz, who was a veteran. He had bought the house through VLA [Veterans Land Act], and had had the land cleared by the government – a couple of D7 Caterpillars. There was* *a lot of stumps they tried to get out and couldn't – there were lots of broken gears lying around out here! Then Schultz sold it, and we bought it. Vi says, Glen had too much junk to move! All the deer horns and trophy heads... all his machinery....*

To finish clearing the property, Glen resorted to the time-honoured use of stumping powder. *I knew how to do it – my dad always kept a box of stumping powder around. If he needed to blow something on the farm – well, we didn't have bulldozers then, so he used stumping powder. And when I worked at the Kootenay mine, I did some blasting there. By that time you were supposed to have a certificate, but the guy who had his papers could see that I knew what I was doin', and I didn't mind doin' it either! So I got some stumping powder from the mill and blew our stumps out. That was about the last blasting I did.*

Their three sons were born while Glen and Vi lived in the old house. Gordon, the eldest, was born in 1959. He died young. *It's heartbreaking... hard to talk about.* William was born in 1961, and David, in 1962. Both boys married and settled with their families close to home.

Glen and Vi built their present house in 1982. Vi says, *The old house we bought from Schultz sat right beside this one. It had a second storey but only a crawl space for a basement. This house has a full basement. Glen dug it with his bulldozer, and after he'd piled up the dirt, the machine rolled back and hit the corner of the old house and damaged it so we really did have to move! On the day they were going to pour the foundations, I had two clotheslines full of washing outside, and I wondered if I should take it in. "Oh, no, the truck won't be anywhere near there." But I took the clothes in anyhow, and it was lucky I did because the long pouring arm on the truck hit the lines and took them both down. Blue skies!! I haven't used a clothesline since. I never had an automatic washer and dryer in the old place – I had an old wringer. And I didn't want to get a washer because I thought it used too much water. But I'm glad I was persuaded to drop that idea.*

In addition to logging, Glen took contracts for earth moving. *Some guys wanted a football field built in the bush. So I dug it out for them. They come out with a transit level: "It's three inches low on this end!" I said, "Well, a football field in the bush – what does it matter if it's three inches low at one end!"*

I did some work for an old guy that had built a barn and wanted it backfilled. I looked at it and figured out how long it was going to take me to do – added up what my machine was worth per hour and a little bit for a cushion, and seeing it was a neighbour, I charged not as much as I told him and did it in less time. Then he wanted a basement dug for a new house, but I was taking my bulldozer back to work the next day, so I went over there after supper and dug the basement for him for $35. I guess $35 then would buy a lot more fuel than it will now! I used to burn at least 100 gallons of fuel a day when we were loggin'. Then it was $25 to $35 worth. Now it would cost $300. I still have a couple of fuel tanks outside. I use diesel fuel for the bulldozer, the tractors, and the pickup. I only use gasoline now for the lawnmower, my welder, my chainsaw and my four-wheel ATV for chasing the cows.

Glen keeps a herd of Black Angus Cross up the mountain on the old farm, which he purchased from his brother Art in 1994. *I had quite a run-around the other day. I usually take a pickup of corn stalks up to my cattle, and they all gather 'round, so I can count and check them and spray for flies. The cows followed me up to where I like to feed them, and here is another bunch of cows with a big Hereford bull, and our bull is gone!* His own cows didn't like the intruders, began fighting and some of them scattered. *I made some phone calls that night and found who owned the bull but he didn't own the cows. He came over, and we separated the bull and loaded him out on a trailer and managed to lock up three of the strange cows and a calf. Meanwhile my cows are up in the bush somewhere and I didn't know if my bull was with them. Somebody told me they'd seen the bulls fighting – I didn't know if he was hurt or if we'd ever see him again! So I spent the next day ridin' around the mountain on my ATV tryin' to find my bull and the rest of the cows.* No luck. *I went up next day to feed corn and here's my bull and the rest of the cows and calves. He'd come home, but he'd been beaten up by the other bull. He's seven years old and the other one was about four.*

On occasion Vi monitored the herd. She says, *Someone phoned that our cows were out on the road. So I got a pail of corncobs from the garden and went up there, and sure enough, they were out. I coaxed them to follow me by dropping cobs behind me, and I got them back inside the pasture and mended the hole in the fence by weaving it with branches.*

One important aspect of Glen's life was his membership from 1962 to 1987 in the Armstrong Spallumcheen Volunteer Fire Department, for which he received a silver cup commemorating his twenty-five years' service. *I started when the Armstrong and Spallumcheen fire departments combined. Spallumcheen was divided into four zones – ten volunteers from each zone – so that even if somebody was away, there would be enough others to respond to the call. It was a way to protect our own community.*

Throughout his life, however, Glen Howard has been happiest when he is hunting. He and Vi are Life Members in the Armstrong and District Fish and Game Club. *We have a thirty-nine-acre shooting range on Reservoir Road below Memorial Mountain, but our main purpose is to protect wildlife. We worked hard to bring pheasants back to the area. One year we raised 500 to 1,000 birds and turned 'em loose.* Vi doesn't shoot; she cooks for the banquets.

Big game, however, presents Glen with a special challenge. In their home beautiful and immense trophy heads populate the living room. One can imagine the size of the animals lurking beyond the walls. *I still love hunting – mountain goats and bear and elk and moose. That elk there is the biggest of twenty that I took in my day. I got quite a few moose around this country – Falkland way, Monte Lake. Jim Nelson and I went hunting antelope a couple of times in Wyoming. I've harvested mule deer for years and never got one mounted. Two years ago I took one that probably makes the BC re-cord book, and then I got one this year that looked even better, so it's at the taxidermist.*

Another hunting partner is his son David. *David and I were hunting grizzly one spring in the Kootenays. We climbed over 7,000 feet right up into the alpine – no timber up there, and still snow. If we'd gone up far enough, we could have looked down the valley and seen the mine I'd built road for. We didn't get a grizzly but we saw caribou. So that fall we went back for one. Since it was the middle of September, we didn't think to take fly dope with us. The insects just* **ate** *us! The only place we could get away from them was up in the alpine snow patches and, needless to say, the caribou weren't there – they were walking through the thick brush at the timberline to get away from the flies. (Cattle do the same thing.) So after about two or three days' hunting, we bailed out and came home.*

I've only ever heard a cougar once. David and I used to go hiking up the trails on Rose Swanson Mountain in the evening, and we were comin' down just about dark. The cougar was below us in the thick cedars, and I guess he thought we were another cougar on the trail, and he roared like a lion. But I worked in the bush all my life, and I could count on one hand the number of cougars I've seen. Then I saw a little one last year [2005]. The dog had it treed in the small pine tree on our lawn just before the end of May. (I remember because the neighbour cut his hay that day and it was the only hay he got down until July because it rained all June.) I didn't realize it was a cougar, and the dog was goin' crazy, and I was wonderin' how I was going to get the dog to shut up. But before I got to do anything, the animal dropped to the ground and I realized it was a cougar. The dog tangled with it – ki-yi-in' from both of them and that was the end of it – I never saw it again.

And then I saw a big one here later in the summer. A white-tailed deer was runnin' across the field and I went inside for my binoculars to see if it was a buck, and by the time I got outside again, all I saw was the rear end of a cougar goin' into the City of

Armstrong at the back end of our property. Where it came off the body, the tail was about ten inches around. I think that big one got a lot of the fawn deer last year between this place and our old farm because a lot of the does didn't have fawns with them. Deer range miles and miles, and they range from here to the old farm. I can tell them by their horns – they're up there one day and down here the next.

Certain wildlife, however, has nothing to worry about. *There's lots of quail around – I don't know of anybody that would eat them though. They used to live around Vernon and haven't been up here that long. There's quite a few up at the old farm but they don't winter there – they disappear in the fall and show up near the end of April. Their escape route was a big pile of orchard prunings we'd piled up. I hated to burn that pruning pile in the fall – I liked to watch them – I put it off until they had gone.*

My son Will and his wife, Leanne, run the orchard on the old place. Fruit growing lasted up there because it doesn't get as cold as in the lower elevations. The soil is rocky, loamy, and underlaid with clay, which holds the moisture. We still grow good apples there.

In the old days quite a few of the old varieties went through the packing houses, but we also shipped Duchess, Wealthy, Wagner, Jonathan, Rome Beauty, Snow, and Wolf River. The earliest apples were Transparents, followed by Duchess, and then, Wealthy. Everybody had Wealthies; they're gone now. The Wagner was a small type of tree that they used in early days as a filler – when the main row got to a certain size, then they'd remove the filler row. Wagner and Jonathan were late apples. We still have Rome Beauty but a lot are Red Romes. Snow was a small apple with real white flesh that the packing house always wanted for a Hallowe'en apple. They were sweet – a nice-tasting apple. Wolf River was a big cooking apple.

The present varieties are McIntosh, Spartan, Delicious, Rome Beauty, and Winter Banana. Spartans are popular but I like 'Macs' best. It's got to be red to be ripe. I can pick one off the ground that's been under the tree for two weeks, and it's quite soft and sweet. Winter Banana is coloured like a banana and supposedly tastes something like one. There's new varieties out now; such as, Gala and Fuji. Will has planted some of these too.

Besides pears, apples, and some plums, they've got probably 150 cherry trees. They hire cherry pickers, mostly kids. They're paid by the pound, so if they're good pickers, they can make fairly good money. He's comin' nine now, but when he was six, my little grand-son Harley was pickin' cherries, and got paid the same as the others. He ended up with five ten-dollar bills. So he traded with his brother Jason for a fifty-dollar bill and was tryin' for the second one. He's kind of a jokin' kid, so I showed him a 100-dollar bill and said, "How'd you like that?" "Yeah!!" "Well," I said, "you got to get two of those fifties before I give you this one." He came back to me with his orange fifty dollar bill and an orange Canadian Tire bill and said, "I got it!" No flies on that boy!!

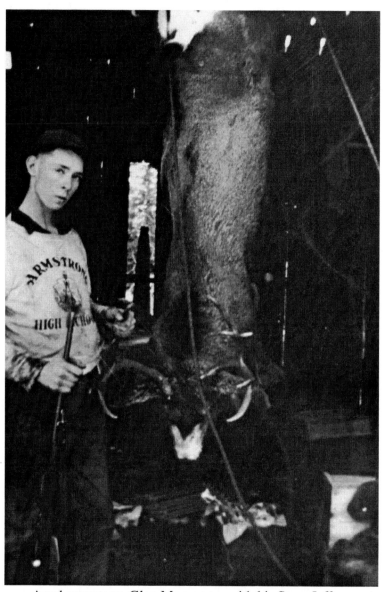

Aged seventeen, Glen Maw poses with his Steyr Jeffrey
Mannlicher rifle and a mule deer he has taken

Chapter Seven

Work and Friendship

Jack Wesley Noble

I was reading some family papers the other night. One story out of Ontario was hard to believe! After John Setterington took up his homestead [1817], his wife came down with consumption and died, and she left him with three young children. One morning he told them he was going away for six days and gave them six loaves of bread to tide them over. He left, and he never came back! Finally, someone went into town and reported that these kids were running wild in the bush – no clothes on – and they tracked them down. Clarinda Setterington, Jack Noble's paternal grandmother, was a descendant.

Our family came to British Columbia from Leamington, Ontario, in 1908. They went first to Abbotsford in the Fraser Valley where they stayed about a year, and in 1909 they moved to Armstrong and bought this eighty acres that we're on now [4195 Noble Road]. They were the only ones of the family that came west. The rest of them are still back there. I never knew my grandparents – they were both dead when I was born. His grandparents were Andrew Jackson Noble and Clarinda Setterington Noble.

The names Noble Road, Noble Tractor and Equipment Ltd., and Roedorack Farm, an enterprise now farming almost 500 acres [spring, 2006], along with several generations of descendants who have remained in the area, mark close to a century of involvement in the community.

When Andrew Jackson Noble brought his wife and four children to Armstrong Spallumcheen, he was already forty-eight years old and Clarinda, forty-six. Fortunately, their children were young adults and largely self-sufficient. Maude Beatrice, the eldest, was twenty-one. *She married an Irishman who was a CPR steam locomotive engineer. [Two years younger], Belle [Ida Belle] never married. She lived at the Coast and owned some neighbourhood stores down there.* Milton Stanley, Jack's father, was sixteen and his younger brother, Angus Ross, fifteen. *Ross was the first teller in the Imperial Bank here in Armstrong. He was transferred out to Tabor, Alberta, and got typhoid fever and died young.* Thus, Stanley would farm with his father, and both would discover that agriculture in Spallumcheen was somewhat different from their earlier experience.

My dad came out of an area in Ontario that specialized in row cropping – tomatoes, vegetables, tobacco. So they were row crop vegetable farmers, not hay farmers. And I think most of the land in the area had already been selected – Lansdowne had been laid out in the 1880s, and some of the big places like Stepney Ranch and O'Keefe Ranch, even earlier than that. In fact, the relatives who remained in Ontario held a jaundiced view of Andrew Noble's prospects. *I know when I was about ten or twelve years old, I was horsing around one day in an old, one-car garage out beside the house – there was all kinds of junk in there – and I found pieces of two old revolvers – and I showed them to Dad: "What are these?" A relative had heard wild stories about the West and armed them before they left. I don't know* why *they left – it was something I never asked.*

Jack's family records supply possibilities. They show that Andrew Jackson Noble was one of twelve children and the eldest of eight who survived into adulthood. When their father (himself one of thirteen children) died in 1906, his will among other bequests left all his property (amounting to at least 330 acres) to the youngest son, who was living on the home place, and the sum of one dollar to Andrew Noble. Andrew in 1885 had married Clarinda Setterington and lived on what was known as the William Henry Setterington farm, 130 acres. One wonders if this farm was inadequate to support the family and, having no share in his father's estate, Andrew decided despite his age to head west. He may have felt too that he had a good knowledge of farming.

From what I read about the Noble family back in Ontario – there was a whole batch of them – they all were quite successful farmers – some of 'em had 300 acres. And it was bush – absolute bush country – when the first one came there from England [1837]. And they were on the school board and so forth, so they were [civic-minded] and good farmers. They were also accustomed to hard work, as were their wives and children.

I think 100 years ago people would starve to death if they didn't work – there was no welfare or anything like that. Dad said they had to cut down some trees on this *place before they could turn the horse and buggy around! That may not be quite accurate, but very little of it was cleared – you can imagine clearing it by hand! Women were out there with the men picking these darn tree roots.* It was strenuous, boring work. *This farm is made up of about five parcels and they were all bought separately and cleared.*

They'd bought twenty acres over where Jeanne is [4184 Noble Road], and there was a fence between them and Frank Young's place [4196]. I remember Dad saying he and Mom were over there picking roots, and just for fun Dad would take the pitchfork and rake the wire, and Mrs. Young would holler over, "Quit that, Stanley, I saw you throw that root over here!" About every hour he'd rattle the fence with his pitchfork just to get her going! Mrs. Frank Young sold insurance. *She might come at 9 o'clock at night and you'd have to go to bed and leave her sitting there at 3 o'clock in the morning. She just outwaited you.*

When Dad came to this area, there were big farms, but there were lots of small farms too – forty to eighty acres. Along this road on the forty acres where Wieringa has his dairy [4149], Wilbur Scott, and before him the Freemans, also raised cows. (Maude Freeman married Howard Spears, who used to run the Armstrong Egg Pool. He is now [2006] almost 100 years old.) Where Galuska lives [4136], that was McRosti. On MacDonald Road where Dave Harrison lives [4214], there was a dairy – Lindsays [4262] had cows, MacDonald

[4312] had cows, Ericksons too – Flora (MacDonald) and Joe – who had a house on the MacDonald place before they moved to Otter Lake Road [1768]. All these little places were sustaining themselves with cows, chickens, eggs, maybe some pigs. Nobody had a lot of them – people made a living and a little more. The eggs went into town and you sold the stock. The stockyard used to be across from the [government] liquor store on Railway Avenue, and they shipped one day a week to Vancouver or Calgary. Evans – who first worked on the Prairie and later became the magistrate here – was the agent for Burns Meats and owned the stockyard. You could call Evans and say, "I've got twenty pigs," or maybe some cattle, and when he got enough calls, he'd order in one, two, or three railway cars depending on how many he thought he needed. He'd weigh the cows and pay you so much a hundredweight. Then they'd go out on the train that day. The pigs had to be graded when they reached the city, so you got that money later.

Andrew and Stanley Noble learned to do likewise. *At first they would have developed some sort of a herd of cows, and raised just enough feed to keep them, and they kept growing and adding, and it took quite a long time to be able to do this. Like I said, everybody had to have chickens and pigs and cows and eggs. By the time I was growing up, this farm always had two or three hundred chickens – laying hens and meat hens. And we always had pigs. We showed Yorkshire pigs in the Vancouver Exhibition [Pacific National Exhibition] for years – we'd take a carload down on the railway. We took purebred Jerseys and Yorkshire pigs to the Armstrong Fair. I won the cup in the swine Open Class so many times in a row that they finally gave it to me.* This two-handled silver cup is a significant artifact, since it identifies itself with the North Okanagan Fair, which preceded the adoption in 1930 of the name Interior Provincial Exhibition. The engraving on the cup continues, "Presented by Armstrong District Yorkshire Breeders for best Yorkshire Sow over 5 months. Won by J. Noble."

From an early age Jack Noble had participated in Junior Farmers, later known as 4-H. A family photo catches him with his prize-winning, purebred Jersey calf. The calf and the boy look equally young. As a teenager at the Pacific National Exhibition in Vancouver, Jack captured the Pym Trophy, awarded to the best aggregate livestock judge among contestants from 4-H clubs throughout British Columbia. In one marathon day participants judged seven classes of livestock: beef, dairy, poultry, swine, swine carcasses, sheep, and horses. It was a prestigious achievement, as competition was intense.

In order to maintain financial stability, settlers needed more than one iron in the fire. *Maybe they logged on their own property or worked in the sawmill. Dad and Don MacDonald did some logging up on Rose Swanson Mountain in the wintertime, and they used to go down to Otter Lake and saw ice and haul it into town for the use of the packing plants. They stored the ice in sawdust in big sheds next to the packing houses along the tracks and it kept through the summer. I have a photo of Dad and Don geared up and heading out for one of their jobs off the farm – trying to make enough money to keep going. Dad worked on the [CN] railbed for the track when it came through in the early twenties. Virtually all they used then was a horse and a slipscraper. A slipscraper has two handles and a long, scooped-out bucket, and as you run it along behind the horse, it fills itself. When it's full, you tip the handles down and slide it on a pan to where you want to dump the dirt, then lift the handles. It catches itself, tips over, and dumps. It holds about half a yard of dirt.* Spreading dirt was patient, plodding labour but, according to Johnny Serra's *The History of Armstrong* (p 97), it paid three dollars a day for the man (and, customarily, something extra for the horse).

In addition to one's own enterprise, however, in Jack Noble's view the secret of success lay in the neighbourhood. *Everybody around here used to neighbour back and forth. You visited on Sundays. If you were sick, people would look after you. Otter Lake District twice a month had a card party in town – Glaicars from the [Grandview] Flats, people from Otter Lake. Noble Road had a party twice a year. It was the same with all the neighbours – MacDonalds were that way – Lindsays – all of them. That doesn't happen any more. There are more new people – places changing hands all the time – that didn't happen years ago.*

And you never really worked alone. You grew corn for silage even in the dry land and it turned out not bad, so there was a group that had a machine for chopping and blowing it into a silo – Mr. Gill... MacDonald... McKechnie... Page-Brown... Dad. The machine sat beside the silo, and you fed the corn into it. Knives beside the blower inside the machine cut it up, and the blower blew it into the silo. They'd rotate this machine around the farms and go around with it and help everybody out – four or five people bringing in the corn. Take threshing – you didn't have a threshing machine so you got somebody in to thresh, and later to combine.

Albert Haller used to come quite often to help with the haying. On the front of his tractor he had a big sweep 12-foot wide, and he'd go around and pick the hay coils up. It lifted real high and he could stack with it. Field stacks were built in various places, and then somebody would come in during the winter and bale those stacks with a big stationary baler. Then you'd haul the bales down to the railway and load it in railcars and ship it to the Coast – 100-... 110-... 120-pound bales – every one weighed and ticketed. You lugged every bale down the length of the car and you started stacking them. And to put those bales up ten to twelve feet high in those rail cars – it's some workout, I'll tell you! I was doing that when I was fourteen or fifteen years old. Not 'til we get into the early '50s did we have any sort of labour-saving equipment. (We had tractors in the late '40s but they didn't make things much easier.) But there was always somebody in the area in the '40s and '50s – like Dan Popowich and Albert Haller – that did custom work for you. They followed a certain route every year.

The weather, of course, was always a factor and encouraged a stoic attitude. *It's bad for haying this year [2006], but we've had rain like this before. I can remember as a kid, you couldn't see those black, mouldy, first-crop coils in the field because they had sunk down in the rain and the second crop had grown up so high around them – it was that sort of year. We'd just throw them in the bush and burn them.*

Milton Stanley Noble met Florence Hope Binkley at a Methodist sleigh ride party in Armstrong – *he was a Presbyterian and she, a Methodist, and then the churches united [1925].* Stanley was tall and good-looking; Hope, petite and pretty. *Mother was born in Souris, Manitoba, and in 1913 her family moved to Armstrong – her father and mother, herself, and four brothers.* Hope was sixteen at the time. *She worked here as a receptionist for Dr. Van Kleeck. She wasn't a nurse, but I guess in those days you did all kinds of things. She probably had to work to survive because I don't know what her parents did when they were in Armstrong.* (Grandfather John W. Binkley died several years before Jack was born and Grandmother Alice Gunby Binkley, when he was two.) *Two of Mother's brothers, Mansell and Glenn, ended up as undertakers in Saskatchewan – a pretty good business. A younger brother, Melvin, was a schoolteacher, became an accountant, opened a business in Vancouver and did quite well. Ward was killed in the First World War – shot down in Germany. A war history somewhere in the house mentions his name.*

Stanley Noble married Hope Binkley on March 12, 1919. The *Okanagan Commoner* of May 9, 1919, records the event:

Binkley-Noble Nuptials

A quiet wedding was solemnized at the home of Mr. and Mrs. J.W. Binkley, Wood Avenue, on Wednesday, March 12th, at two p.m. when their only daughter, Flossie Hope, was united in the bonds of matrimony to Mr. Milton Stanley Noble, son of Mr. and Mrs. A.J. Noble, Armstrong. The ceremony was performed by Rev. J. Wesley Miller. The bride was attended by Miss Isabelle [Ida Belle] Noble, sister of the groom, while the groom was supported by Mr. Stanley Cary.

The bride entered the drawing room leaning on the arm of her father, and was attired in a dress of white crepe de chine, trimmed with satin and silk fringe, and wore the customary veil and orange blossoms. She carried a bouquet of white rose carnations, and maidenhair fern. The bridesmaid wore a dress of blue silk and carried a bouquet of pink carnations.

After hearty congratulations a dainty buffet luncheon was served. The bride's travelling suit was of nigger brown serge trimmed with military braid and she wore a satin hat to match. We join in wishing Mr. and Mrs. Noble all the blessings afloat on the matrimonial sea.

Their first child, Stanley Roy, was born on January 14, 1921. He was by way of a birthday present for Hope, herself born on January 5th. Daughter Doris Loreen arrived on May 25, 1923, and in 1934 Jack Wesley completed the family on November 5th, Guy Fawkes Day, wildly celebrated in Britain as the day in 1605 when Guy Fawkes was captured in a basement room of the British Parliament with enough barrels of gunpowder to send the House of Lords to oblivion. When Jack was born, his mother was thirty-seven and his father, forty-two.

I grew up in a houseful of adults, basically. I'm eleven and thirteen years younger than Doris and Roy. By the time I was old enough to do much, they were sixteen and eighteen years old. And there were no other kids on this road until later on in school when Gordon Danallanko lived on the hill. The MacDonalds were over on MacDonald Road – Jeanette and Norman. Jeanette is the same age as I am – we went to school together – and Norman was a few years older, but Norman got polio [1941] so then I wasn't allowed over there either. We went to town, but the people my father went to see were old people too. No young kids! It wasn't 'til I was five and started school that I got exposed to other children.

Luckily for Jack, summer brought an influx of new faces because the blackcurrants were ripening. *We had all these blackcurrants out here – from the house to the road on both sides and more in the back – ten acres. They planted them in crisscross rows in the '20s and pruned and cultivated them – a single horse pulling a little cultivator that you walked behind.* Andrew and Stanley Noble had finally achieved their row crop. *It was the only major patch of blackcurrants that I know of. Some people had a row or a quarter of an acre, but in those years ten acres was significant. People used to come from quite a ways up and down the valley and buy them for jam. We sold lots locally – shipped them to the cannery for processing – tons... and tons... and tons of blackcurrants. They were a real good income for years and years.*

They were picked in late July and we used to get natives, mostly from Head of the Lake – some from Enderby. We'd hire Dan Popowich. He lived down at the bottom of the hill here and he had one of the only trucks in the area – a little two- or three-ton flatdeck truck that he hauled milk on. We'd go down to Head of the Lake a week or two before the crop was ready and say, "Are you going to come?" And they'd say, "Yeah," and when we came back, six or seven native families would be ready to go. Bedrolls and tents, and pots and pans, three or four kids apiece – and they'd gather up all these belongings and load the natives on the back along with them and haul them up because that was the only way they could get here. I knew lots of them, of course – some kids were born here – I grew up with a lot of them. They'd camp here so I used to hang out with them. My mother wasn't too sure about that because TB [tuberculosis] was going around then. And they ate things that I ate with them, and she wasn't too impressed with it – bread they dipped in oil [bannock]....

There'd be thirty... forty... fifty pickers here – people used to come out from town too. It was a lot of work picking one berry at a time... you had to pick them with no stems on... and it was 100 degrees out there at times. I've picked the darn things! My mother ran the blackcurrants job. There was an 8- x 20-foot shack on skids that the horse pulled along to various locations. It had a scale in it, and about twice a day they came there with their pails or lugs of currants and she'd collect and weigh them. She kept a tally of the weights – each family picked as one. We didn't pay by the day – we paid at the end of the job – otherwise, they left – and some we kept back to buy groceries for them. I don't remember what it was – but if you got four cents a pound when you sold them, you paid two cents a pound for picking. Mom had to be at the shack at various times during the day, so she'd send me out into the blackcurrant patch to pick too. That was her idea of babysitting!

The blackcurrant acreage disappeared suddenly. *The folks went back east for three months in 1952 – their first holiday. It was the year I got out of school, and Roy was here on the farm for a bit. While they were gone, we ploughed all the blackcurrants out. Dad came back and said, "Well, I'm glad somebody did that!" They'd pretty well run out – and it was tough by that time to get pickers. Like a lot of things, you know, they'd kind of run their course.*

The civic gene that flourished in the Noble family in Leamington, Ontario, re-emerged in Armstrong Spallumcheen. From 1931 until 1952, that is to say, three years before Jack's birth until the year he graduated from Armstrong High School, his father was a member of Spallumcheen Municipal Council, his first four years as alderman followed by seventeen years as reeve. During his time of office Spallumcheen celebrated its Golden Anniversary, 1942, and its Diamond Anniversary in his final year. *It was continuous once he started. I remember as a kid the phone calls – everybody got some grief or complaint – and Mom and Dad would talk about it. I heard this day in and day out, and as a teenager I thought to myself, 'I'm not having any part of that! I've seen enough of that already!'* Hope Noble recounted that she and Stanley routinely drove about the large municipality on Sunday afternoons, first in a horse and buggy and later by car, to check out the state of the roads and prioritize improvements, as settlers needed to get themselves and their produce to and from town. *Potholes would develop in the gravel roads, and all they had to fix them was hand shovels – they later bought an old truck.* Important but less in the limelight were Stanley Noble's contribution to the formation of the Armstrong Cheese Co-operative Association which built the Armstrong Cheese Factory in 1938, his Life Membership in the Armstrong Spallumcheen Board of Trade, and his trusteeships on the Otter Lake Water District and on the Armstrong School Board.

Hope's forte was to be the excellent cook and manager of a busy farm household, her husband's confidante and advisor, and a

262

good neighbour to newcomers and old friends alike. She never referred to these friends as anything but 'Mrs...,' and she never came to visit without a present: fresh strawberries or cherries, cookies or cake. In her eighties she continued to drive her car, although she preferred the back roads. For many years Hope belonged to a social and supportive group of twelve women who called themselves the Cheerio Club and always began their meetings with a funny story.

When Jack turned five, World War Two had newly begun, and the training of the local militia supplied him with curiosities. *On the north side of the B.F. Young place across from us on Noble Road, there was a half-mile federal rifle range with markers for 100, 300, and 1,000 yards, and five large targets that went up and down on big pulleys. During the war hundreds of men from the Vernon army camp used to come out and spend three or four days hammering away with guns out there. And they'd sometimes come to the house to get some milk or eggs – they were half starved and wet – lots of times it was raining. When they left, I'd go over and pick up shell casings and other leftovers by the box. One day I found a whole bunch of blank shells crimped at the end – they had powder in them but no shot or bullets. My room was in the top storey of the house (it was coal oil lamps and candles until 1947 when rural electrification came), and that night I was admiring one of these shells over the candle. BANG!!! I'm just lucky I didn't have my head over it! It bowled me over and scared the hell out of me! My mother figured I'd shot myself!*

Oh, I remember the war. I remember the blackouts we used to have – going down the road at night and no lights on. I remember the rationing. You couldn't get a tube of toothpaste unless you had an empty tube to exchange for it. Butter and meat were rationed. Of course, on the farm we did fine because we shot lots of pheasants in the winter and had cows and chickens, lots of milk and eggs. We butchered, but some of the things you <u>had</u> to buy in the store – gasoline – and the paper to cover the windows when they called for a blackout.

In fact, Jack for a time was an undercover agent. *Webers lived just west of us – they were Austrian, I think – nice people. He was considered a little odd – he used to disappear for hours and days and nobody would see him. On the [Spallumcheen] Council, Dad had some responsibility to be on the lookout for anybody who was against the cause: conscientious objectors, deserters, and so forth. So there was some thought that Weber might have a radio out in the bush and be communicating with somebody... someplace... they didn't know who... so I was told to spend time over there and see what he was doing! I was quite welcome so I went. Well, the poor old guy was building a set of kitchen cabinets up in the top of his house – and that's what he was spending most of his time at. He was a cabinetmaker – an Old Country craftsman. He eventually had to take off the top of the house to get them out because he couldn't manoeuvre them down the stairs!*

As local people enlisted, farms and businesses experienced a shortage of labour. *I remember at the start of the war we used to go downtown and try to get the men riding the rails. Another time we had three or four servicemen from the Vernon camp come and help us hay for four or five days or a week. You applied to get them, and you'd put them up and feed them. Afterwards, the ones we had were sent to the Aleutians, the islands that run off the coast south of Alaska, and one of them was killed.*

A fixture on Noble Farm, however, was a distant relative. *My mother had a second cousin named Herb Binkley that came in 1931 from Manitoba to visit. It was the Depression. He drove out in an old Model A car, and the visit was forever! He stayed so long they finally built him a cabin out in the yard – didn't want him in the house – he was a miserable old devil – real cantankerous. But he helped in the barn – he ran the horses – and he was a blacksmith. He made all the singletrees and doubletrees – all the hardware for the equipment. (I still have some of his tools – they're antiques today.) His car used to sit in the old horse barn – still had the Manitoba licence on it – 1931 – because he never drove it here. One day in the summer of 1949 he was putting the horses away. He had a bit of a bad attitude toward horses sometimes – and one of them decided he'd had enough. He reared up in the stall and beat him to death – killed him right there.* Herb's visit had lasted nearly twenty years.

The summer of 1949 brought another change. *Mother and Dad built a second house on the place – I was fourteen, and I wheeled cement for the foundations and pounded nails all summer. The house was for my brother, Roy. Roy was an agriculturalist. He started his degree at UBC and finished it after the war.* At the age of twenty-one, Roy had enlisted in the air force, graduated in 1942 as a flying officer, became a bombardier, and by 1945 had won the Distinguished Flying Cross. The citation read in part:

> *[He] completed numerous operations against the enemy in the course of which [he has] invariably displayed the utmost fortitude, courage, and devotion to duty... His sorties included many major targets such as Essen, Stuttgart, Dortmund, Bottrop, Emden, Russelheim, Bremen, Brunswick, Hamburg, and Wesseling, as well as special French targets which required precision bombing, such as Bois de Casson, St. Leu, Forêt de Chantilly, and La Pallice. On each occasion Flying Officer Noble bombed successfully and has secured many good photographs.*

Like many veterans Roy found the transition to civilian life difficult. *He would never talk about the war.*

Roy was the agriculturalist at the Summerland Research Station for a few years. Then he went up to Savona to grow potatoes with his father-in-law on sixty acres of bottomland along Dead Man's Creek. That fall he trucked them to Kamloops and put them in storage and, of course, the market went to nothing, so that was a one-year deal. So he was coming back to work the farm with Dad.

Stanley and Hope Noble had named their farm Roedorack, an acronym comprised of the partial first names of their three children. Doris's career, however, focused her in larger centres rather than close to home. Denied entry to the nursing profession because recurring eczema might interfere with her ability to 'scrub,' she enrolled in Home Economics at the University of Manitoba, majored in nutrition, and achieved First Class Honours along with the highest fourth-year-student award, 'Lady Stick,' i.e., Faculty President and University Women's Association Vice-President. She then embarked on a successful and varied career of graduate education, administration, travel, writing and speaking engagements, mainly in nutrition, in both the federal and provincial health services and in the private sector. An achievement in B.C., for example, was to set up a provincial helpline of professionals called 'Dial a Dietitian.'

Roy's decision, therefore, to return to the farm was welcomed. *But Roy and Dad didn't get along that well, and after about a year and a half, Roy decided to go on to other things. He sold insurance in the Fraser Valley and had an office in Cloverdale.*

Roy's departure left Jack to take his place. However, production on Roedorack Farm was about to change.

The farm had always raised pigs and dairy cattle. The pig barn was located very close to where the office in the shop is now. Then about 1950 or so, the pig barn burnt down and we lost half the pigs – we couldn't get them out of the barn – it was awful. Some of them survived and were fine – some of them survived and we should have shot them – they were no good. And so we went out of pigs.

The dairy barn is the old barn that is still in the yard. We had maybe thirty-five or forty cows – not that many – but in the later '50s that number was quite a few. For nearly all the years we had pure-bred Jersey cattle, and for the last two or three years we'd bought a few Holsteins – the butterfat from the Jersey milk was too high, and you were paid more for volume than butterfat.

Dad had a second farm on MacDonald Road where he ranged cattle up on the mountain and kept a small feedlot – fifty... sixty... eighty at various times. We had to dehorn and vaccinate them. We had no chutes, so I used to have to go in there and "rassle" them like a cowboy – see if I could get the best of them – and half the

time they got the best of me! Two immigrants – a Hungarian and a
Czechoslovakian – lived in a shack there and looked after the place
– the cattle, the fencing and so forth. One was a bit handicapped
and they were both getting old. They worked and died there – they
found one of 'em out in the hayfield with his feet in the air one day.

I liked the cattle but they didn't fit with me. I was allergic to the
hair on them, I think. When I was around them a lot, my eyes swelled
up and got sore. It showed maybe that cattle weren't my thing, and
Dad wanted out of them too – he was getting older by then – so he
sold them. I think we sold the quota for five dollars a pound – not
very much – they're talking now that if you want to milk thirty cows,
you have to spend around half a million.

For the first time in its existence, Roedorack Farm was no
longer a stock farm. The old routine of cows, pigs, chickens, and
eggs had passed away. The farm needed a different focus. When in
September, 1955, not quite twenty-one, Jack Wesley Noble married
Carolyn Anne Hoover, the two would work together to discover a
new formula for making a living on the land. With the passage of
the years, the right fit would become a combination of farming and
a farm machinery dealership.

Like the Nobles, Carolyn's family had a long association with
Armstrong Spallumcheen. Her great-grandfather George Hoover arrived with his wife and children in 1904, and her grandfather Charles
Hoover was a successful grain farmer and sawmill owner and, in the
thirties and early forties, owned and operated Inland Flour Mills in
town. *We both grew up in Armstrong... went to the same Sunday*
School... but she was sixteen months younger, and I wasn't looking
for girls – I was afraid of them! We saw each other at school dances,
and in my last year we started dating. When Carolyn and I were
married, we lived in the old house right here, and Mom and Dad
moved into the house we'd built for Roy. On their first anniversary
in 1956, their daughter Brenda Cheryl was born, followed by Jeanne
Marie in 1958, their son Gordon Douglas Jack in 1959, and daughter
Lesley Loreen in 1962. An outgoing and fun-loving woman, until

her sudden death in 2005, Carolyn was a strong and supportive force behind her husband and children.

Carolyn and I were best friends and we worked as a team. She was always involved. She worked in the office – any place she was needed – she earned a Class 1 licence for driving trucks. Even if some of my decisions weren't perfect, she supported me in whatever I did. The family grew up in the business too – the kids were around the shop when they were young, and the farm and the shop were integrated nicely – farming and farm machinery – the same type of business. The kids all worked on the farm. They ran tractors and swathers. They were all in 4-H.

In fact, except for Lesley, who is the vice president and chief financial officer of an oil and gas company in Calgary, Alberta, his other children Brenda, Jeanne, and Gordon are all employed in the family business. They say, *That's one thing Dad made sure we learned – how to run equipment, how to weld, how to fix all kinds of machinery in case we ever broke down in the field. It didn't matter if you were a boy or a girl – he made sure that if we were going to be in the business, we'd better know the mechanics. We learned how to drive backwards for miles before we ever got to go forwards! He said you have to know how to back up or you may as well not be driving.*

In the early years Jack tried putting various aspects of farming together at the same time. *I went into hay and grain farming, and I started welding and fabricating haying equipment, primarily bale-bunchers, in the old board shop here and selling to dealers and people in the area.*

The bales were handled in a couple of different ways. The simplest was to hammer together a platform of four or five 1- by 6-inch boards to make a wooden sloop very close to the ground and pulled behind the baler. You stood on the sloop next to the baler and piled the bales behind you as they came off – two on the bottom of the sloop going one way and two on top going the opposite way until

268

you had eight or ten bales in four or five layers – and then you stuck a bar between the boards into the ground and the bales slid off as the sloop moved forward underneath them. They stayed in a stack because they only had to slide a short distance until they caught the ground, and the hay made the boards as slippery as greased paper.

So, like some other people, I built a device that was similar to a forklift but instead came in at the sides of the stack and squeezed the bales so you could pick it up. It had a rack at the back so you could tip the stack slightly and drive away with it, load the stack on your trailer and unload it later as well. It was all welded together and had a hydraulic cylinder on it, and most people didn't have welders or cutting torches or the ability to use them. That was around 1958.

I also made a bale buncher that improved on the simple wooden sloop so it didn't need anybody working on the back of the baler. The bales would come off the baler and fall freely into it. But when you had six or eight in there, you pulled a rope to trip a gate on the back of it, and again the bales would just slide off randomly. You'd always drop them in a row across the field so they'd be easy to collect. If the hay was a little tough, some people might stook the piles for a while. Others just came with a wagon and threw them on and hauled them to the barn. But because they were in a row, in any case the bales were easier to deal with.

One long-time Noble employee was Lester Odiorne, who ran the farm operation for twenty-five years before he retired. His was a regular figure on farm equipment in the field season after season.

Most of the work I did, though, was repairs for people. I also installed a lot of hydraulic truck hoists, and lengthened truck frames for these hoists, and made truck boxes, both wood and metal. Years ago the area was predominantly in grain – more grain than hay – so farmers were buying combines and had to have a way to haul their grain. Silage was becoming more common too. So somebody would bring a truck to the shop and, of course, it was a used truck he had bought someplace, and half the time it wasn't long enough, so we'd first have to lengthen that truck frame – put a piece in – and change the drive shaft. Then we'd buy a hoist and install a PTO [power take-off] and a pump to make the hydraulic work, and then you'd build the box on it with a gate, and a floor, and sides that came off so you could use the truck for hay or grain – a bigger size for silage. We put on dozens of truck hoists and boxes.

And then I took on a line of equipment manufactured in Winnipeg – Versatile Equipment – for about two or three years. I'd completed a diesel mechanics course by correspondence in 1959 and worked under a mechanic in the wintertime for a while. But, honestly, Carolyn and I were finding it tough to exist – we had nothing when we started. So in 1963 we took on a dealership for J.I. Case, which was a big leap for us – a <u>big</u> leap! We didn't have a lot of money, and you have to invest in parts – inventory – and so on. But the company was really easy to get along with – they cooperated with their dealers – and the first couple of years we did really well, but then we were stuck for a good many years because the cash flow didn't grow as much as we needed it. There was machinery to lay out money for... and accounts receivable... and parts....

In setting up the business, however, Jack and Carolyn Noble had two advantages. The first was that having lived so long in the area, the families were well known. The second was Jack's belief in the value of neighbourliness. *Service has built our business. If somebody came in the yard at eight o'clock at night and wanted something fixed, I worked until midnight, or whenever, to get it done. Somebody would break down in the field on Saturday or Sunday – Carolyn would bring the kids and we'd go out and do the repairs.*

So Jack's children learned by watching and doing. Brenda says, *Dad was determined to get things done, and Gordon is just like him. Dad would go out to deliver equipment after work – or on a weekend – for a customer who needed it. It might be over to Edgewood (where a coffee shop made great pie!), or out along the west side of Okanagan Lake before the road was finished. We'd be hanging over the side of a cliff in our little old truck, or a semi with equipment on the back, and he'd say, "Have we enough room to get around the corner?" "No, you have to back up." "Okay." And he'd back up and we'd eventually make it around the corner! Oh, my goodness! But he was determined to get it there and make sure that the customer was happy. Most of his customers were friends as well, and to him that's what the business has always been – helping your friends.*

Another asset has been Jack's inventiveness and adaptability. *Dad reads a lot. He was always bringing up something he'd read or heard about and saying, "Now this business tried* this *and it didn't work, but if we changed it to* this*, do you think it would work? Let's try it." He was always learning – going out and seeing what else was out there. So part of our joy in this business is that each day brings something different – something new to learn.*

Jeanne laughs. *I remember one time Dad and I were shot at when we were repossessing a tractor. We'd made the road trip to the ranch to pick it up and had it loaded on the truck. Then the guy started to shoot at us and Dad began pulling out, and I'm still trying to get the beavertail back up and running to catch up with him!*

Brenda remembers, *We went to 100 Mile House one time. A customer had told us that a unit had fallen through the ice on the lake, and if we wanted it, we'd have to go up in the spring when the ice melted and dig it out! One of our farm workers had been up there selling hay, and he said to Dad, "I don't think that's true." So Dad gave him time off to do a little investigating and he came back and said, "I think I found it!" So we went up there late one night and gathered at a coffee shop about 3 a.m. because the fellow always left home at 5 a.m. and came back at 8 a.m. It was twenty-five miles on this goat trail to reach his place, and we took the truck in as far as we could and found the tractor. And on the way out with it, we met him coming back! We waved, and Dad kept looking in the rear view mirror: "Is he coming after us?" "No, it's fine!" But the guy was quite amiable – he phoned up – "You found it – I guess it's yours!" Afterwards he came back to buy more stuff, but* cash *this time. And his sons still do business with us.*

Gordon adds, *In the course of a transaction, a good customer wanted Dad to take his vintage tractor.* Jack has a sense of humour. *It's Dad's tractor now,* says Jeanne. *A number of people have looked at it and wanted to purchase it but he won't let it go. And it was a Noble Road tradition that if you showed up at our house on Hallowe'en, the dog would be in costume, and Dad wearing something to match.*

One piece of equipment, however, caused Jack some anguish. *We sold snowmobiles for years and, though it was always illegal, sometimes people would take a quick tour through town. Dad had his snowmobile in town one night. He and an RCMP member had been imbibing at a local watering hole, and being a Good Samaritan, Dad said, "Oh, I'll give you a ride home," and he put his rather inebriated friend on the back of the machine. Well, when he drove around the corner at Okanagan Street, the guy rolled off and Dad thought he'd killed him! He just sat on the steps of the Hassen building with his head in his hands! Then he heard a moan and realized the fellow was still alive, so he loaded him back on and finished the trip.*

Fire is a hazard during a hot summer, but the expertise of the whole family in operating machinery pays off in security. A spark from a working combine set the grain field behind the shop on fire in 2002, but quick action from the Nobles, work crews, and the volunteer fire department protected adjoining neighbours. Brenda says, *I remember my grandmother [Hope Noble] telling me that the year my dad was born, the whole mountain was on fire. And one memory I have when I was about three or four and Jeanne about two, was of the mountain being on fire again, and Dad and a crowd of men out there with shovels and burlap sacks and a tank of water to wet them down, trying to smother the embers falling around the barns. Then I remember him gathering us up and stuffing us in the car, and my mom driving us away to safety.*

Although Jack Noble was never interested in holding municipal office, he was a dedicated member of the Spallumcheen

272

Volunteer Fire Department and recalls that experience with pride. *The Municipal office used to be in the same building with the City office [Bridge Street], but for years and years, as far as I know, there weren't any joint ventures or committees. For example, the City had a fire department but Spallumcheen didn't have one. The City fire truck was made by Art and Bill Clayton at the Armstrong Machine Shop, and it was down at the Fire Hall until about eight or ten years ago – not active any more but still there.*

I was on the first municipal fire department. It was 1962 and Spall got its own pumper truck – a big, International Hub pumper truck – a pretty nice truck in those days. It's the one that carried the hose... the pump... ladders... but it held only about 500 gallons of water and would be used up in about ten minutes, and there was no money in the budget for a tanker. Gordon Sidney was on Spall Council at the time, and he asked me if I could help him solve this dilemma. So he and I decided to make a tanker truck for packing the water because there were no water hydrants in Spallumcheen at that time.

The method the two used was commonplace, but the scale of the endeavour was not. *Most people had gas tractors in those days, and it was not uncommon for fuel tanks to have holes in them – get rusted out. So I'd throw some carbon tetrachloride in the tank to produce some non-explosive vapour, and start welding. You'd see the fumes coming out of the top of the tank and know it was safe to work on. It's not an approved method, but I used to do it often. You should be wearing a gas mask too, but you don't have your head in the tank when you're doing this! Some people used to attach a car exhaust to the gas tank because carbon monoxide fumes won't explode either, but that method wasn't very safe.*

Gordon Sidney found an old 1,000-gallon gas and fuel tank that we changed into a water tank. (1,000 gallons is about 10,000 pounds so that is about all a single-axle truck can carry.) We poured a gallon of carbon tetrachloride into the tank, tipped it, and heated the bottom with a torch to activate the chemical. I cut a hole in the top for the water fill and welded two baffles [metal plates] inside the tank to divide the space into thirds, and they sit about six inches from the top and bottom. Otherwise, when you're driving, especially when the tank is not quite full, the water will slosh back and forth and make driving unsafe. Then in the hole we inserted a metal fill with a lid, and at the back we installed a valve with a quick drain. We strapped the tank onto a truck frame, and that's all there was to it! We used it for years.

The Spallumcheen Volunteer Fire Department serviced four areas – Otter Lake, Hullcar, Stepney, and the east side of Highway 97. We didn't go to the City fires. Part of the problem was that some Spall firemen lived out in Grandview Flats and Hullcar, and by the time they got to town, fifteen or twenty minutes might have passed – I lived close enough to town to respond to most of the area fires. So what happened is that most of the City guys responded to the Spallumcheen fires and were supposed to call the Spall members, but maybe they would and maybe they wouldn't. Members of the Spallumcheen fire department lost interest because they weren't being involved. It went on that way for about six to eight years. Then it became a joint department where we shared equipment, trained together, and responded to all fires. When Jack Noble retired from the Armstrong Spallumcheen Volunteer Fire Department, he had served for thirty-two years. Gordon Noble carries on the family tradition. In 2006 he received a medal commemorating his first twenty-five years of service as a volunteer fireman.

In 2002 in recognition of their longstanding support, Jack and Carolyn Noble were honoured with Life Memberships in the Interior Provincial Exhibition, the largest agricultural fair in British Columbia. It runs in Armstrong each fall for the five days preceding Labour Day and is currently [2007] in its 108th year. Jeanne Noble is a director. She says, *Anytime we ever needed anything at the IPE, Mom and Dad were always there and gave more than we needed. Moving stages... lending equipment.... One year the person that was supposed to look after the performers – see that they each had food and refreshment, a spot to change their costumes, a chair to sit on – whatever they required – at the last minute was unable to do the job. I lent Mom my golf cart and she took over on the spot. She was so enthusiastic. She got everything organized and had them all eating out of her hand: "When is your mom coming back!" It was the same in every case – they'd dig right in and help: "We need this to happen!" "Okay, we'll do it." I can be phoning from the middle of the fairgrounds at 3 a.m: "Help!! We need....!" And somebody will bring it down. I've done the grounds layout for the last couple of years and Dad has helped me do all the measuring – fitting everything in. And Mom would drop by when it got dark and take us out for supper.*

Civic enthusiasm made Jack and Carolyn founding members in Armstrong Spallumcheen of the Kinsmen and the Kinettes, a philanthropic organization, while their business acumen won them prizes from J.I. Case Ltd. that included cruises and a memorable trip to Haiti during one of that country's ongoing periods of unrest. *When they were in Cap-Haitien, one of the locals offered his services as a guide, and they visited an orphanage. The children were running around calling, "The Canadians – they're here! The Canadians – they're here!" The nuns came out and hugged them because they hadn't seen any newcomers for six months. Mom and Dad had some great adventures on their travels.*

During these latter years, Jack has been devolving more of the business of the farm and dealership to Brenda, Jeanne, and Gordon and spends several months each year away from Armstrong Spallumcheen. He enjoys grandchildren and great-grandchildren and has followed up several new interests.

I took up cycling in earnest about ten or twelve years ago when we went down to Arizona in the wintertime. I started out cycling on the irrigation canals by myself, and after a couple of years, I found a cycling group and joined them. We've been roadbiking down there ever since. We cycled across Iowa last year with about 12,000 other cyclists – 500 miles in seven days. And I've just come off a ten-day cycle trip in the Silver Triangle in the Kootenays and the Coeur d'Alene area in Idaho, where we had anywhere from twenty-five to thirty cyclists. And this summer [2006] another fellow and myself walked the West Coast Trail on Vancouver Island with full pack – forty pounds – from Port Renfrew to Bamfield in a little over five days. We had to carry everything we needed – sleeping bag, water, dried food. It was pretty good for a seventy-two-year-old!

For our last anniversary the children gave Carolyn and I the ride from Kamloops to Armstrong return on the old steam train. We saw people we knew waving to us at the side of the track, and passed by all the farms of the people we knew or had done business with over the years – Monte Creek... Monte Lake... Westwold... Falkland.... It was a wonderful *trip. I remember all the time I was growing up, the neighbours were absolutely important. Your neighbour was always your best friend – you looked after each other, you worked together – that's the way it was.*

[On January 20, 2007, in Armstrong, Jack Wesley Noble married Joan Zeimantz Van Veen, a widow with four adult children, whom he met through his cycling group.]

Jack Noble at age sixteen

Chapter Eight

Dragonheart Finds Gold Mountain

Louie Non Chip Jong

I was born on August 7, 1924, but when I came to Canada
there was a problem because the Chinese [lunar] calendar is cal-
culated differently, and what is August 7 in China is not August 7 in
Canada. I decided to keep August 7 as the date so my birth certificate would match my other Canadian papers.

*I was born in Xinhui [county] – the Guangdong province of
Canton – in a village about the size of Armstrong. Everybody in
my village has the surname Louie, but they are not necessarily related. In China the family name is always given first, [so] my name
was Louie Non Chip. I was probably named Non Chip after my
grandmother.*

*I came from a small family – two boys – I was the only girl.
My oldest brother, Bak Yung, was nineteen years older than me. He
was married and had four kids. They lived with us. The custom is
for the woman to live with her husband's family – she looks after
his parents, her husband and children. My other brother, Bak Fai,
was just a year older than me. There were some children born between my older brother and my younger brother, but they all died
young – there were no doctors in those days and much hardship.
When I was very young, my father went to work in Mexico – I don't
know what he did there – but when he came back, he bought two
undertaker shops in his district. He died when he was forty-nine.*

Louie Non Chip was treated differently from her brothers. *In
China boys are more important than girls – if you didn't have a son,
you adopted or bought a son – it could be a relative. So I was not
taught to read or write. [Instead] I gathered straw and sticks for cook-*

ing and heating. I helped with the farming – the soil was red clay. We planted rice, sweet potatoes, taro root, bitter melons, Chinese melons – anything the family could eat. We ate very little meat. We raised chickens to eat, but if we raised a pig, we sold it because we could not afford to eat it ourselves. I [also] looked after the ox. Every family had one. It did the ploughing. I'd walk it out to pasture on the mountain and spend the day taking care of it. It was the prize possession. Our lives were mainly hard work. I don't remember much fun.

Festival days were a welcome change. The celebration of the Chinese New Year was especially important. Firstly, the calendar indicated the prospects that the coming year might hold, and secondly, the family honoured the ancestors, who had brought them into the world. *The Chinese New Year lasts for several days. You make special dishes, go house to house. You go to the neighbours and give them best wishes. You go to each of the relatives and bring gifts of oranges and dumplings. In the open air in front of your house, you burn incense. Every house has a room with an ancestral shrine where you remember your ancestors and give offerings to the gods. If you had a good year, you can make a better offering. These [ceremonies] are what the ancestors learned that people should have and pass on from one generation to the next.* Other special occasions might be a wedding or the birth of the first son. At any of these festivities, Louie Non Chip might receive Lucky Money. *Relatives give it to children or unmarried [relations]. You bring oranges or goodies with you, and half are given back to you with some Lucky Money. In the old days it was red tissue paper folded up with money inside.* In such ways as these, inspired by Confucius and other philosophers, the solidity of hierarchical family relationships was revered and maintained.

Then in 1931 when Louie Non Chip was seven years old, her world changed. *The Japanese invaded my village and burned it down. They burned my father's two undertaker shops and we lost everything. We ran and hid in a cave in the mountains. We knew the Japanese were coming because people could read the old characters [language] on the [flyers] the Japanese sent ahead of them. They*

[Japanese] had a central headquarters and invaded all around it. Some Chinese collaborated – they accepted bribes to bring them into the village. The Japanese used the villagers to carry things [forced labour] and they burnt everything in their path that they didn't kill. I saw executions. Lots of people lost their lives at that time. There weren't many people left but they fought back – they didn't have good weapons either. We were lucky to have a meal after the invasion. My family survived [but] a lot of people starved to death – they couldn't farm because of the fighting. Even when the war ended, there was [turmoil] in the country.

When the Japanese withdrew in 1939, Louie Non Chip was aged fifteen and World War Two began. She was twenty-one when that war ended. She had lived fourteen of her twenty-one years in the shadow of war. *My oldest brother died in 1940 and I had to babysit his children for almost ten years.*

In 1948, however, her prospects changed. She met her future husband, Jong Yoi, who was visiting his family after years in Canada. Like thousands of his countrymen, he had left China seeking economic opportunity, characterized during the mid-nineteenth century gold rushes in California and British Columbia as 'Gold Mountain.' Daughter Mary adds details about that period in her father's life: *His father was working in the United States and bought official papers [paid head tax] for my dad to come over. My dad travelled from China by boat to Victoria.* The year was 1910. *My grandfather had a brother in Los Angeles and wanted my dad to join them there, but he decided to stay in Canada. They never saw each other again.* A small booklet belonging to her father holds his passport picture and a red stamp inscribed:

Consulate General of the Republic of China, Vancouver, B.C. Jong Yoi. Birth: December 26, 1887.

Yoi is pronounced 'You-ee'; hence, in Canada, he discovered his given name had become 'Hughie.' *And all his other documents say he was born in 1888.*

In China Dad was a scholar and a teacher. In China at that time, the designation 'scholar' had a special meaning. Confucius taught that the purpose of education was to produce a moral man, and that an educated man, no matter how poor or powerless, commanded more respect than the merely wealthy or powerful. *The brightest boys, whether rich or poor, were given schooling that they didn't have to pay for, and when they graduated, they were called scholars and were eligible for government jobs. When Dad got to Victoria, he couldn't get a job as a teacher because he couldn't speak English, so he took up the trade of bricklaying. His first job was putting up some of the buildings in Chinatown.*

In general, Jong Hughie would not have found British Columbia a welcoming place. In the 1880s during construction of the transcontinental railway, the Chinese had been considered useful, often essential, labour: they were hard working; they usually spoke little English so were less likely to complain; they put up with more primitive working conditions and received lower pay packets than other workers, as they were perceived to have a lower standard of living and therefore fewer economic needs. After the railway was completed, however, local labour accused Chinese of undercutting their jobs. Furthermore, Chinese were not Christian, and by sending savings to support their families in China, they were also seen as unpatriotic. Consequently, Chinese were unwanted as permanent settlers, and laws passed in the provincial legislature treated them differently from other nationalities.

In 1911 in his early twenties, Jong Hughie left Victoria for Armstrong Spallumcheen. *Dad told me that working on road construction brought him into the [Okanagan] Valley.* Local history supports his statement. The first dozen years of Johnny Serra's *History of Armstrong* provide numerous examples of the settlers' demand for roads to link the farms within and outside the town. *1911 - Settlers still clamouring for more roads,* Serra observes; his excerpted council minutes are laced with the names of teamsters and labour costs. Serra also reports (p 181) that Jong Hughie worked for Sam Fruno on Powerhouse Road chopping trees and clearing bush. Mat. S. Hassen, a ninety-one-year-old local resident [2006], knew Fruno: *He was an Italian whose house burned down, so he built himself a cement house – it's still there.* Another of Jong Hughie's jobs was growing vegetables on the rich, drained bottomlands around Armstrong that in 1910, Serra says, produced 400 tons of celery. Head lettuce was introduced in 1912 [*Okanagan History*, #16], and over the years double cropping of both early and late lettuce and celery increased productivity. Two of Jong Hughie's working relationships were with Harry Sing Lee, who farmed J.H. Wilson's CNR lease along Otter Lake Road between Wood Avenue and Deep Creek, and with Lee's uncle, Lee Bak Bong, who owned land along Okanagan Street and in the flats south of Patterson Avenue. [See map, p 11]

Louie Non Chip Jong recalls that Jong Hughie talked little about the thirty-seven years he spent on his own in the Armstrong Spallumcheen district. *They were years of hardship and he did not want to share that with us.* However, the following excerpts taken from the *Armstrong Advertiser* and from Serra's history give a flavour of the area in which he chose to live between his arrival in 1911 and his introduction to Louie Non Chip in China in 1948.

> *April 13, 1911 – The Health officer was instructed to inspect all Chinese boarding houses as to overcrowding of inmates.* These boarding houses were located mainly along the junction of Patterson Avenue and Okanagan Street; they were Chinese-owned and catered to 'bachelor' Chinese who, because of the $500 head tax imposed by the Canadian government in 1904 on all Chinese immigrants, would work for years to pay to have their wives and children join them.

> *February, 1912 – There was a fracas... on the street near the Armstrong Hotel between a white man and a chink over a sum of money alleged by the Chinaman to be owing him... A heavy piece of gas pipe was the instrument used by the celestial to try to make the white man disgorge his ducats. The white man is still carrying his sore head and his coin.* The writer's choice of the word 'ducats' (W. Shakespeare: *The Merchant of Venice*) implies that the victim of the assault was mercenary; and 'coin,' that the amount in question

was small. Such confrontation is also unusual and therefore treated as a joke.

April 4, 1912 – Chung Yuen has bought out the Royal Café and will serve meals at all hours of the day or night. Chinese looked for small business opportunities open to them; such as, a laundry or a store.

November 30, 1912 – A deputation... requested that the curfew bell be rung again and that the curfew law be enforced... that Sunday observance be duly kept... a check be made on the selling of merchandise on Sunday. Chinese-owned buildings were often multi-purpose: on the ground floor, a business or two, and on the upper floors, dormitories where men bunked during the winter season especially in preference to a small shack on their rented acreages. Some local residents objected to the congregation of Chinese outside these buildings, located in the centre of town, as both a nuisance and a factor in lowering property values in the neighbourhood.

Mary laughs, *I can understand that. You have all these men smoking pipes and congregating outside on a hot summer's day, speaking a strange language, and playing mah jong. I can just visualize them [locals] thinking, "What are these people doing?"*

The Vernon News Holiday Number, December, 1912 – Armstrong is the largest cabbage shipping point in B.C. Cabbage on low lands yields 10 to 15 tons per acre; on high land, 5 to 9 tons per acre. They can ship cabbage singly in railcar lots or in mixed shipments including potatoes, beets, carrots, turnips, parsnips, and onions. The same article states that beets, carrots and turnips yielded 8 to 20 tons per acre. Adequate labour was essential and Chinese were available.

May 1, 1913 – The Vernon News – ...In the Armstrong council chamber several witnesses gave evidence before the [provincial] Labour Commission concerning the conditions of labour in the Armstrong district. The Mayor, Mr. James Milton Wright, postmaster, was the first witness... [He stated], The Chinamen seem to be working among them-

selves at the bottom of the town. They rent celery and cabbage land at from $50 to $60 an acre per year... it certainly helps in the produce raised here.... Mr. Frederick Taylor Jackson, produce merchant, was the next witness. He said that at times farmers could not get all the help they required. The employment agencies at Vancouver did not handle the class of men required for farming.... There are perhaps 60 or 75 [Chinese]... employed on the land.... Commissioner: If a Chinaman raises a better article than the white man, wouldn't he get a better price for it? He does not, because the white man gets the preference now.

May 26, 1913 - ... brought before the Council the question of Chinamen working on Sunday... on July 21 the Constable was instructed to ask the Chinamen to desist from working on Sunday. Economic reasons for the delay in enforcing Sunday observance were that local transfer wagons stood idle, railway express orders were delayed, store shelves lacked fresh produce, and perishable produce, such as celery and berries, was put at risk if Sunday observance were strictly kept.

June 5, 1913 – The Royal Commission on Agriculture visited the Okanagan to gather information on such topics as farm costs, labour supply, and "the Oriental labour problem." One witness,...Mr. H.A. Fraser gave testimony gained from personal experience of about twenty years in the district. Wages had practically doubled in the last fifteen years... Last year he had to pay $2.50 to $3.00 per day... there was such a scarcity of labour. He had received 5 cents a pound down to 3½ cents a pound from local dealers [shippers] for washed and packed celery... had it not been for Chinese competition, the price... would not have dropped below 5 cents a pound.

Mary says, You had to sell through the packing houses. If you didn't like the price offered, what would you do with the vegetables? If there was a surplus and they lowered the price to the Caucasians, then the Chinese produce would go for next to nothing. My dad said it wasn't worth cutting the vegetables. They left them in the field to rot.

June 26, 1913 – ... an announcement of the Parisian Laundry, a new industry for Armstrong. Mrs. Field, the proprietoress, promises to do her best to give entire satisfaction to patrons, and employs nothing but white labour. Two Chinese laundries operated on Okanagan Street. Some aspersions were cast about lack of sanitation.

A recurring theme over the years reflects the cultural differences that encouraged tension between Chinese and other residents:

December 15, 1924 – The Law made a raid on Armstrong's Chinatown. As a result 14 Chinese were up before Magistrate Groves... the Keeper of the House was fined $50 and costs, and the other 13 were fined $20 each and costs. Occasionally, disgruntled letters to the newspaper complained that men couldn't have a drink or "turn a card" past a certain hour in the local hotels whereas no such rules applied in "the gambling and opium dens" in Chinatown.

Mary adds, *Dad told me that a couple of unexplained murders in the Chinese community were probably caused by unpaid debts.* No one was prosecuted.

The real issue, however, was the fear that Chinese might come to own blocks of bottomland. They might then compete on an equal footing with local market gardeners instead of either renting from them or working for them, and, given their demonstrated talent for co-operative initiatives, they might put local growers out of business altogether, or dispense with the services of local packing houses and organize their own marketing outlets. Mat. Hassen says, *Yut Fong Co. was a store located behind the Fire Hall on Patterson Avenue. We always called the guy Yut Fong but it was a co-operative. The room behind the store was a kitchen and the two floors above held cubicles for members.* Wong Chog's business on the east side of town was also a cooperative.

In 1913 the issue heated up:

November, 1913 – eight acres were sold to a Chinaman at $745 *an acre.* For bottomland, $500 an acre was average. This deal reflects the need for the security of land ownership rather than tenancy. The reaction is hostile and quick.

November 10, 1913 – A resolution was proposed to City Council to regulate the further sale of land within the City to the Chinese.

November 13, 1913 – City Council passed a resolution against the policy of allowing Chinese ownership of lands. The resolution cited the undesirability of large communities of Chinese in small Anglo-Saxon communities... language... culture... impossibility of assimilation... would not tend to the social, economic, and moral benefit of the community. In response to a largely signed petition, a public meeting was called by Mayor Wright for the following evening in the Opera House.

November 27, 1913 – [Residents of Armstrong and Spallumcheen] in open Meeting [on November 14]... passed an unanimous resolution... not to sell land for five years to Chinese and Orientals, and [after expiration of present leases], not to lease land to [them].... We... request... that an act be passed by the B.C. legislature preventing Chinese, Japanese and other Orientals from owning farmland within the province.

January 29, 1914 – [A meeting of twenty-five produce growers] was held in the... fruit packing warehouse of the Armstrong Growers' Association... to arrive at some solution of the vexacious labour problem of the district... as it affects the market gardener. [One proposal was]... if no land was rented or sold to Chinese, then produce growers could get Chinese labour at as low as $20 a month. [One speaker had] paid off his Chinese labourers last fall at $1.10 per day and they had raised no objections. [The following resolution was]... carried unanimously: That all white men owning bottomlands agree not to pay more than $40 a month without board or 17½ cents an hour without board to Chinese labourers.

By now, Jong Hughie had worked in Armstrong Spallumcheen for three years.

The beginning of World War One sidetracked this discussion because of the labour shortage caused by local enlistment. Instead, the dehydrating plant set up in town to process root crops such as potatoes, carrots, and onions for shipment to soldiers overseas employed over 100 Chinese, and despite pleas in the local newspaper that the job of vegetable peeler was eminently suitable for white women, the majority of peelers were Chinese. In 1917 Serra reported, *The evaporator is running day and night.* Local residents could discern by the smell which vegetable was being processed, onions in particular.

Once the First War ended, however, the economy sagged. The dehydrating plant closed, returning veterans needed to be reintegrated into civilian life, and the debate about Chinese renters resumed. An August 15, 1918, article in the *Okanagan Commoner* [a combined newspaper for Armstrong and Enderby] declared in "Facts We Must Face" that without Chinese involvement in agriculture, ...*our productivity would drop.* The same newspaper on March 6, 1919, reported that... *the Armstrong Board of Trade [Chamber of Commerce] suggested that the government buy out Chinese landowners and renters and settle returning soldiers on those lands.* A week later the paper noted that in the Armstrong Spallumcheen area, 250 Chinese produced celery, potatoes, cabbage, onions, and carrots on 600 acres of fully cleared bottomland rented from thirty white owners, and another 126 acres, including 80 acres of black peat, along the Canadian National Railway right-of-way. On July 10 this newspaper reported that a resident... *was compelled to sell out to a chink because no white man would help him out.*

The dilemma was that the Chinese were good tenants. They paid rents promptly and bought seed, fertilizer, sacks, and twine through the local packing houses that also marketed their produce. They bought the lumber to build their packing crates from the local sawmill. They used local transfer outfits, such as Warner's or Blackburn's, to haul the vegetables to town.

They were excellent market gardeners. Two or three would share both rent and labour on one or two acres of land. The result was intensive, orderly cultivation accomplished by hands and feet and handmade tools. They shovelled off snow in early spring and started seeds in homemade hotbeds. Sticks and string laid out the long, straight rows. A man jumping on a wooden celery stamper, for example, punched a double row of holes in which another placed the celery plants. A wheeled hoe loosened the soil between the rows. Careful fingers endlessly picked weeds into pails and carried them off the field. Soil hilled against wide boards propped beside the adult plants blanched the stems white prior to harvest. A heavy knife slashed the root and trimmed the leaves for packing the 50-pound crate.

During the growing season the norm was an eighteen-hour day. Mat. S. Hassen recalls, *When I was a young buck, I would be going home at eleven or twelve o'clock at night or three o'clock in the morning. The Chinamen would be in the fields at eleven o'clock at night and back in the fields again at three o'clock in the morning. I can remember going into the bank in the fall of the year. There was a desk over on one side with an abacus on it, and two or three Chinese men would come in and go to the desk and work with the abacus and then go to the teller and buy so many Hong Kong dollars. All their knuckles were sticky-taped up – chapped from harvesting in the wet. I often thought of those guys working like that – suffering – the misery – they had to be sore... sore... sore... and then sending their money over to their wives in China.* As F.T. Jackson testified to the Labour Commission in Vernon on May 1, 1913, *If I had a piece of land I wanted put in good condition and wanted to be sure of getting the rent, I would rent it to a Chinaman.*

Mat. Hassen shares a similar opinion with regard to their character. *They were the finest people – bar none – that ever came to this country, and many people here missed their greatest opportunity because they didn't get to know them or invite them into their homes. Oh, they knew them through their connection with the land or the market, but they never did anything for them except for the odd one that rented land to them. That kindness was [returned] because they used to shower their landlords with gifts at Christmastime – silks and fruits and nuts. They were generous people – you could never get ahead of a Chinaman. If you gave him a cigarette, he gave you seven pounds of tobacco. And he never forgot you. I was notary public for thirty-five years and the Chinamen and the local Indians [natives] used to come to me. I never charged a Chinaman five cents for anything (or the Indians either) but I was certainly more than well repaid because that grew into a connection where Rose and I were invited to all the festivities and social events in Vernon and Kelowna because we were friends of the Jongs or the Chins, or whoever it was.*

Serra's history reports Louie Chin's arrival in Armstrong in 1912, a year after Jong Hughie. The Hassen family had a long association with the Chins: *Chin lived in a little shack on Deep Creek just north of Wood Avenue, and Dad would stop in there for vegetables. I was very young, and he'd give me a dime to get some celery. So I'd have this dime between my finger and thumb and the Chinaman would say, "Hold your arms out," and he'd pile celery in my arms, and on top of it, lettuce. Then he'd take the dime out from between my finger and thumb and put a nickel back. All the load that a small boy could carry for a nickel!*

You couldn't tell by lookin' at a Chinaman what his background might have been. A bunch of them used to rent land down at Head of the Lake country in the heyday of tomato-growing and they were shipping to the canneries. I used to go down there to buy early tomatoes and peppers. I would go to their places – a shack, or even just a tent on bare ground – and the guy would be dirty… dusty… always in work clothes. And then I'd go to one of their social functions and the guy would be in a tuxedo and his wife in the latest fashion. And their manners were polished – there was nothing 'rube' about them. They are wonderful people – they are so darn deep. I went to school with a few of them – Harry Lee and Wong Chog, the son – and they were always the best spellers and the best writers. No one could touch them for handwriting. They were expected to excel.

When World War One ended, Jong Hughie had been working

in Armstrong Spallumcheen for seven years. He wrote letters for men to send to family back in China and read to them the replies. Celery production had resumed after the war. In September, 1920, Serra reported, *On account of such heavy express shipments, the northbound train had been late every day; great quantities of celery were still being shipped from here.* In the 1920s and '30s the number of Chinese in Armstrong was at its peak. Around 500 persons, they totalled nearly half the number of local residents.

Within a year of each other, two disasters occurred in the Chinese community. On June 29, 1922, Armstrong's Chinatown along Okanagan Street burned to the ground along with the City's Fire Hall and Wong Chong's brick block on Patterson Avenue. Rebuilding began immediately; Lee Bak Bong's new home and place of business, still standing in 2007, was built of locally made brick. The second event had deeper consequences. On July 1, 1923, the federal government passed the Chinese Immigration Act, also known as the Chinese Exclusion Act, which with few exceptions prohibited further Chinese immigration. As a result, Chinese men in Canada no longer had any hope of bringing their families to join them. For the next twenty-four years the only Chinese wife in Armstrong Spallumcheen was Mrs. Lee Bak Bong, whose husband and father-in-law, Lee Nye, had earned enough money by 1920 to pay the head tax and bring her into the country.

Ironically, Depression in the 1930s had the unexpected result of drawing economic segments of the community into closer rapport. When the rapid loss of markets introduced discussion of a central 'pooling' system for the sale of fruits and vegetables, including celery, both local and Chinese growers were opposed. The August 7, 1930, *Armstrong Advertiser* reported the following position by the three local growers [Frank Marshall, Otto Lane, William Boss]: *...Celery is too expensive a crop to raise and too hard to regulate in supply for the market. If we are not able to sell our celery for a cash price on delivery to the warehouse, we feel we shall be forced to discontinue growing celery.* The letter from the thirty Chinese growers stated, *...Unless we receive a cash price for our celery on delivery to the warehouses,* *our celery will stay in the ground.* The total celery crop of the district in 1929 was recorded in the article as having been 970 tons.

December 8, 1932 – A large advertisement in the *Advertiser* pleaded:

Align Yourself with Constructive Community Movements
and
Support the Local Workers for Your Welfare

Four of the businesses named were Wong Chog & Company, vegetable and fruit shippers; Sing Lung, laundry; Lee Bak Bong, vegetable grower and shipper; and Yut Fong Co., groceries.

June 15, 1933 – A deputation consisting of J.H. Wilson, W.S. Cooke and Wong Chog, representing in an informal way the shippers and growers of truck produce in the Armstrong district, went down to the Coast last week to enquire... as to the causes of the hold-up in the disposition [sale] of this year's lettuce crop. They were accompanied by Fruit Inspector Pothecary. The group discovered that lettuce grown by Coast Chinese was both equal to Armstrong lettuce in quality and available earlier in spring; hence, the 'soft' market. The loss of sales was marked. Serra notes, *In 1930 Armstrong shipped 34 carloads of lettuce [and] large quantities by express; in 1933 but one car[load] was sent out and express shipments were practically nil. Prices received in many cases were cut in half.*

The community suffered. From the 1930s to the 1960s, Depression and post-war recession stories were rife. Mat. S. Hassen recalls, *Shu Bing Shong [locally, Soo Sun] had two acres where the City's sewer lagoons are today [Adair Street]. He used to go into George Taylor's Golden Gate Café and have a coffee every morning, and George would read his statements for him. One day I was in there and George told me that Shu had brought in his statement from the packing house, and after all the deductions for sacks and string and hauling and everything else, that year his two acres had netted him twenty-eight dollars.*

I remember Joe Glaicar had early spuds – in February he'd be *told by the packer: "$80 a ton." He'd go back in March: "Not so good - $60 a ton." Go back in April: "Not so good – $40 a ton." And the first shipment he had ready he took to Dolph Browne's in Vernon: "Not so good – I can give you $20 a ton." And Joe had to turn around and drive home and stop the harvest because he was paying his pickers more than he was going to get for the potatoes. Joe was friendly with a storekeeper in Williams Lake. That guy was rationed to one 100-pound sack of potatoes a week at $5 a sack – that's $100 a ton. And he wasn't allowed to have two sacks! Somebody was makin' money and it wasn't the grower!*

Express shipments or railcar-lot sales were also not immune from tampering. Mat. continues, *The packing house would sell on consignment to Winnipeg or Toronto and they'd get a wire back: "The vegetables were poor quality or all bad." R.W. McDonald was a shipper, and he took the train out several times to see for himself. "Show me the bad stuff!" Well, they'd either sold it all, or if there was any left, there was nothing wrong with it. They did the same damn thing in the lumber business. The sawmill would ship a carload of lumber somewhere, and they'd claim it was 'short.' Now that stuff was counted into the car – so many 2x4s, 2x6s, 2x8s – so they knew how much was in there and it wasn't short!*

In his years in market gardening, Jong Hughie had also seen some unfortunate incidents. Mary Jong recalls, *Some trainmen were bad. My dad used to say they would leave whole shipments of lettuce behind to rot in the heat – they just wouldn't hook the [box]car on. It stayed on the tracks the whole day. It was devastating to the Chinese growers.*

However, in 1947 Chinese in Canada received some good news. As a result of Chinese enlistment in World War Two and their support of the war effort, such as, the purchase of Victory bonds; lobbying by Chinese community leaders; and a change in public opinion, the Chinese Exclusion Act was repealed. Wives and unmarried children under the age of eighteen could now immigrate to Canada. That year Serra noted the contributions of thirty-six Chinese, including Jong Hughie and Lee Bak Bong, among subscribers to the

Armstrong Spallumcheen Hospital Fund. In 1948 Jong Hughie returned to Canton to look for a wife and met Louie Non Chip. *I met Jong Yoi when things settled down after the war and he came back to visit his family. The Jongs lived in the next village and my mother introduced us. He had other girls but we 'clicked.'*

When Louie Non Chip met Jong Yoi, he was a widower. A family photograph depicts him and his first wife dressed formally and seated on either side of a small lace-covered table in their home, the elder son standing beside his father. His wife died in 1940 during World War Two leaving two sons and a daughter.

Jong Yoi was a handsome man and, despite many years' difference in their ages, his education, good standing in the community, and prospects in Canada made him a suitable match. *We married in 1949 and lived with his parents in the Jong village. He left again in the spring of 1950.* Their first child, Allan, was born that October. *He worked on my papers for two years, and I flew into Vancouver on January 16, 1954.*

Louie Non Chip Jong felt positive about the move. *This country still had a lot of opportunity. China had gone through fourteen years of war – there was devastation... hardship... starvation.... I remember those years! Even if there was hardship in Canada, it could be no worse than what I had already lived through.* This optimistic attitude would over the years stand her in good stead. So would her radical independence in deciding on a course of action and following it through to a successful conclusion.

Jong Hughie had always travelled to and from China by boat. Bringing his wife and son to Canada by plane was an auspicious beginning. However, Louie Non Chip Jong remembers vividly that Allan, who had just turned three, was not impressed. *He had to wear shoes here. He had never worn shoes before – he kicked them off and refused to wear them! Lee Bak Bong's oldest son, Quong, drove his mother, his sister May, and my husband down to Vancouver to meet the plane. We went first to Nanaimo to visit Alice Lee Wong, Lee Bak Bong's oldest daughter, and her husband, Gunner Wong. They had a TV and other [appliances] that I had never seen before and didn't understand. (The Lee Bak Bongs here in Armstrong had a television too. I thought they were rich.)*

When we drove into Armstrong, everything was covered in snow. Quong took the Jongs to Jong Hughie's place of employment on Otter Lake Road, Harry Lee's acreage. *We had a little room off the Lee house that had just enough room for one bed. I had to use the outhouse and I kept falling in the snow because I wasn't used to walking in snow and my slippers had no [grip]. I wasn't used to the food either – bread and butter – so I couldn't eat much.*

In the main part of the house were Harry and Elizabeth [Lizzy], his native wife, and their two small sons. *Allan was not allowed to play with Harry Lee's boys or with their toys either. He was considered a lower class because we were working for them. One day the kids were playing with their tricycles and Allan used a little chair to hop around with.*

Having arrived in mid-winter, Louie Non Chip Jong was within a couple of months preparing and seeding hotbeds, watering and thinning plants, and transplanting into the fields. *I took Allan to work with me and put him in a box, and he had to stay in that box. When it rained, I covered him with a potato sack. The Lees had a few people working with them – not many – most of them had left because the packing houses were shutting down.* In fact, the 1950s were witnessing the demise of the vibrant market garden economy that had once existed in Armstrong Spallumcheen: Californian produce undercut local prices; the last packing house closed; the last CP rail passenger/mail service ended; after decades in the area, many old Chinese market gardeners had died or moved away.

Louie Non Chip Jong made a second unpleasant discovery. *My husband had worked for Harry Lee for about ten years. And for those years he never got paid – was always promised "Next year's crop...." "Next year's crop...." But he never saw a penny! We were going nowhere. No matter how desperate we were – no matter what it took – we had to get some money together and get some land of our own. Lee Pon acted as go-between, and we quit Harry Lee and went to work for a year for Lee Bak Bong.* Lee Pon had a shoe repair outlet in the Yut Fong Co. building on Patterson Avenue.

We moved into a shack on twelve acres that Lee Bak Bong owned just across from Colonial Farms [3830 Okanagan Street]. The shack is still there. It was a storage shed for vegetables. It had just room enough for a bed and a little stove – I got the stove secondhand. Kerosene lamps. Allan slept on the table. He was four and Mary was just a baby. Mary had been born in November, 1954, during her mother's first year in Canada. In naming his eldest daughter, Jong Hughie began the tradition of including the word 'moon,' a reference to the legend of the Chinese moon goddess, in each daughter's full name. It was a way of distinguishing the generations.

To get a little money together, the Jongs worked every day. Louie Non Chip Jong remembers: *We were criticized for working on Sunday. If we didn't work on Sunday, we didn't eat. I got seventy-five cents an hour – we didn't make enough to even spend. It was eight to five most days, sometimes earlier, sometimes later. Planting – weeding – anything that had to be done. Harvesting for [shipping] orders meant we worked until it was finished... cabbage, celery, Chinese vegetables, potatoes, head lettuce. The train came by every night at five o'clock. If the whistle blew at the sawmill or the train came by and I hadn't gotten home, Allan would stand at the door crying because he was scared I wasn't coming at all. When it got dark, he had no lights – just kerosene.*

Mary adds, *We went to Dad's grave in Highland Park Cemetery the other day, and as we were driving home, we passed the shack and my brother Allan began to reminisce. When he was about five, he remembered my mom and dad going to work and leaving him at home to babysit me, just a baby. And he broke the baby bottle. It was glass and he put it on top of the wood stove without setting it in water, and I was crying to be fed. He said my mom could not afford another one – she didn't have forty cents – and she had to rig up a makeshift. Finally, she borrowed a dollar from Lee Pon and bought another bottle.*

Another time while Allan was babysitting me – I was still quite young – it got dark, and Mom and Dad hadn't come home. Suddenly, we saw a face in the window – somebody peering in at us! Allan and I were so scared we hid under the table!

Joan was born in the fall of 1955. In 1956 the Jongs were able to make a deal to buy some acreage. *A woman called Mrs. [R.L.] Lidstone owned the land. She worked at the Armstrong Hotel. Lee Pon introduced us and acted as go-between. We made a very small down payment, then paid it off little by little because the bank wouldn't loan us any money – until later – because we had no [collateral].* In 1957 the City tax roll lists Jong Hughie as the owner of 7.79 acres on [3800] Pleasant Valley Road.

Success was bittersweet because now they owed money and had to go back to working for Lizzy and Harry Lee, as Lee Bak Bong couldn't provide enough hours. Necessity and tradition dictated the decisions made about the children. *Allan was nearly six and old enough to look after Mary and Joan. Every noon hour I walked from Otter Lake Road back to the shack to check on them. A lady saw me do this and she began to give me a ride. I was so grateful. I didn't speak English so I never knew her name. I wish I had.*

When Allan started school, I put Mary and Joan in a [play] wagon and pulled them with me to work wherever I could find it. Somebody might have a big [vegetable] order and I'd go there to help fill it. I'd dig potatoes and put them in the wagon with the kids. [Most nights] I would get two baskets full of kindling from the saw-mill here and take it home to burn for cooking and heat.

Mat. Hassen recalls the same image: *I used to be friendly with the station agent on the CPR, and the first I knew of Mrs. Jong, she would come up along the platform pulling a kid's coaster wagon filled with vegetables to be shipped express to the Prairie. She didn't speak a word of English, but he knew enough to get the information straight.*

Luckily, on her travels she spotted a building that with some elbow grease would do very well for a house. *I found a henhouse that the owner didn't want any more and I moved it onto our property. So in 1957 we moved out of Lee Bak Bong's shed into our own house. We added on to it a few years later. It is still part of our old house next door.* In the short space of three years, Louie Non Chip Jong had her own home on her own land. On the eight acres she could grow the family's food and engage in market gardening.

I had no education. I had been growing vegetables since I was a small child, so it was one thing I knew how to do. My mother taught me the importance of land – she invested in land herself when my father had money – and she said the land would never [depreciate], and it would always give you something to eat. Even if you went into debt for it and you had to work hard, you were working for yourself.

To compensate in part for the lack of wages while they had worked for him, Harry Lee gave the Jongs an old truck to transport their produce. *It wasn't good enough to drive on the road, but Allan learned to drive enough to get it around the field to pick up the vegetables. We kept it next to a vegetable storage shed beside the house, and one night someone came and set fire to the building. So the truck burned up too. There was a lot of prejudice then.*

At this juncture in their lives, Louie Non Chip Jong needed all her fortitude. She would have another three children. In 1957 Margaret was born; Jeannie, in 1958; and Danny, in 1959. In wintertime during those years, she was forced to apply for assistance. *Betty Lee, Lee Bak Bong's third daughter, drove me to Vernon to get a bit of welfare money – to interpret for me. I didn't want to go on welfare but it was desperate times. Welfare was hard to get. They would give it for a while... then it would stop... we would struggle... we would get it again.... It was so difficult. My husband was too old. In 1959 he had a stroke. I was making payments on the eight acres. Very seldom would we go to see the doctor but Dr. Haugen was really good. He didn't want money. All my kids except Allan were born in the Armstrong [Spallumcheen] Hospital. He never charged me a penny. We gave him vegetables, of course, but everybody did – how much could he eat?*

There were other good people.

Jack Laursen owned the meat locker on Okanagan Street south of the Armstrong Hotel. *I couldn't afford to buy the meat, so I asked him, "If you have any fish heads to throw away, would you give them to me?" So he gave me all the fish heads and I used them to make soup. Then he said, "If you don't have the money now, you can charge it." So that's what I did and he kept a little tally of what I bought.*

In those days I carried the vegetables in from our field on my shoulder in two wicker baskets on a pole – one basket in front and one behind. Oh, my shoulder was sore! The owner of the [equipment dealership] next door watched me, and one day he said, "Here is a tractor free of charge for you to use." Allan was still young and had never driven a tractor. The first day it ended up in the ditch! They dragged it out and said I could still use it. We could load the vegetables in the bucket. It was a [blessing]. Kineshanko operated the Massey-Harris dealership beside the Jongs.

We couldn't afford to buy a tractor – only Lee Bak Bong owned a tractor – so we hired Dave Blackburn to plough our field for us. For a long time City Council wouldn't let us have a driveway from our place onto Railway Avenue – we had to take our vegetables out the alley onto Patterson Avenue [Grey, 2290]. So Dave Blackburn went to the council and spoke for us, and they changed their minds.

Rose Hassen too has a special place in her memory. *When my kids were away from home, or too busy on the farm, Rose drove me to Kelowna for my doctors' appointments. She was so kind.*

Being the oldest child, Allan was expected to assume early responsibilities in the family business. *He was nine. I needed to adver-*

tise my vegetables, so I gave him samples of all the different kinds to take to Vernon to sell. I gave him the money to pay for a ride in the Rocky Mountain freight truck. He paid for the ride down – not very much, but for us at that time, quite a bit. Then he lost his money for a return trip so he had to walk home. He was gone a long time and I was worried! Somehow, halfway between Vernon and Armstrong he found a place with a phone and phoned [Kineshanko], and they brought me the message that he'd be late.

For both Allan and Mary, who broke the ice for the younger ones, school tended to be a trial. *Because Allan was the only boy, he tried to figure out different [routes] to get to school because the other kids would beat him up.*

Mary didn't like school at all. She says, *Every day the teacher checked for clean fingernails and asked if we ate from the Five Food Groups. My nails were always dirty because I worked in the garden before school started, and I didn't eat from the Five Food Groups, I ate rice porridge [congee]. So the kids in my row blamed me because we never got a gold star. Louie Non Chip Jong tried to help. Mom went into the meat store and asked what went "between bread." The clerk said, "Butter." So we ate bread and butter lunches for months! Another time the clerk said, "Bologna." So we ate bologna sandwiches for a year!* In time the situation improved.

Cultural differences also separated the Jongs from the community. Mary remembers, *When we were little, church groups would come to our house and want to take us to church. They thought they were going to save our souls. It's funny now but it was serious then. They didn't understand we had another faith.*

The Salvation Army used to give us used toys at Christmas, but they never seemed to be complete: one roller skate in good condition and one that wasn't, a doll's bed but no dolly.... Most of the time we spent Christmas with the Lee family [Lee Bak Bong]. Once Mom went into the bush with Allan and got a little tree. We put it in the middle of the table. We have a picture of me on the table with the tree.

One Christmas Mr. Upper gave us each a little purse. It was new, *and I thought it was the best thing I had ever got! We used to ride the train to Vernon to celebrate the Chinese New Year. We'd be early. Mom would be visiting, and she was very strict. Kids must never be heard! So we'd sit outside on the bench very quietly, and wait... and wait... and wait... until the big banquet with all the speeches – so boring. But after the meal the men would give out Lucky Money. So I brought my purse, and I'd wish I was brave enough to go around twice! We were very poor then, so when you got one or two dollars, it was a lot! My mom told me in those days she could afford only one set of clothes for each of us and that's when we got them – she made all our overalls from hand-me-downs.*

Louie Non Chip Jong has some dark memories. *Somebody gave us a big bag of winter clothes, and I spent a lot of time patching holes in the pants and making everything good to wear. That summer I stored them in an old barn that used to be on the property. When I went that fall to get them, they were gone. When I think back on this, I could cry. We were so poor. Even some of the Chinese community looked down on us – too poor and too many kids. When I went to visit, I had to leave the children outside – the people were scared they were going to have to feed everybody!*

In 1962 at the age of seventy-five, Jong Hughie had a second stroke that left him partly paralyzed and his back permanently hunched. He could no longer work. Louie Non Chip Jong recalls, *He was in hospital for many months. Rocky Mountain Transport used to give me a ride in the truck to Vernon to visit him. I had to hire some Chinese ladies from Vernon to come down and work in the field.* They worked alongside the children: Allan, twelve; Mary, eight; Joan, seven; Margaret, five; Jeannie, four; and Danny, three. *The ladies would test them. They'd say, "That's a weed. Pull it!" And the kids would answer, "No! That's a vegetable!" And the ladies would tell me afterwards that my kids could tell a vegetable from a weed!*

At age thirty-eight Louie Non Chip Jong faced the fact that in addition to her six children, she had an invalid husband to care for. *It was very difficult in those years because of the Vegetable Marketing Board. They were very strict. We couldn't go outside our district to sell vegetables or they would [confiscate] them.* Armstrong and Vernon, for example, were in marketing zone #2; Revelstoke, in zone #7. Other regulations made little distinction between root vegetables, which stored well, and Chinese vegetables, which tended to have a short life. In addition, some vegetables required the purchase of an identifying tag. Tagged vegetables included cucumbers, tomatoes, peppers, onions, and potatoes.

One letter dated August 11, 1965, from the British Columbia Interior Vegetable Marketing Board cautioned the Jongs:

Mr. Jong Hughie,
Armstrong, B.C.

Dear Sir:

On July 26, 1965, we wrote to you outlining our regulations and advising you not to ship regulated vegetables to Revelstoke. Yet on July 31, our inspector found 150 lbs. of cucumbers being unloaded from a Rocky Mtn. Transport truck in Revelstoke at the Super Value store. We have copies of the bills of lading to prove they were shipped by yourself. This is the last warning we give you in this regard. If we discover one more shipment of tagged vegetables being made by yourself to Revelstoke, we will seize the shipment and we will launch prosecution in the courts against you under the B.C. Natural Produce Marketing Act.

Yours very truly,
(signed) *F.N. Magee*
Secretary-Treasurer
Interior Vegetable Marketing Board

A letter of the same date to the manager of the Super Value store in Revelstoke that had accepted the Jong vegetables was equally severe.

In the early sixties Jong Hughie placed his camera on a tripod, arranged his wife and children on the sofa and snapped a family photo that included himself. Despite the effects of the stroke, he still looks handsome. Louie Non Chip Jong is smiling. On her blouse she wears a round pendant of Chinese jade with a small gold centre. The girls in dresses are perched along the top of the sofa behind their parents and the two boys. Danny, the youngest, can barely sit still. Like his father, Allan is wearing a bowtie on his white shirt and a suit. He is beaming. *We borrowed that suit from Mackenzie's menswear to wear for the day and then returned it because we couldn't afford to buy it. It took us ten years to pay off the debt on our land. But then I could make some headway – sell vegetables and keep the money for ourselves.*

1967 was a celebratory year. It was Canada's 100th birthday, and an odd series of events introduced a large Chinese restaurant into downtown Armstrong. *The building that used to be the Overwaitea store was vacant and I wanted to rent part of it to sell vegetables. But the owner, Mr. Laursen, didn't want to rent – he wanted to sell the building. So to get some space, I had to buy the whole thing. Then people in town said, "The Chinese bought the building. They must be going to open a restaurant."*

Allan and a friend went upstairs in the building to check it out and fell through the floor, so I decided to take a gamble. I had Maddocks Construction tear the building down and put up a new one. I went to the bank and asked to borrow the money to open a restaurant and I used our land for collateral. The Chinese community said, "You're going to open a restaurant? This community is too small – you don't need more than a dozen cups and saucers because that's how many people you will get. You will lose everything you have!"

On May 15, 1967, Jong Hughie and Louie Non Chip Jong opened the Shanghai Restaurant. *I hired two cooks.* The *Armstrong Advertiser* reported a banquet for eighty guests on the evening before the opening. Mat. and Rose Hassen were there, Dr. Roy and Edna Haugen, the Sabys, and other friends. *Actually*, says Mat. Hassen, *there were two banquets – one for the whiteys and one for the Chinese. Rose and I were at both of them. The tables were set for ten people and one person acted as the host for the table. They were feasts – the most exotic meals you ever ate in your life. We had bird's nest soup. Rose wasn't sure she'd like it but she sent her dish back twice – it was delicious!*

I knew Jong Hughie very well. He was a very smart man – a delightful man – he would never say anything to upset anybody. After they opened the restaurant, in the evening he would sit at the counter and I'd sit with him and talk to him and get all kinds of stories – ask questions and get all kinds of answers – until Mrs. Jong had finished, and then they'd go home together.

Louie Non Chip Jong decided their present acreage wasn't large enough. *We were selling vegetables to the stores in town, and the Rocky Mountain freight truck took our vegetables all over the Okanagan and even up to Revelstoke. We were supplying the restaurant and shipping Chinese vegetables to Calgary. So we rented the piece just east of us for a few years. Then the ten acres south of us went on the market but we couldn't afford it. It went off the market. When it was put up for sale again, we bought it. The Chinese community said we were crazy to buy more land – all we'd be doing was pay taxes! But I knew that if we got into trouble, we could always sell off a piece and live on the rest.*

Inevitably, the Jong children had a role to play that was both traditionally Chinese and essential to the success of the family enterprise. Mary says, *We all had to quit school early and help out. I never finished grade eight – I was twelve when I started to manage the restaurant because Allan was working for the CPR in Lillooet, Dad was too old, and Mom couldn't speak English. Most of us went back to school when we were older. I upgraded at Okanagan College and then went to U.Vic [University of Victoria] and Simon Fraser [University] and got a degree in Fine Arts and teaching. Joan went to UBC for a degree in Dietary Science, was a cook at the Enderby Hospital until it closed, and is now the supervisor at the extended care facility, Parkview Place – nearly twenty years all together.*

Allan came home to be near the family when Dad was older. He works for Kenkraft RV in Lavington in building and maintenance. Margaret manages Cole's bookstore in Vernon, Jeannie works in town at Shepherd's [Home] Hardware, and Danny is a computer analyst at NAIT [Northern Alberta Institute of Technology.]

Jong Hughie died in 1977 at the age of ninety. Louie Non Chip Jong continued to operate the restaurant until it closed in 1995. Her legs were bothering her. Mary says, *Mom had to have her knees replaced this year [2006] – all those years kneeling in the garden. But even when we had the restaurant and we'd be going home late at night, she could outwalk me – I could not keep up with her.*

Louie Non Chip Jong's direction of the family's market garden has never flagged. In the growing season the level, eighteen-acre field behind the house burgeons with produce. When they were growing up, each of her children had a responsibility to supply and sell Jong produce at one of the weekly farmers' markets in Armstrong, Vernon, Kelowna, and Salmon Arm. Although fewer family members are involved today, the tradition continues. Louie Non Chip Jong participates vigorously – weeding and hoeing, coaxing the flowerbeds into perfection, braiding garlic ropes for sale. She treats the Armstrong Farmers' Market as a social event – a pleasant walkabout to greet people she knows in the town where she has lived for fifty-three years.

Jong's vegetables continue to win largely each fall at the Interior Provincial Exhibition, and baskets overflow with winning ribbons. Mary says, *Mat. Hassen persuaded us to exhibit at the Fair. We used to load vegetables into the back of a tractor-trailer, park it on the corner of Bridge Street and Pleasant Valley Road, and sell out of it. The school was there and the City and Municipal Hall, and it was a busy place. Mat. said, "Why don't you enter your vegetables in the IPE?" and that's why we started.*

Louie Non Chip Jong remains an indefatigable source of strength and indomitable will. For the last ten years she has lived in the new house that Allan built for her, a high-ceilinged, spacious, two-storeyed home. Stone lions guard the carved front door, and carved dragons rampage on the newel posts of the stairway to the upper floor. It is a welcoming place.

In the summer of 2006 on her new legs, Louie Non Chip Jong, along with Allan, his wife Penn, their small daughter Alayna, Joan, Jeannie, Mary, and Mary's daughter, Asia, took a trip to China. It was her third visit since her arrival in Canada in 1954, and she noticed many changes. Mary says, *In 1979 we visited China together, and people were poor and hungry. In 1992 Mom took my brothers and sisters to visit me when I was teaching in Chongqing [Chungking], and we thought the people were better off. This past year we found the economy thriving. The main reason for this third trip was to visit Mom's brother and the family of my dad's first wife because, having married into that family, she has an obligation to them. She had a house built near where she was born, and that's where we stayed. While Mother visited, the rest of us took a tour of and around Beijing – the Forbidden City, the Ming tombs, Tiananmen Square, the Temple of Heaven, the Emperor's summer palace, and the Wall of China.*

In 1954 Louie Non Chip Jong undertook a difficult task. To immigrate to a new country is never easy. To emigrate from East to West with no education and minimum skills and yet survive and suc-ceed was a feat. *I am lucky,* she says. *I have good kids. My kids are good to their mother.* She runs upstairs and returns with a closely-knit wool toque. *I saw a lady knitting a toque like this on the plane when I first came to Canada. I watched what she did. I can't read a pattern. I just look at what I want to knit and figure it out. I make sweaters the same way.*

In the Jong home, three tall, wood, richly painted male figures known as "The Three Immortals" bestow good luck on the house-hold. Luk represents high rank and affluence, the achievement of good things with ease; Fuk brings happiness and prosperity; and Sau promises health, longevity, and wisdom, that comes with age.

Family photograph taken by Jong Hughie in the early 1960s
Left to right, rear: Margaret, Jeannie, Mary, Joan
Front: Allan, Louie Non Chip Jong, Jong Hughie, Danny

Index

ISBN 142511709-0